The **Poker** Player's Bible

The **Poker** Player's Bible
How to Play Winning Poker

LOU KRIEGER

BARRON'S

A QUARTO BOOK

First edition for North America published in
2004 by Barron's Educational Series, Inc.

All inquiries should be addressed to:
Barron's Educational Series, Inc.
250 Wireless Boulevard
Hauppauge, NY 11788
www.barronseduc.com

International Standard Book Number
0-7641-5788-4
Library of Congress Catalog Card Number
2004100208

QUAR.PKP

Conceived, designed, and produced by
Quarto Publishing plc
The Old Brewery
6 Blundell Street
London N7 9BH

Project Editor Paula McMahon
Art Editor/Designer Peggy Sadler
Assistant Art Director Penny Cobb
Editor Richard Geller
Assistant Editors Kate Martin, Mary Groom
Picture Researcher Claudia Tate
Photographer Martin Norris
Models Graham Stones, Kelly Thompson
Indexer Joan Dearnley

Art Director Moira Clinch
Publisher Piers Spence

Color separation by Modern Age Repro
House Ltd, Hong Kong
Printed by Midas Printing Ltd, China

9 8 7 6 5 4

CONTENTS

Introduction 6

SECTION 1 **Poker Basics 10**
What is Poker? 12
Choosing Your Game 18
  Texas Hold'em 20
  Omaha 22
  Omaha Eight or Better, Hi-Lo Split 24
  Seven-Card Stud 26
  Seven-Card Stud Eight or Better,
    Hi-Lo Split 28
Hand Rankings 30
Common Poker Terms 34
Reading Your Opponents 36
Analysis at the Table 40
Etiquette 44

SECTION 2 **The Mechanics of
the Game 46**
  Texas Hold'em 48
  Omaha 56
  Omaha Eight or Better, Hi-Lo Split 62
  Seven-Card Stud 68
  Seven-Card Stud Eight or Better,
    Hi-Lo Split 74

SECTION 3 **Starting Hands 82**
Texas Hold'em 84
  Starting hands 84
  Pairs you can play in any position 88
  Early position hands 90
  Middle position hands 91
  Late position hands 93
  Complex situations 94
  Selectivity—the key to winning play 95
Omaha 96
  Recommended starting hands 104
  The very best Omaha hands 107
  Very good hands 108
  Unplayable hands 109
  Fit or fold 110
  Omaha flops 111

Omaha Eight or Better, Hi-Lo Split 114
  Recommended starting hands 116
  Fit or fold 120
  Very best Omaha/8 hands 121
  Very good hands 122
  Playable hands 123
  Judging your hand 125
Seven-Card Stud 130
  Very good hands 130
  Overcards 143
  Ante stealing 144
Seven-Card Stud Eight or Better,
  Hi-Lo Split 146
  Starting standards 146
  Recommended starting hands 154

SECTION 4 **Playing Your Hands 156**
Texas Hold'em 158
  Your position in the betting order 158
  Odds and outs 161
  Implied odds 165
  Deception 167
  Semi-bluffing 168
  Defending 169
  Raising 171
  Free cards 176
  Slow-playing 177
  Reading your opponents 178
Omaha 180
  Your position in the betting order 181
  Odds and outs 183
  Implied odds 188
  Deception 189
  Semi-bluffing 189
  Defending 190
  Raising 191
  Free cards 192
  Slow-playing 193
  Reading your opponents 194
Omaha Eight or Better, Hi-Lo Split 196
  Your position in the betting order 196
  Odds and outs 199
  Implied odds 205
  Deception 205

Semi-bluffing 206
Defending 207
Raising 207
Free cards 209
Slow-playing 210
Reading your opponents 211
Seven-Card Stud 212
  Your position in the betting order 214
  Odds and outs 216
  Implied odds 218
  Deception 219
  Semi-bluffing 220
  Defending 221
  Raising 222
  Free cards 224
  Slow-playing 225
  Reading your opponents 226
Seven-Card Stud Eight or Better,
  Hi-Lo Split 228
  Your position in the betting order 232
  Odds and outs 234
  Implied odds 239
  Deception 240
  Semi-bluffing 242
  Defending 243
  Raising 243
  Free cards 245
  Slow-playing 246
  Reading your opponents 247

Glossary 248
Resources 252
Index 254
Credits 256

INTRODUCTION

Poker is changing in a big way. While some folks still have an image of poker straight out of the movies, where poker games are played by Mississippi riverboat gamblers with pencil-thin moustaches, fast hands, and a derringer hidden up their sleeves, or by gunfighters of the Old West—men like Doc Holliday, Wild Bill Hickok, and Bat Masterson—that picture is 120 years old and aging.

The film The Sting *provided us with an enduring image of poker.*

The classic film *The Sting*, which starred Robert Redford and Paul Newman, gave us an image of poker played by 1930s Chicago mobsters: A round table, a low-hanging lamp illuminating thick cigar smoke, guys with shoulder holsters and snub-nosed 38s, a bottle of cheap scotch on the table, and someone the size of a heavyweight boxer stationed by the peephole at the door.

There's a kinder, gentler version too. This is the image of Uncle Jack and Aunt Maggie playing poker with their children around the kitchen table for pennies.

Poker has been all of these things and more. But in recent years it has undergone a renaissance. Like bowling and billiards before it, poker has moved away from the seedier side of its roots and out into the open; not only is it flowering, but it has become a staple on television. The advent of the "lipstick camera" makes it possible to show the viewing audience what the competitors cannot see: each player's concealed cards. This has turned poker into a spectator sport of sorts, made heroes of dozens of poker players who up until now toiled in obscurity, and created an interest in the game. As a result, thousands of new players are flocking into casinos seeking to emulate the pros.

Why you need this book

If you've never played poker seriously before, you might wonder why you need a book about it. Why can't you just sit down at the table with a few friends, watch what the pros do on television, or visit the casino and learn as you go?

Well you can, but there are better ways to go about it. The school of hard knocks can be expensive, and there's no guarantee you'll ever graduate.

Poker has never been more popular. With the advent of personal computers a great deal of research about the game has been done in recent years, and some of the tried-and-true concepts have been changing. Players need to keep their knowledge up to date or run the risk of being left behind.

This book explains the basic rules for the most popular variations of poker and provides a sound strategic approach so you can learn to play well in the shortest amount of time possible. Furthermore, its richly illustrated format makes learning easy and fun, too.

Many poker players have never picked up a book on the subject. Some even disdain this new breed of studious poker player. Although a few self-taught players are quite skillful, the majority of them are not. While they may have been playing for 20 years, they've probably been making the same mistakes day after day, month after month, and year after year.

Until you become aware of your mistakes, it's impossible to correct them. And don't think your opponents will rush to your aid by pointing them out either. After all, your opponents want to win as much of your money as you're willing to risk at the table. Whenever an opponent finds a weakness in your game, he'll exploit it for all it's worth—literally. After all, you'd do the same to him. Wouldn't you?

Poker is famous for having its own lingo. Some of the phrases and expressions such as "the buck stops here," "showdown," and Kenny Rogers' classic, "You gotta know when to hold'em, know when to fold 'em…" have migrated into general usage. While you'll learn lots of cool poker expressions from this book, we've written it in plain English, and where card jargon is used, we've clearly defined the terms for you. If you're going to become an expert poker player, you might as well sound like one too.

Even if you don't live near a casino or card room, these days it's easy to find a poker game and you don't have to venture any farther than your computer.

Assessing the strategies of poker players on television could improve your game.

You can download any one of a number of internet poker sites and compete—for play money and real money—against opponents who might be located anywhere in the world. The only difference between Internet casinos and the traditional brick and mortar card rooms and casinos is that online poker rooms are located in cyberspace, and your opponents might be in France, Finland, Zimbabwe, and Canada—or right across the street. Internet poker is a growing phenomenon, and its popularity is skyrocketing.

This book has something for everyone. Absolute beginners will learn to play relatively well in a short period of time because there is enough strategic information within these pages to jump-start much of your learning. Plus, even experienced players will gain new insights from the book as some of the concepts are quite sophisticated.

How to use this book

Each game in this book is described in a self-contained unit that has most of the information you'll need to know about that particular version of poker to set you well on your way to becoming a skilled, winning player. In addition, information common to all forms of poker supplement these game-specific chapters.

While you might not be ready to invest $10,000 to buy into the main event of the World Series of Poker, you'll find tournaments where the entry fee, not to mention the competition, is more modest. Casinos frequently hold tournaments where the cost to play is $50 or less. Many also have daily tournaments you can enter for as little as $10. You get to play against opponents at a variety of skill levels, and all you can lose is your initial investment. Tournaments are a great way to learn new games because you can limit your losses to the cost of the entry.

How this book is organized

This book begins with the basics. It explains what poker is and how to choose the game that suits you best. Whether you decide to specialize in Texas hold'em, Omaha, Omaha eight or better, hi-lo split, seven-card stud, or seven-card stud eight or better, hi-lo split—the five most popular games played in card rooms and casinos all over the world—or whether you'd like to learn and play all of these games, this book is for you. An overview of each game will help you understand the differences and similarities between these popular forms of poker and guide you as you begin to learn and expand your poker playing skills.

You'll learn hand rankings for all of these games. If you didn't know whether a flush beats a straight (it does), you'll learn why and how hand rankings were developed and you'll never confuse them again. This book will also teach you how to read your opponents and how to analyze your own hand and the possible hands held by your opponents at the table. You'll learn poker etiquette too, and along with it you'll become familiar with the mechanics of the game. Players in casinos want a smoothly flowing, efficiently dealt game, and knowing the game's mechanics along with common poker etiquette will ensure that your game progresses smoothly.

For each of the five games discussed in this book, you'll learn betting structures, what kinds of starting hands you ought to be playing, and which starting hands to fold. You'll also learn about the importance of your position in the betting order, as well as the odds and outs associated with various hands and drawing opportunities. You'll learn some fairly sophisticated strategies too, such as implied odds and semi-bluffing. This book will show you how and when to check, bet, raise, and reraise, when to fold, how to bluff, and how to defend against an opponent's bluff. You'll learn when and how to disguise a strong hand by "slow-playing" it, and when and how to get a free card.

There's a wealth of information for beginners and experienced hands alike, all easily understood and presented in a richly illustrated format. Each game is presented in a different color, so you can flip through the book and find the game you want to know about.

Texas Hold'em
Omaha
Omaha Eight
Seven Card Stud
Seven Card Stud Eight

There's also a full glossary of all the poker terms that you need to know (see page 248), and an easy-to-use key on the back jacket flap so that you can understand all the symbols used in this book. All this is guaranteed to take you from poker novice to skillful player in the quickest time possible.

With a bit of study you can leapfrog far ahead of players who may have years of experience yet are unfamiliar with some of the very sophisticated concepts presented in this book. It's all here— well most of it, anyway. To become a really skilled player you'll have to supply the dedication and effort; we can't do that for you. You'll have to read and reread this book as you think

about the game. Each time you play poker you ought to review the ideas and concepts presented in this book. This will help you to square the theory you've learned with the reality of a live poker game. It will also facilitate integrating the principles of good play into your game. But to be a winning player you'll need discipline too. While we stress the need for disciplined play throughout this book, that's all we can do. You'll have to supply the actual discipline yourself, because if you play an undisciplined game, you'll probably lose money in the long run regardless of how much you know about poker.

But enough about negatives. Just believe in yourself. If you are willing to supply the necessary discipline, we will provide the know-how you need to become a strong, winning poker player. We guarantee you'll enjoy winning a lot more than losing. Everyone does. So give it a go, dig into this book, and become a winning poker player along the way.

Internet poker is becoming more and more popular. Players from all corners of the globe play one another in cyberspace.

1

Poker Basics

WHAT IS POKER?

Poker isn't just one game. It's really a group of related games that have a number of common elements, including hand rankings, checking, betting, calling, folding, raising, bluffing, and a few other things too. Poker has been described as a game of money played with cards, and that's truer than you might realize at first glance. If money wasn't a major element in this game, poker wouldn't be a test of will and skill. It would be a game of luck, with each player retaining his or her hand until the very end, when the best hand would always win. If this were the case poker would be a game for children or a simple game for adults with very short attention spans. But it's not, and it's the element of money that makes poker the exciting game that it is.

The object of the game

Players win money by capturing a *pot* that contains all the wagers made by various players during a hand. Matching a bet is known as calling. A player bets because he believes he has the best hand, or he does so to give the impression that he holds a strong hand. When he has a weak hand but is representing a strong

A POT CAN BE WON IN TWO WAYS:

- **By showing down the best hand** When two or more players are still involved in a hand after all betting rounds are over, they show down their hands by turning them face up. The player holding the best hand wins the pot. Here's a quick tip for you. Although it's possible, but not very common, for a professional casino poker dealer to misread your hand at the showdown, always announce your hand to minimize the chances of this occurring. If you play online, the winning hand will always be correctly rewarded. As long as you've called all bets in the final round of wagering—or gone all-in, meaning you've put the remainder of your money into the pot in the course of the hand—the game's virtual dealer automatically awards the pot to the winning player, or whatever portion of it the winning player is entitled to if he or she has gone all-in.

- **When all your opponents fold** If all your opponents relinquish their claims to the pot by deciding not to match your bet, they fold—and you win. If you win because your opponents fold, you may have had the best hand, or you may have been bluffing. It doesn't matter. If all of your opponents surrender their claim to the pot, the pot belongs to you.

one, he's *bluffing*. He is hoping his opponents will relinquish their hand and along with it any claim to the money that comprises the pot by *folding*.

There's an old poker adage that says, "Money saved is just as valuable as money won," so knowing when to fold a hand that appears to be beaten is just as important as knowing when to bet.

In poker, regardless of how many cards you're dealt—and the number of cards dealt to each player varies from one form of poker to another—the best combination of five cards is the best hand.

THE BASICS

Depending on the game, any number of players—typically from two to ten—can play. Most casino games are set up with eight players for games like seven-card stud and seven-card stud eight or better, hi-lo split (which we'll call "seven-stud eight" and abbreviate to "seven-stud/8"). Typically there are nine or ten players for Texas hold'em and Omaha.

In casinos, most poker games use a standard 52-card deck. But for lowball and draw poker, a joker, or "bug," is usually added. It's not strictly a wild card since it cannot represent any card, as is so often the case in home games. Instead, the bug can be used to complete a straight or a flush, or as an additional ace in draw poker. In lowball, it's used as the lowest card that does not pair your hand. For example, if you held 8-7-5-A-joker, it would be the same as holding 8-7-5-2-A, since the deuce is the lowest card that would not pair another low card in your hand.

Because it's easier to count chips than to count various denominations of bills, chips are used for wagering. Different

Poker chips come in many different colors, styles, and weights.

denomination chips are assigned different monetary values and are manufactured in different colors, which make them easier to distinguish than money. Chips also make it easier to ensure that the pot is correct. In most American casinos money plays, but often only $100 bills are accepted, though it does vary, and those bills are usually exchanged for chips at the end of the hand. In other casinos, money never plays, and chips must be bought before the start of a hand.

Chips also contain edge spots for security reasons, and the colors usually follow a traditional arrangement. In Las Vegas, dollar chips are white, five-dollar chips are red, twenty-five dollar chips are green, one-hundred dollar chips are black, and five-hundred dollar chips are purple or lavender. The colors differ in California—which, based on the number of poker tables, is the poker capital of the world—and they vary in other countries. Internet games use virtual chips rather than real ones, but except for play money games, these virtual chips nevertheless represent real cash.

In games like Texas hold'em and seven-card stud the best hand is a high hand. In other games, like lowball and razz, the best hand is a low hand, and the best possible low hand is 5-4-3-2-A, which is known as a bicycle or a wheel. The next best low hand is 6-4-3-2-A, followed by 6-5-3-2-A, and so on. A wheel cannot be beaten; it can only be tied, in which case there would be multiple winners who would split the pot.

You'll also find split-pot games in many casinos. In these games multiple winners can split the pot. In seven-stud/8 or Omaha eight or better, hi-lo split (Omaha/8), the best high hand and the best qualifying low hand split the pot. A hand qualifies for low if it's composed of five unpaired low cards with a rank of 8 or lower. If there is no qualifying low hand, the high hand wins the entire pot.

Where it all began

While Western movies and gunfighter ballads have convinced the world that poker is a quintessentially American game, its roots go back hundreds of years before the Wild West. The Persians were said to play a poker-like game centuries ago. A bluffing game called "Pochen" was played in Germany as early as the sixteenth century, and later there was a French version called "Poque." The French brought this game with them to New Orleans, and its popularity was spread throughout that area by the paddle wheelers who traveled the Mississippi River.

Poque soon became known as poker, and the rules were modified to allow cards to be drawn to improve one's hand. Stud poker, still very popular today, appeared at about the same time.

Poker is played all over the world today, and hundreds of unique versions are played in home games everywhere.

Poker has been played in one form or another for centuries.

It's also played in casinos and poker rooms in most of the United States, England, Ireland, France, Holland, Austria, Germany, Finland, Australia, New Zealand, Aruba, Costa Rica, and many other countries. People play for pennies at home and professionally for hundreds of thousands of dollars.

WINNING RATHER THAN LOSING

Poker sharpens the intellect and, when played well, nourishes the wallet. Above all else, it forces us to think and change strategy. Players who choose to ignore these realities are usually the ones who lose consistently. Rather than face the deficiencies in their own game, they place the blame on fate, on the dealer, on that deck of cards, or on anything else handy—except themselves.

It was Jonathan Swift, some 250-odd years ago, who said, "Satire is a sort of glass wherein beholders do generally discover everybody's face but their own." The same analogy holds true for losing poker players. They see flaws in everyone's game but their own and fail to examine their own shortcomings.

Perhaps British author and poker player Anthony Holden said it best. In *Big Deal: A Year As A Professional Poker Player*, he writes: "Whether he likes it or not, a man's character is stripped bare at the poker table; if the other players read him better than he does, he has only himself to blame. Unless he is both able and prepared to see himself as others do, flaws and all, he will be a loser in cards, as in life."

Unless you are prepared to examine your poker skills and your character— and your better opponents do this every time you play them—there is little else you'll be able to do that ensures success.

That's your challenge for as long as you aspire to play winning poker: Be willing to strip your own character bare, examine and analyze it, repair it, and do it over and over again—as long as it takes to become a winner—in cards and in life. If you can stand up to this challenge and have even a modicum of talent, you will become a winning poker player.

When a player wins, she sweeps in all the chips in the pot.

PLAYING POKER

Poker is a simple game to learn, although you can spend a lifetime trying to master it. The objective of the game is to win money, which is accomplished by winning pots—the money or chips wagered during the play of each hand.

Each poker hand begins as a chase for the blind bets or the antes. If antes are used, each player must post this token amount of money in order to receive cards. If blinds are employed, one or two players are required to post a bet or a portion of a bet before the hand is dealt. This requirement rotates around the table so that each player has to pay his fair share.

Each time a round of cards is dealt, it is accompanied by a round of betting. If no one has bet and it's your turn to act, you may check or bet. If someone has already bet, your options are to fold, call, or raise. Any time a player decides to forfeit his interest in the pot, he may release his hand when it is his turn to act. When a player folds a hand, he is not required to place any additional money in the pot.

If you bet or raise and no one calls, the pot then belongs to you, the cards are collected and shuffled, and the next hand is dealt. If there are two or more players still active at the end of the hand, the best hand wins.

While there are different rules for each specific version, poker really is this simple. Yet within its simplicity lies a wonderfully textured game structure that is always fascinating and enjoyable.

Essential strategic considerations

Poker is all about strategy, and strategy is what makes the game interesting and exciting. After all, if you have no basis for making decisions about whether to call, fold, raise, or reraise, you might as well play the lottery. Strategy and knowledge provide control over your destiny at the card table.

Strategy is always based on achieving an objective of sorts, and in poker that objective is to win money. It's not to win pots. If your goal is winning the most pots, that's easy. Just play every hand until the bitter end and you'll win every pot you possibly could. But you'd lose money—and plenty of it—along the way.

Since you can't play every pot without losing your shirt, you have to be selective about the hands you decide to play. There's no need to play every hand, and you shouldn't even consider it. The very best players play relatively few hands, but when they enter a pot they are usually aggressive and out to maximize the amount they win when the odds favor them.

Here's the essence of winning poker, and it's simple: Anyone can win in the short run, but in the long run when the cards and luck even out, the better players win more money with their good hands and lose less with weak holdings than their adversaries.

Poker is a game of strategy, and there's so much available in the way of poker strategy that it is important to develop a perspective that allows you to put each piece of information, each droplet of data, each factoid, into a structure. Without this, you run the risk of being unable to see the forest for the trees.

So what's important? One way to sort through all the information that will soon be at your fingertips is to look at the decisions you make frequently. Even if the amount of money attributed to a wrong decision is small, it will add up to a tidy sum if the same error is made frequently. Always defending your small blind in hold'em or Omaha is a good example, since you have to make this decision once every nine or ten hands. If you always defend your blind, regardless of the quality of hand you've been dealt, you are investing a portion of a bet on those occasions when it is probably unwise to do so. At the end of a year, the cost of those mistakes—any one of which only involves a token sum of money—begins to add up.

DECIDING TO CALL OR FOLD

Costly decisions are also important, even if they don't come up all that often. Here's an example: Suppose you can't decide whether to call or fold once all the cards are out, and your opponent bets into a fairly large pot. This is an important decision, but it's one that's unbalanced when you stop to think about it. While you may feel it's 50-50 as to whether you or your opponent has the best hand, or maybe there's a 60 percent chance that he has the best of it, you're only considering the cards, not the money. But you really need to simultaneously consider the cards and the money involved.

After all, if you call and your opponent holds the best hand, you've cost yourself a single bet. While that's an error in judgment on your part, it's not catastrophic by any means. But if your opponent bets and you fold the best hand, you've cost yourself the entire pot—perhaps nine or ten bets, or even more—and that is a catastrophe.

While you certainly shouldn't call each and every time your opponent bets, deciding to call rather than fold really ought to be your error of choice. If the cost of a mistaken fold is ten times more costly than a bad call, then calling doesn't have to be correct too often. When that's the case, you only have to be right slightly more than 10 percent of the time to make calling worthwhile.

MAKING THE RIGHT CHOICE

Choices can also be important depending on where they occur in a game. Decisions that are first in a sequence of subsequent choices are always important because an incorrect decision up front can render each

It is important to make the right decision with your cards—bad decisions can be very expensive.

subsequent choice incorrect, regardless of whatever else you might do. That's why the choice of which starting hands you play in any poker game is so important, and usually much more critical than decisions made on subsequent betting rounds. After all, whenever you start with weak cards, you're usually doomed to play a weak hand. Most of the time there's not much you can do during subsequent betting rounds to extricate yourself from mistakes and bad judgment made earlier in the hand.

If you adopt an "any cards can win" philosophy, you will play yourself into losing situations that even the world's best players can't overcome in the long run.

CHOOSING YOUR GAME

While the number of home poker games is nearly infinite, this book concentrates on the five most popular games you'll find in card rooms, casinos, and in cyberspace, where poker can be played online for play money and real money too. Each variation is different, and some games may appeal more to certain players than others.

The games at a glance

We recommend that you learn all the games. Variety is, after all, the spice of life. You have to begin somewhere, and these guidelines will help point you in the direction you want to go.

TEXAS HOLD'EM is the most popular form of poker played in the world. It's the game used to determine each year's world champion during the World Series of Poker in Las Vegas, and is the form of poker you're probably used to seeing on television if you've watched the World Poker Tour, Late Night Poker, or the World Series of Poker.

Texas hold'em can be played at fixed limits, as a pot-limit, or a no-limit game, and is equally popular as a cash or tournament game. Texas hold'em is deceptively simple and can be learned in minutes, though it takes a lifetime to master. You'll need a variety of skills to play it well, and those who have mastered the game know all the percentages, and are also expert at "hand reading," that arcane art by which one player is able to determine what his opponent is holding. Pros do it with an accuracy that can be scary.

Some other forms of poker require a prodigious memory, but Texas hold'em is not one of them. In stud games, by comparison, players receive seven cards in their hand (some up, some down) and have to be able to recall cards that were folded in order to determine the likelihood that they, or their opponent, have made a particular hand. But in Texas hold'em all the exposed cards are there for each player to see. The exposed cards are community cards that belong to each player active in the pot and are combined with each player's personal cards to form the best five-card poker hand. These cards are never removed until the hand is over.

So if your memory is less elephantine, Texas hold'em is the game for you. In fact, we recommend you learn this game first. Not only is it the most popular game played in casinos, but also it provides a baseline for understanding and comparing other poker games.

OMAHA AND OMAHA EIGHT OR BETTER, HI-LO SPLIT (OMAHA/8) are closely related to Texas hold'em. The major structural difference is that in Omaha each player receives four personal cards instead of two, and players must form their hands by using precisely two cards from their hand—no more, no less—and three community cards. In Texas hold'em you can use two, one, or none of your cards to form the best five-card poker hand, but not in Omaha. While Omaha is played for high only and Omaha/8 is a game in which the best high hand and the best qualifying low hand split the pot, they are structurally similar to hold'em. Where they differ is in the strategies for successful play, and there they are nothing alike.

SEVEN-CARD STUD AND SEVEN-CARD STUD EIGHT OR BETTER, HI-LO SPLIT (SEVEN-STUD/8) are very different from hold'em and Omaha. While hold'em and Omaha use community cards that belong to each player, each stud player receives his or her own hand, and if they determine their hand is not worth playing, they toss it in the pile. This forces active players to track discards, so they can better estimate their own chances of making a straight or flush, while they simultaneously calculate the odds surrounding their opponents' hands. Tracking exposed cards is a required skill for playing stud games, and just like gin rummy, you'll never become much more than a mediocre player if you have no idea of the cards that are no longer in play.

If seven-card stud appeals to you more than Texas hold'em, go ahead and learn it first, by all means. But outside of the eastern seaboard of the United States, where stud has always been the game of choice—though hold'em is making inroads and may already have surpassed it in popularity even there—you won't find nearly as many stud games in casinos. In fact, in some casinos you might not find a game at all unless you're willing to try hold'em.

But if you have no preferences, we suggest that you first get a solid grounding in Texas hold'em, then learn seven-card stud. Once you have each of those forms of poker under your belt, go where you feel most comfortable. Most players in the United States gravitate from Texas hold'em to Omaha/8, while in Europe, many players go from Texas hold'em to pot-limit Omaha, or they skip Texas hold'em altogether and begin with Omaha. But Omaha's structure is rooted in hold'em, and Texas hold'em is more easily learned than Omaha.

Other players learned seven-card stud before learning hold'em. Many make the transition to Texas hold'em and never go back to stud, which seems rather tame after a few sessions playing hold'em. Others gravitate from seven-card stud and take up seven-stud/8, because the high-low split aspect of the game creates bigger pots and much more action. It is a livelier, more exciting game than seven-card stud, and one that's grown in popularity in recent years.

Regardless of which game you learn first, it's certainly advantageous to learn every form of poker. As you learn other forms of poker, you'll find new insights accruing in your primary game. Besides, it's more fun to become a well-rounded player who can play a variety of games.

Texas Hold'em: The Rules

Two players immediately to the left of a dealer button place blind bets: A "small blind" to the left of the dealer button, and a "big blind," to the small blind's left. The small blind is usually a fraction of the big blind, while the big blind is almost always the size of a small bet. With $4 and $8 dollar betting limits, the blinds are usually $2 and $4.

Once the deck is shuffled and the blinds posted, two cards are dealt face down to each active player. These are the only "private cards" each player will be dealt. All other cards are dealt face up on the table and are the communal property of all players in the hand. Each participant, starting with the player to the left of the big blind, may fold, call the big blind's bet, or raise.

The player posting the small blind has an option to fold, call, or raise, but only after everyone at the table except the big blind has already acted. The player posting the big blind acts last on this betting round, and may check if no one has raised his blind bet, or he may raise. If an opponent has raised, he may fold, call, or reraise. In most games a bet and either three or four raises are permitted on each betting round.

On the second, third, and last round of betting, the small blind acts first and may check or bet. Once a player bets, others either relinquish their interest in the pot by folding, or may call or raise. The player with the dealer button acts last on the final three betting rounds.

When the first betting round is complete, three community cards, called the "flop," are turned face-up on the center of the table, followed by another round of betting. A fourth card, called

HAND MOST LIKELY TO MAKE A STRAIGHT

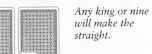

Any king or nine will make the straight.

HAND MOST UNLIKELY TO MAKE A STRAIGHT

Any two or seven paired with a four will make the straight but most players would fold with these cards.

NUT FLUSH

This is a hand that cannot be beaten.

the "turn," is dealt face-up and there's another round of betting. A fifth and final community card, called the "river," is turned face-up on the table followed by a final round of betting. If at least two players remain at the conclusion of all betting rounds, a "showdown" determines the best hand.

If the communal cards are Qc-Jd-Ts-8h-Ah, it's a lot more likely that one of your opponents has made a straight than if the communal cards on the board were Kh-6d-5h-3c-As. In the first example, anyone holding either a nine or a king in their two private cards would have a straight, while in the latter a straight requires a player to hold either a four and a deuce, or a four and a seven. Not only are two cards required to complete a straight, but most players are not going to stick around with hands like that. After all, hands like 7-4 or 4-2 are weak starting hands, and most players would fold them before the flop.

In the first case, I'd be very worried about an opponent having a straight and would probably fold my hand if it did not contain a king. But in the latter example I wouldn't even consider the possibility that an opponent held a straight. It's that unlikely.

HOW TO SUCCEED
You need to learn to be aware of when you are holding the nuts, which is how poker players describe the best possible hand. If you're holding Ad-Td and the common cards are 9d-5s-7d-8c-3d, you have the nut flush. With that combination of your two personal cards combined with three diamonds from the five communal cards, you have a hand that cannot be beaten.

Because of the communal nature of the cards, if you hold bigger cards than your opponent, you'll be starting out with a better hand and you'll usually have a better hand at the showdown.

Omaha: The Rules

Omaha is a poker game that was derived from Texas hold'em and the rules are identical, with the following two exceptions:

- You are dealt four private cards in Omaha, whereas in Texas hold'em each player receives only two.
- You must use two cards from your hand—no more, no less—in combination with three from the communal board cards to form a five-card poker hand.

This second rule gets new Omaha players into trouble, and Texas hold'em players must exercise caution in evaluating their hand as they make the jump from hold'em to Omaha. If four diamonds appear on the board and the ace of that suit is the only diamond in your hand, you do not have the best possible flush. In fact, since you must use two cards from your hand, you don't have a flush at all. That's very different from Texas hold'em, where an ace of diamonds in your hand combined with four diamonds among the five communal cards in the center of the table would give you the best possible flush.

BIG HANDS

In Omaha your four private cards can be combined to make six unique two-card starting hand combinations. Hold'em players only have one two-card combination, so big hands are a lot more likely in Omaha than hold'em. In hold'em, players form the best five-card poker hand from a combination of seven available cards: two in their hand and five community cards. But in Omaha, players form the best five-card poker

hand from a combination of nine cards: four in their hand and five on the board.

In Omaha, any hand that is possible given the configuration of board cards is also quite probable. That's not the case in hold'em. For example, if the board contains three hearts, that doesn't necessarily mean that one of your hold'em opponents has made a flush. But if those three hearts appear on the boards in Omaha and you're facing two or three opponents, one of them probably has a flush. While that hand isn't a certainty, one of your opponents will make a flush often enough so that you should condition your play as though it is a sure thing. And if you can't beat the flush you think your opponent is holding and you don't have a draw to a better hand, your best course of action is to fold.

When hold'em players are drawing to a straight, they're usually hoping to catch one of eight cards. If my two private cards are J-T and the flop is 9-8-3, I've got eight outs, and I'm hoping for either a queen or a seven to complete my straight. The chances of that happening by the river are 33 percent. But if my Omaha hand has all four of its cards in close rank proximity, I can have as many as 20 outs to a straight. That means my draw is favored over an already made hand, because with 20 outs I'll complete my straight 70 percent of the time. Not every straight draw is that good, but 20-, 13-, and 17-out straight draws happen regularly in Omaha. A 17-out straight draw will be completed 62 percent of the time, and a 13-outer will be made 50 percent of the time. Draws in Omaha can be very potent holdings.

PLAYABLE HANDS

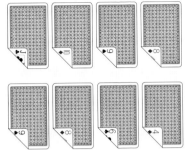

Four cards to a straight with no more than two gaps are playable.

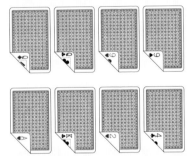

Two pair, as long as both pair are eight or higher, are playable, as are ace-king double suited to two smaller cards.

Because of this, you should play only those hands where all four cards are coordinated and work together. Four cards to a straight with no more than two gaps, such as J-T-9-8 and 9-8-6-4, are playable. So are two pair, as long as both pair are eight or higher. You can also play ace-king double suited to two smaller cards, such as Ah-Kc-2h-4c.

Big hands are frequently made in this game so you should have either the nuts or a draw to the nuts on the flop. Omaha is not a game where you want to draw to hands that are easily beaten, and if you persist in drawing to hands such as

jack-high flushes you're setting yourself up to make the second-best hand—and that's often expensive.

BEWARE BIG DRAWS

Omaha can also be deceptive because some of the time you'll flop the best hand with nothing else to go with it and your hand will be susceptible to big draws. If the flop is 7c-6c-5d and you're holding 9s-8h in your hand, you have the best hand at the moment. But any club can give an opponent a flush, and an eight or a nine might provide an opponent with a higher straight than yours. Moreover, an opponent might have a full house if the board pairs. Your hand is vulnerable. You'll find yourself hoping that neither the turn nor the river cards are clubs, that the board doesn't pair, and that neither a nine nor an eight jumps out of the deck. You'll want to see an ace, deuce, trey, four, ten, jack, queen, or king on the last two cards—as long as none of them are clubs and the board doesn't pair either. That's not too much to ask, is it?

If you suspect that big draws are likely, cautious play is best. This is very different from hold'em. When you flop the nuts in hold'em, you should be aggressive because it usually holds up.

Players new to Omaha are often surprised when they flop the second-or third-best set (three-of-a-kind), and wind up losing. In Texas hold'em, sets are big moneymakers. But in Omaha set-over-set is not unusual; you'll often see one full house beat another. Many hands that are moneymakers in hold'em are extremely vulnerable in Omaha, and should be played with caution if they are played at all. But don't worry, because you'll make your share of big hands too.

Omaha Eight or Better, Hi-Lo Split: The Rules

Omaha eight or better, hi-lo split (Omaha/8) is structurally similar to Texas hold'em. The rules are identical, with the following three exceptions:

- You are dealt four private cards in Omaha, compared to two in Texas hold'em.

- You must use two cards from your hand—no more, no less—in combination with three from the communal board cards to form a five-card poker hand.

- Omaha/8 is a split-pot game, with the best high hand winning half the pot and the best *qualifying* low hand winning the other half. Low hands must contain five unpaired cards with a rank of eight or lower to qualify. Two of them must come from the player's private cards and three from the community cards.

One player can win both the high and the low halves of the pot. This is called *scooping*. You may use any two-card combination, or combinations, to form high and low hands. Straights and flushes are ignored for low, and an ace can be used as either the highest or the lowest card in the deck—or both.

As in Omaha, Omaha/8 players should exercise caution in evaluating their hand as they make the transition from hold'em. Every Omaha/8 hand must comprise two cards from your hand and three of the five community cards in the center of the table.

The same ground rules about potentially big hands that were discussed in the preceding section on Omaha apply to Omaha/8. If a hand is possible, there's a good likelihood it's probable. Your four private Omaha/8 cards can be combined to make six different two-card starting hand combinations, and the array of these starting cards can allow you to try and build the best high hand, the best low one, or both.

Just as in Omaha, Omaha/8 players can have as many as 13, 17, and even 20 outs to a straight. But the difference is that in Omaha/8 making the best possible straight doesn't guarantee you the entire pot. You may make the best high hand, but wind up splitting the pot with an opponent's low hand.

A good guideline to follow is to play only those hands in which all four cards are coordinated and work together in some way. Because Omaha/8 is a game

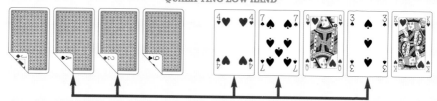

QUALIFYING LOW HAND

Low hands must contain five unpaired cards with a rank of eight or lower to qualify. Two of them must come from the player's private cards and three from the community cards.

where very big and very small hands are desirable, you're better off staying away from mid-range cards. The best starting hands contain ace-deuce, ace-trey, ace-deuce-trey or four, or four big cards. If you were to watch an Omaha/8 game long enough, you'd see these cards in most of the winning hands, and eights and especially nines (nines are the worst card in this game) in the hands of the losers.

An ace is very powerful and is akin to having two cards in your hand for the price of one because it is simultaneously the highest and lowest card in the deck. It is so powerful that many Omaha/8 players won't play any hand that doesn't contain an ace. While our advice is not that restrictive, it's important to realize that a potential low hand or a potential high hand containing an ace is usually a lot stronger than a high or low hand without one.

KNOW THE BOARD

Reading the board is the key to determining the value of your own hand. In order for someone to make a qualifying low hand, the board must contain three low cards with the rank of eight or lower. Once three low cards appear on the board, your high hand loses some of its value, because now you are vying for only half the pot, while the cost of betting and calling is still the same as it was when you had a shot at winning the whole shebang. Not only that, when three low cards appear on the board, there's also a chance that one of your opponents has made a straight in addition to a low hand and might snatch the entire pot right out from under you. But even if you've made a high hand that can't lose, such as the

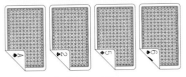

An ace and deuce

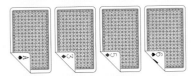

An ace and a trey

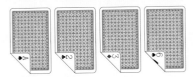

An ace, deuce, and trey or four

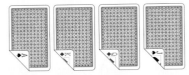

Any four big cards

best possible full house or four-of-a-kind, whenever three low cards appear on the board that sound you hear is half your pot flying away.

When you are fortunate enough to make a very big hand, one virtually guaranteeing you the high half of the pot, you must bet or raise at every opportunity to eliminate anyone drawing to a low hand, or else make it as costly as possible for them to draw for a chance to win half the pot. After all, in the event a low hand never materializes, you'll win the entire pot, and scooping is the name of the game.

Seven-Card Stud: The Rules

Seven-card stud differs dramatically from Texas hold'em and Omaha. Before cards are dealt, each seven-card stud player posts a fraction of a bet, called an ante. Players are then dealt two cards face down and one face up. The player holding the lowest-ranking exposed card is required to make a small bet, called the bring-in, to start the action. The player to the left of the bring-in has three options: fold, call the bring-in, or raise to a full bet. The next player in line has the same options, but if the first player to act raised to a full bet, the next player's options are to fold, call the full bet, or raise again.

Players then receive three more face-up cards and one final card that's dealt face down. There's a round of betting after each card is dealt. In fixed-limit games, the cost of bets and raises usually doubles with the fifth card (called fifth street). The only exception to this is when an open pair appears on fourth street, when any player may make a double bet. As in most forms of poker, the best five-card high hand wins.

Seven-card stud is an intricate game requiring lots of patience. Because each player has his or her own hand, there's a greater likelihood that an opponent will draw out on you. This can be very frustrating when you have the best hand all the way, only to see it go down in flames on the river.

Seven-card stud is a game of *live* cards. Because you'll see players folding their hands on various betting rounds, it's important to recall the exposed cards they held because these cards can affect your chances of making a hand. Suppose you're dealt Ac-3c/8c. You have three clubs and a nice start to a flush. But just how good is it? If you don't see any clubs among your opponents' exposed cards, you have a good chance of completing your hand because the clubs you need are live. But if you see three or four clubs staring up at you from your opponents' hands, your chances of completing your flush are so compromised by those three or four dead clubs that you should fold and save your money for a better opportunity.

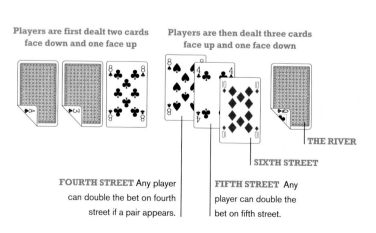

Players are first dealt two cards face down and one face up

Players are then dealt three cards face up and one face down

THE RIVER

SIXTH STREET

FOURTH STREET Any player can double the bet on fourth street if a pair appears.

FIFTH STREET Any player can double the bet on fifth street.

PAIRS

If you're fortunate enough to be dealt a premium pair (tens, jacks, queens, kings, or aces) you'll want to play. But big pairs do better against a smaller field than a large one, and you should bet or raise in order to eliminate any opponents who might otherwise stick around in hopes of making a flush or a straight. On the other hand, if you're the one who has three to a straight or a flush and the cards you need are live, you'll want as many players in the pot with you as possible. After all, straights and flushes are big hands, and while you won't make them too often even when you begin with live cards, a gaggle of opponents usually ensures that one or two will stick around to pay you off whenever you're fortunate enough to complete your hand.

You have just received your first three strategic guidelines for seven-card stud:
- Play live hands.
- Play big pairs against a few opponents.
- Play flush and straight draws against a large field.

Small and medium pairs are not nearly as good as premium pairs, and how you play them usually depends entirely on your side card. If you have a side card bigger than any of your opponents' up-cards, and it's live, you can play. But the key card is your kicker, not your mid-range pair. You'd like to pair your kicker or make three of a kind, but you're not nearly as well situated as you would be if you had a big pair from the get-go. However, if you have a small or medium pair and you catch big, live cards on fourth and fifth street, it's okay to chase an opponent who seems to have one bigger pair than you, or even two pair, as long as your other cards are live and bigger than his largest pair.

KNOWLEDGE AND ASSUMPTION

When you're playing seven-card stud it's always important to remember exposed cards, and to know which of your cards are live. You also have to make some assumptions about cards your opponent might need to help his hand. For example, if your first three cards were 9c-Js/Th, you have a good start at making a straight. If you look at the exposed cards your opponents are holding and don't see any eights or queens, you should continue with your draw, since all the cards you need are live. But if you saw those needed cards among your opponent's up-cards, your hand ought to be released.

Because seven-card stud is a game of live cards, it makes sense to only play hands that have a good chance to improve. Sticking around with a weak hand and hoping for a miracle is a prescription for disaster.

Seven-card stud is a game of strategy, and it requires an ability to understand your chances of making the hand you're drawing to, based on the exposed cards you've seen. Expert seven-card stud players know how to deduce what their opponents might have based on a combination of folded hands, exposed cards, how aggressively their opponents are betting, and how their opponents react to other players' bets and raises. Once you learn this and you have the patience required to play this game, you'll do just fine in seven-card stud.

Seven-Card Stud Eight or Better, Hi-Lo Split: The Rules

The mechanics of seven-card stud eight or better, hi-lo split (seven-stud/8) are similar to seven-card stud. Each player posts an ante before being dealt two cards face down and one face up. The player holding the lowest-ranking exposed card is required to make the bring-in bet, to start the action. Once that round of betting is complete, players receive three more open cards and one final card, which is dealt face down. Again, there's a round of betting after each card is dealt. Most games are fixed-limit or spread-limit games, in which the cost of bets and raises usually doubles with the fifth card (called fifth street). Unlike seven-card stud, no double bet may be made if a pair appears on fourth street. The best five-card high hand and the best five-card qualifying low hand—to qualify a low hand must contain five unpaired cards with a rank of eight or lower—split the pot.

HIGHS AND LOWS

Seven-stud/8 differs from seven-card stud because players are trying to make high hands, low hands, and sometimes both. As in other split-pot games, straights and flushes are ignored for low and an ace is simultaneously the highest and lowest card in the deck. Because an ace can take a player in two directions at once it is an incredibly powerful card, and more valuable than any other card in this game. Suppose you've been dealt 8c-6d/4h. You have the makings of a low hand. However, it's a one-way hand because there's little chance of making a straight or flush with that combination of cards. What if you're raised by a player showing an ace? You can't tell

QUALIFYING LOW HAND

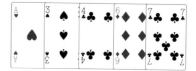

The qualifying low hand must be five unpaired cards with a rank of eight or lower and splits the pot with the high hand.

whether he's trying to build a high hand or a low one, and you might be on shaky ground if you contest him. Actually, his ace gives him a higher hand than you at this point, and if he has a low draw, it's probably better than yours too. His ace has you surrounded in both directions, and even though you're starting with three low cards, you'd probably be better off not playing.

Seven-stud/8 is similar to seven-card stud where exposed cards are concerned. It's important to know which of your cards are live, and which cards your opponent presumably needs. For example, if your first three cards were 5s-As/7s, you have a good start at making a flush as well as a low hand. If you look at the exposed cards your opponents are holding and don't see a spade or any low cards (deuce, trey, four, six, and eight) that will help your hand, you should continue with your draw, since all the cards you need are live. But if you see three spades among your opponent's up-cards as well as several low cards that you need, you're a long shot for making a flush, a low hand, or both.

Like seven-card stud, seven-stud/8 is a game of live cards, and you should only play hands that have a good chance of

GOOD STARTING HANDS

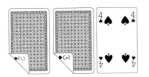

Three cards to a small straight or flush is a good start for both a high and low hand.

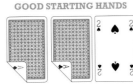

Two aces and a low card is a good start for both a high and low hand.

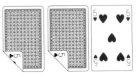

Rolled up trips won't make a low hand, but a low hand isn't always made; and when it isn't, your big hand will scoop the pot.

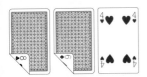

Shows a good start at making a low hand, but if you are raised by a player with an ace, you'd be better off folding.

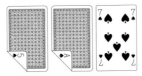

Shows a good start at making a flush as well as a low hand. Playing on depends on the other players' cards.

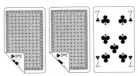

Big pairs are also good starting hands but be wary if you see an ace on the board.

improving. It is also a game of singularity. If you are the only player with a low draw, you'll do well if you make your low against two or three players who are vying for the high end of the pot.

DON'T SPLIT, SCOOP

As in all split-pot games, the general idea is to scoop the pot, not split it. You should look for starting hands that have the potential of winning both the high and low side of the pot. These would include rolled-up trips (they won't make a low hand, but a low hand isn't always made; when it isn't, your big hand will probably scoop the pot), three cards to a small straight or flush, and two aces with a low card.

You can also play starting hands like big pairs, such as kings or queens, but be wary if you see an exposed ace on board. You might be beaten for high as

well as low, and if an ace raises, you would be better off releasing that one-way pair of kings. The general pattern of betting is that high hands drive the action early on because regardless of how good a low draw may appear, it cannot be completed until fifth street. However, once a low hand appears to be completed, the high hands generally slow down, particularly if it appears that the low hand might also be freerolling to a high hand by combining a straight or flush with their low cards.

If you have experience playing seven-card stud but are frustrated because you don't seem to often be dealt hands you can play, you might want to try seven-stud/8. This game has lots of action because of the split-pot nature of the game. With players going in two different directions, pots can often get quite large.

HAND RANKINGS

Poker is played with a standard 52-card deck composed of four suits: spades, hearts, diamonds, and clubs. There are thirteen ranks in each suit.

The ace is the highest-ranking card, followed by the king, queen, jack, and then ten through deuce. In split-pot games, an ace is also used as the lowest-ranking card for forming a low straight or a low hand. In such "split" games, aces are like two cards in one, simultaneously the highest- and lowest-ranking card in the deck. Because of this, an ace in your Omaha/8 or seven-stud/8 hand is a decided advantage.

In draw poker and lowball, a joker (or bug) is usually added to the deck. This is not really a wild card, but one that serves as an extra ace in draw poker, as well as a card that can be used to complete straights and flushes. In lowball, it is the lowest-ranked card not in your hand, so if you held 8-5-3-A-Joker, the bug would be used as a deuce to make the low hand 8-5-3-2-A.

Hand rankings are arranged in order of probability. The rarer the hand, the more valuable it is, so the higher it is ranked. Here are the rankings, shown in descending order from highest to lowest:

ROYAL FLUSH

A♠-K♠-Q♠-J♠-T♠
A♥-K♥-Q♥-J♥-T♥
A♦-K♦-Q♦-J♦-T♦
A♣-K♣-Q♣-J♣-T♣

A royal flush is an ace-high straight flush. It's the best possible hand in poker, and there are only four of them.

You can go a lifetime and never get a royal flush, but we hope you do.

STRAIGHT FLUSH

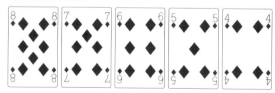

This thrilling holding is made up of five sequenced cards, all of the same suit, such as 8♦-7♦-6♦-5♦-4♦ or Q♣-J♣-T♣-9♣-8♣.

In the unlikely event that two people have a straight flush, then the rank of the highest card decides the winner.

FOUR-OF-A-KIND

Four-of-a-kind, or quads, is a five-card hand containing four cards of any rank, plus one unrelated card, such as 9♠-9♥-9♦-9♣-3♥.

The higher the rank, the better the hand. For example, four queens easily beats four deuces.

FULL HOUSE

Three cards of any given rank with a pair of another is a full house. A hand like J♠-J♥-J♦-4♣-4♥ is referred to as "jacks full of fours." If you held 4♣-4♠-4♦-J♥-J♣, it would be called "fours full of jacks."

The rank of a full house is determined by the three cards, not the pair.

FLUSH

Any five cards of the same suit make a flush. The cards do not have to be sequenced—if they were, you'd have a straight flush.

If there are two or more flushes at showdown, the winning hand is decided by rank order. For example, an ace-high flush is better than one that is king-high.

STRAIGHT

Five sequenced cards, not of the same suit, make a straight.

If there's more than one straight, the high cards in each sequence determine the winning hand, for example a nine-high straight beats a six-high straight. A five-high straight is also known as a "wheel" or "bicycle."

THREE-OF-A-KIND

Three cards of the same rank plus two unrelated cards is called three-of-a-kind.

Sometimes you'll hear players refer to it as trips, or a set. If your best five-card hand was K ♦ -K ♥ -K ♣ -2 ♠ -4 ♥ , you could call it "a set of kings," or "trip kings." It's all the same hand.

TWO PAIR

Two cards of one rank, two cards of another, and one unrelated card make two pair.

If two players each have two pair, the holder of the highest ranking pair is the winner. If each player has the same high pair, the rank of the second pair decides the winner. If both hold the same two pair, the rank of the side card determines the winner.

ONE PAIR

One pair is composed of two cards of one rank plus three unrelated side cards. If two players hold the same pair, the highest side card, or "kicker," determines the winning hand.

NO PAIR

No pair is five unrelated cards, with the rank order determining the winner. For example, if player one has A-K-8-5-3 and player two has A-J-T-7-3, player one wins—A-K is higher than A-J.

RANKINGS OF LOW HANDS IN SPLIT-POT GAMES

The best low hand composed of five unrelated cards with a rank of eight or lower captures half of the pot when you're playing Omaha/8 or seven-stud/8. A hand like 7♠-6♠-5♥-3♥-2♦ beats 8♠-5♦-4♦-2♣-A♣, but loses to 7♥-5♠-4♣-2♥-A♥.

The worst possible qualifying low hand is 8-7-6-5-4, while the best low hand—called a wheel or a bicycle—is 5-4-3-2-A. A wheel can be tied, in which case all players holding wheels split the low end of the pot, but it can't be beaten. Because a wheel is also a 5-high straight, it stands a good chance of being the best high hand as well as the best low hand. If it is, and it's the only wheel, the proud holder of that wheel "scoops" the entire pot.

COMMON POKER TERMS

You will find a full glossary at the end of this book, but here are a few terms you'll need to get you started in a game. Each of these terms are common to most poker games.

ante A mandatory bet made before any cards are dealt.

bet A wager of any sort; the action required by a player whose turn it is to act and who wishes to wager money on his poker hand.

betting round The phase in a hand in which each active player has the option to fold, bet, call, or raise. This phase almost always follows the appearance of a new card or cards in players' hands or on the board. A standard betting round consists of one bet and three or four raises, depending on house rules.

blind A bet made by a designated player or players in games such as Texas hold'em and Omaha, before the initial deal. A blind becomes part of that player's bet if he comes into the pot, as compared to an ante, which is a separate bet.

board The five community cards in hold'em and Omaha, or a player's four exposed cards in seven-card stud or seven-stud/8.

bring-in The amount required to open a pot. In stud games it is a token wager—something less than a full bet—made by the player with the smallest exposed card. In a $20–$40 seven-card stud game, the antes are usually $3 each, and the bring-in, or first forced bet, is $5. Players acting in turn must then either fold, call the bring-in, or raise to the amount of a full $20 bet. In a no-limit game, a statement such as, "I'll bring it in for $50" implies a wager that exceeds the minimum bet, and is the same thing as saying "I'll open for $50."

call To match a bet made by another player. By calling, a player retains his interest in the hand and is eligible to win the pot as long as he calls each bet to the showdown.

check To make no bet, but to still hold your hand. A check is, in essence, a bet of nothing. If John is first to act, he may check and he retains his option to fold, call, or raise when the action gets back to him. The only time a player may not check when first to act is when there is either a blind bet on the first round of a hold'em or Omaha game, or a forced bring-in bet on the first round of a seven-card stud or seven-stud/8 game. Then he must fold, call, or raise in order to remain in the hand. After the initial betting round, the first player to act may always check. And if he checks, so may each additional player in the betting order, until someone wagers. If all players check, another card is dealt and another round of betting takes place.

check-raise To check initially and then raise an opponent who bets behind you.

community cards Cards that are dealt face up on the table and which belong equally to each player active in the hand, as in Texas hold'em or Omaha.

door card In stud games, the first exposed card in each player's hand.

down card Any card dealt face down to a player; a hole card.

flop The first three board cards in games like hold'em and Omaha.

fold To withdraw from participation in the hand and surrender any equity in the pot. A fold is tantamount to saying, "My hand probably won't win so I'll surrender all I've contributed thus far and while I won't be eligible to win the pot, I won't have to call any additional bets either."

heads-up Playing one-on-one, head-to-head, mano-a-mano; when there are exactly two players in a game, such as in a tournament when only two players remain.

hole cards Any cards dealt face down to a player and which are for that player's use only; a down card.

pot limit A betting structure in which the size of a player's bet is limited only by the current size of the pot.

pot odds The ratio of the size of the pot compared to the size of the bet a player must call to continue in the hand. For example, if the pot contains $10, and you must call a $5 bet; this gives you pot odds of 2-to-1.

raise To increase the wager. In a game with fixed-betting limits, such as $4–$8, this means adding a bet equal to the betting limit. In a no-limit game it means increasing the bet by any amount equal to or greater than the previous bet or raise. In a pot-limit game it means increasing the bet by any amount equal to or greater than the previous bet or raise, up to an amount equal to the size of the pot. In a spread-limit game it means adding a bet of any amount within the betting range. For example, if

the spread was $2–$10, a player could raise anywhere between those limits.

reraise The act of raising the bet of a player who has already raised. In limit games, the size of the reraise is defined by the betting limits, but in spread-limit, pot-limit, and no-limit games, the size of the reraise must be at least equal to the size of the raise that preceded it. For example, if Tom bets $2, Joe raises $4, and Mary reraises, the amount of her reraise will be $4 in a game with fixed limits (meaning that the next player will have to fold or match the $10 total of Tom's bet, Joe's raise, and Mary's reraise), but in a spread-limit game Mary's reraise may fall anywhere within the structure as long as it is $4 or more (in a $2–$10 spread-limit game, she is eligible to raise anywhere from $4–$10). In a pot-limit game, she may match her opponent's raise of $4 and then raise any amount up to the size of the pot, and in a no-limit game she is eligible to reraise anywhere from $4 to any amount of money Mary has in front of her on the table.

the river The final card that precedes the last round of betting in a given hand.

showdown The point in a hand when all the betting is over and the players still vying for the pot turn their cards face up to determine the winning hand or hands.

street A betting round in poker which follows the introduction of a new card or cards during a hand.

the turn The fourth community card to be revealed in games like Omaha and hold'em.

READING YOUR OPPONENTS

Some players are like open books; others as inscrutable as a foggy night. If you knew what your opponents' cards were, you'd almost never lose because you'd always make the right decision. You still wouldn't win all the time because any player can get lucky and beat you if the deck delivers the card he needs at just the right moment. Nevertheless, the better you are at deducing what your opponent is holding, the better your results will be.

Watching body language and strategies

Figuring out your opponent's hand is often a combination of two skills:
- Picking up "tells"—those voluntary and involuntary physical signs that suggest when a player is bluffing and when he really has the goods.
- Deducing your opponent's hand or determining a broader range of hands that he might have, based on what he does with the cards he's dealt.

Both of these skills presuppose that you've spent time playing against your opponent because body language, as well as betting and raising patterns, are quite individualistic. A reraise from a conservative player usually means something quite different from a reraise from a loose, aggressive player.

Reading opponents is a delicate blend of skill and art. To accurately read players, you have to watch them play. The best time to study your opponents is when you're not involved in a hand. Many players who have difficulty picking up tells and can't accurately predict an opponent's probable hand are those who don't pay attention when they are not playing. They're easy to spot because they're usually chatting to someone, or else just oblivious to all the information that is swirling around

them when they're not actively involved in a hand.

If you aspire to excellence in poker, you need to use your free time to your best advantage. You need to study how your opponents play the cards they're dealt, while looking for nonverbal clues and cues about the strength of their hands.

There's no mystery to this. You're simply scouting opponents to learn their tendencies. Do they come out betting from an early position with strong hands, or do they look for opportunities to check-raise and slow-play? Which opponents bet their drawing hands aggressively? Who checks and calls until his hand is complete? Who always bets his big hands, and which opponents are tricky players who try to lure you to bet so they can trap you by check-raising? Does Heather only bluff against three or more opponents? Does Scott like to get the last raise in regardless of whether he has a suitable hand?

DECIPHERING BETTING PATTERNS

By examining your opponents' betting patterns against the hands they reveal at the showdown, you can uncover their playing style. It may surprise you, but good players are more easily read than weak opponents, because a good player's actions are predicated on logic and consistency. Against a logical opponent your job is to uncover the reason behind his action and put him on a hand.

It's tough to accomplish this when you're confronting weak players, particularly those who operate on whim. Sometimes you can figure them out because they give off more tells than stronger players. Other times you won't be able to figure out a hunch-player at all. When that happens, all you can do is play your own hand for whatever intrinsic value it has. If you do that and are aggressive with your good hands, you should regularly beat your opponent.

When an opponent flies by the seat of his pants, good solid poker is all that's required in the long run. And while a weak, whim-based player might get lucky for a while, he won't come out ahead in the long run unless his erratic play puts you off so much that you start to play worse poker than he does.

The easiest way to read a player is to suppose a variety of possible hands that he may hold, based on how he acts initially, and then narrow down those possibile hands based on the cards that appear and how he plays from one betting round to the next. You can also anticipate later plays in terms of how your opponent played his hand on earlier betting rounds.

Shannon raises before the flop. Since many hold'em players always raise when they have a pair of jacks, queens, kings, or aces, or with big cards like A-K, A-Q, A-J, or K-Q, you suspect she might have some of those hands. She bets a flop of 9h-6h-4d. At this point you think she might have a big pair, or else she has missed the flop entirely and is bluffing. You can't tell for sure, but because she did raise before the flop, you're pretty sure the low cards that flopped did not help her.

If the flop helped you, you probably have the better hand because there's a greater chance that Shannon holds two high cards than a big pair. After all, there are only six ways to make a pair of aces, or any other pair for that matter, but 16 ways to make A-K or any combination of two unpaired cards. If you know she would raise only with the cards shown above, there are 24 possibilities that she has a big pair and 64 chances she's raising with big connecting cards.

By using simple arithmetic you know that Shannon is two-and-a-half times more likely to have big cards than a big pair. If you're holding a hand like T-9, you can call or even raise if you think she is trying to steal the pot from you.

If you raise and she calls, she probaby has big cards provided she's a moderately skilled player. After all she would probably reraise with a pair that's bigger than the highest board card. On the other hand, if she's a tough, tricky player, she just might call, hoping to trap you for an additional wager on the next round when the cost of betting doubles.

Suppose an ace comes on the turn and she bets into you. You raised on the flop, so you can assume the ace helped her. She may have a set of aces and an insurmountable lead over your hand, or she may have A-K or A-Q, in which case she is firmly in the lead with one card to come. Unless you have reason to suspect she is continuing to bluff, you'll save money by releasing your hand.

Here's another, very simple example of deducing a player's hand by the betting patterns. Suppose you're holding Ac-Jd and the flop is Ah-9s-4h. Looks sweet, doesn't it? You've flopped top pair with a good, strong kicker. There's no possible straight draw, and it's not the kind of flop that will give someone two pair. Your opponent checks, then calls when you bet. The turn card is 6d and the action mirrors what transpired on the flop. Your opponent checks. You bet. He calls. But now he comes out betting when the 2h shows up on the river, putting three hearts on the board and making a flush possible.

This is a common situation. Your opponent was checking and calling all the way, a pretty good indication that he had a drawing hand. After all, if he had a hand that could beat a pair of aces on the turn, he either would come out betting or would have check-raised once you bet. But he didn't. He waited to bet until the board made a flush possible.

What should you do now? If this player seldom bluffs, you can safely release your hand. If your opponent likes to bluff and does so every time a card appears that supports this sort of play, you can call. If he was bluffing, you've caught him. But if he's a tough, tricky player who bluffs occasionally, you're faced with a dilemma. He could have a flush or he could be bluffing; there's no way to know for sure. If this

is the case, your best option probably is to call his bet. If you err by calling when he has the best hand, you've cost yourself one extra bet. But if you fold the winning hand, you've cost yourself the entire pot. And that's an error of greater magnitude.

STUDYING YOUR OPPONENTS

The trick to reading an opponent's hand is to suppose a variety of hands at the start of play and eliminate possibilities based on his play and the cards he catches. It's deductive logic; the kind made famous by Sherlock Holmes. By the end of a hand you should be able to assess your own chances in relation to what you think your opponent is holding. You don't even need to be all that specific. It doesn't matter if your opponent has a flush, a straight, or two pair, if all you have is one pair.

However, usually it's not that simple, and you're often forced to decide if your opponent has a much better hand than you or if he's bluffing. If all you can beat is a bluff, you need to assess your chances in relation to the size of the pot and decide whether to call or throw your hand away.

There's no magic to reading hands; simply practical logic and a knowledge of how your opponent plays in a variety of situations. Study your opponents, and with a bit of practice, you'll learn to read them.

Tells

Tells are a bit different. They are simply a combination of behavioral patterns; involuntary physical reactions like veins that pulsate on an opponent's neck when someone's holding a powerhouse hand, body language, or vocal patterns. All of these can provide information about an opponent's hand.

These physical manifestations come in two forms: involuntary body language and acting. A player who dramatically takes his chips and pounds them into the table is more likely indicating that he has a weak hand and wants his posturing to convince you otherwise than it is to represent a powerful hand. Acting weak when you have a strong hand and strong when you have a weak one is just that: It's an act. On the other hand, when a player's hand trembles involuntarily as he gathers his chips and tosses them toward the pot, it's usually a sign of a very strong hand.

Understanding tells is enough to turn a break-even player into a winner. That's true even if you're able to spot only one tell every few hours, especially if that tell either wins a hand for you that would have been lost, or causes you to fold when you would have called—and found yourself trapped behind subsequent raises. Tells are too powerful to ignore. Some are obvious; others are subtle. There are some tells you can read with absolute certainty. There are other tells that players emit only part of the time. Moreover, a tell for one person might not be a tell for another.

Consider, for example, the most common of them all. Tell number one: Players holding weak hands act strong,

and when they're strong, they act weak. That's a tell you can rely on with a high degree of certainty in most low-limit games. But it's not foolproof because you'll always find some players who act strong when they are strong and weak when they're weak. Even if this tell is accurate in your game only 70 percent of the time, it's still a significant improvement over a 50/50 guess.

If an extremely tough player suspects you're reading tells, he might toss out a counter tell to confuse you. If he's sharp, he'll act weak when he's strong, and once he figures that you've established a read on that, he'll reverse himself—but only with you—by acting strong when he *is* strong. He knows that you've read him for a weak hand and that you now presume he is bluffing. Once he knows that his counter tells have confused you, he'll probably start randomly interspersing counter tells with his normal style of play so you'll seldom be able to get an accurate read on him.

Even in games where there are other means of discerning what an opponent might have, tells are incredibly valuable tools. When combined with observations about an opponent's betting pattern, an awareness of the cards that have been exposed, and a knowledge of whether his playing style is tight or loose, aggressive or passive, there's lots of information available to make good decisions at the poker table.

Tells along with other information picked up during a game provide the mean for us to divert from the book play in order to make a better play.

ANALYSIS AT THE TABLE

At its core, poker is all about risk versus reward. Decisions regarding risk-reward questions are usually made with incomplete information and precious little time to analyze situations in anything resembling studious detail. Do you bet if your opponent checks you? Do you call if he bets? If you check because you're hoping to raise, what are the chances that your opponent will cooperate by betting?

Making rapid assessments

Lots of time could be spent analyzing these situations, and long hours could be devoted to a post-mortem analysis of your decisions. But when you're at the table, you don't have much time to think about what you might do. You have to move quickly. Chess players are luckier. They have the luxury of spending a long time thinking about their next few moves when they get into dicey situations. As long as they're not in "time trouble," they can carefully evaluate any number of moves. Poker players can take some time on occasion—when you're in a no-limit tournament and are faced with a decision that would require you to commit your entire stack of chips. Most of the time, however, you just can't sit there thinking about what you might do. Poker has a bias for action built into it. Players expect a fast-paced game and there are times when you'll have to make a move even if your mind is pleading for more time to think.

If you're a serious poker player, you know it's tough to win consistently without exercising your mental muscles. The job of a poker player comprises a variety of factors found in every job, though in varying degrees. Whether a job is as simple as sorting the big eggs

from the small ones on a production line, or as complex as nuclear physics, each job requires a specialized knowledge base, as well as some degree of critical thinking, problem solving, and accountability for results. While poker players don't have the headaches that come from supervising others, you alone are responsible for the results you achieve.

As a poker player, your job is really one of gathering knowledge and being able to apply it in the heat of battle. Thinking on your feet, as it were, is where the proverbial rubber meets the road.

So what about poker? Is it a deep-thinking game like chess, or does it demand quick decision-making? It's true that poker requires substantial thought. But it also requires quick decision-making, since you do not have an unlimited amount of time at the table to decide whether to check or bet, or fold, call, raise, or reraise.

Poker requires a reservoir of know-how

In poker the successful player must be able to quickly tap into a vast reservoir of information. Since there's no time for leisurely thought, success demands that you gain all the knowledge you can while you are away from the table. Once you are able to deal with difficult situations in a controlled or simulated environment, you'll be better able to make the correct decision in the real world. By putting that theoretical knowledge into practice, you will mold it into practical know-how.

Decision-making at the table

Poker requires that certain decisions be made in the heat of battle. It's clear that you can't subject each situation you encounter to lengthy analysis. You don't have the time or tools to take a situation and run a 100,000 hand simulation to determine the best strategy. You have to act right away!

Since you have only a short amount of time in which to make decisions, what kind of thinking and analysis should you be doing at the table?

Categorizing your opponents

First, gather as much information as you can. Observe each of your opponents and categorize their play: loose, tight, aggressive, weak-tight, calls too often, prone to bluff, likes to check-raise good hands on the turn, etc.

Since your playing strategy will be guided by the nature of your opponents, you need to categorize their play before you are faced with a decision in which an opponent's playing style is a critical factor.

For example, suppose you raised before the flop with A-Q and by the turn the board shows Q-6-7-8 of mixed suits. You're up against one opponent who called your raise from the small blind. When you bet the turn, he raises!

If you know your opponent to be a very loose, habitually bluffing player who is currently losing and on tilt, you'd call. You might even reraise. On the other hand, if the player who raised was an extremely tight player who seldom bluffed, you'd probably figure him for a big hand and you'd throw yours away!

None of this is very exotic from a strategic viewpoint. But unless you invested the time to categorize your opponents before you played them, you'd have no other option than to guess about their play.

Not only is it important to categorize your opponents play, but you have to keep doing this throughout the game. Most of us don't play the same way all the time. Some play well for the first thirty minutes, then they get caught up in gambling and their strategy slips. When they notice they're almost broke, they either tighten up, or go to the other extreme, betting their last dollars on anything in a frenzy to break even. If they do get even, watch out. That once loose opponent now tightens up—playing well in an attempt to hold on to the money he miraculously won back.

During the play of a hand, you don't have time for much complex analysis. Once you have a lot of game experience, you won't run into many new situations. Most will be analogous to others you've faced before. That's why there is no substitute for real-game experience coupled with theoretical knowledge that you've molded into practical know-how. Expertise at poker comes from a cycle of reading and studying poker, playing, and thinking about the game.

Always be aware of pot odds

Regardless of whatever knowledge you bring to the game, there is always some at-the-table decision-making to do. At a minimum you must always be aware of the pot's size. While it is not critical that you mentally count each pot to the last dollar, you do need to know roughly how much is in the pot at any one time.

If you don't know how much the pot is offering you, then there's no way to properly evaluate the odds against

making your hand compared to the odds offered by the pot.

You need to keep track of the size of the pot to know whether it's sufficient to warrant calling with a less than great hand.

Putting your opponent on a hand…or hands

It is critical that you put your opponent on a hand (in other words, figure out what hand they may possibly have). Many players make the mistake of putting their opponent on a single hand and never change their assumption, but it is better to put your opponent on groups of hands, then eliminate as many as you can based on how he plays on succeeding streets.

Here's an example. No one has called the blinds, and you raise in fifth position with a pair of tens. The player to your immediate left reraises you. No one else calls, except the big blind, who calls for the single additional bet. You call too. At that point, you can put the raiser on any number of hands. Let's assume the raiser is an average player. He might have reraised with any pair from 9's through aces. He could also have reraised on A-K, A-Q, A-J, or even A-10 (though the latter three are not prime reraising hands), as well as with some very marginal hands like K-Q or K-J. If he raised with a big pair, he's in the lead. If he raised with big cards, you have the edge.

Suppose the flop is 9-7-3 of mixed suits. The blind checks, you bet to test the quality of your hand, and your opponent raises. The big blind folds and you call. What kinds of hand can you put him on? You can eliminate his having flopped a set, since he would have called with a hand like that and planned to raise on the turn—when the bets double.

He could have raised with any pair bigger than the highest board card. He might bluff-raise with a hand like A-K, if he suspects you are holding connectors like A-Q, A-J—or even A-K. Remember, he isn't sure what your hand is, either. And he's trying to find out.

With a pair of tens, you're not sure where you stand. If your opponent is playing big cards, you're in the lead. But if he does have a pair, it's undoubtedly bigger than yours. You call. The turn card comes and it is an 8. Now you're holding overpair with a straight draw. You check and your opponent checks after you. Even though there are three sequenced cards on the board, you know your opponent is a good enough player to realize you probably would not have raised before the flop with a hand like J-10, and certainly not with T-6 or 6-5. Consequently, he does not check because you might have a straight.

You now assume he has a hand that probably can't beat two pair and may not beat one big pair. Now you figure him for big connectors, with some possibility that he has a pair of queens or jacks.

Unless a jack or six falls on the river, you plan to check. If your opponent is playing big connectors, he might bet on the river, and you will gain one additional bet by snapping off his bluff. If he checks behind you, you have not cost yourself anything, since he probably would not have called your last bet without at least a big pair.

Even without playing this hand to its conclusion, you can see how you put your opponent on a fairly wide variety of possible hands. Through deductive reasoning based on how the hand is played out, it became possible to define the hand your opponent might have.

In real life, you have one other significant advantage. By knowing your opponents, you will have a strong idea of their strategies. The better you know your opponents, the easier it will be to make the correct decision under pressure, and the more confident you'll be that your decision is correct. That's why you'll seldom see a top player regretting that he threw away a hand. When a marginal player tosses a hand away, he'll inevitably spend time bemoaning the fact that he might have had the bettor beaten. The top player will be quite certain that his hand is not worth a call by the time he discards it. Because of that, he is much less likely to make crying calls that have no chance of winning. As a result, he presents a much slimmer target for his opponents to shoot at—and saves money in the process. And what you don't spend, you don't have to earn!

ETIQUETTE

Poker, like all singular endeavors, has its own form of etiquette that's grown up around the game, and it's something that everyone learns when they begin to play regularly. We all behave differently depending on our circumstances because we've been conditioned that way. That's part of etiquette. And what's considered okay in one endeavor may be considered rude in others.

You're expected to scream your head off at a horse race or boxing match but maintain complete silence while you're standing by the 18th hole, watching a top-notch golfer putt for a championship. Why is it okay to scream at one event when you're expected to remain perfectly silent at another? Who knows? It's just etiquette—that unwritten code of conduct that's grown up around the event. It's part of the culture. And poker, like boxing, horse racing, and how you behave when visiting your in-laws, has a set of unwritten rules all its own.

Rules and protocol

Most of poker's rules and protocol exist to speed things along and keeps the game orderly. The rules of etiquette are part and parcel of poker—just like the cards and chips. In fact, the very first time you venture into a casino or card room, poker's protocol and etiquette may take more getting used to than the actual game itself.

Act in turn Not just protocol, but a rule of the game, each player must act in turn as play proceeds clockwise around the table. This protects a player from providing too much information to opponents. If John bets and you plan to fold your hand, wait your turn before doing so. If you act out of turn, your opponent will have an advantage if he tries to bluff, because he won't consider your course of action before making his decision. If you're playing online, this won't ever happen since the software doesn't allow you to act out of turn.

Keep your cards in plain sight Keeping your cards on the table and in plain sight is another rule that helps maintain the integrity of the game. The best way to protect your hand is to keep it on the table and look at the cards by shielding them with your hands while lifting a corner of each card and peeking at it. If you're playing online, there's no need to worry. No one else can see your cards, not even technicians at the game's headquarters. The cards, or to be more precise, the representations of your cards, are transmitted to your computer only; they do not reside at the host computer, and no one can hack into the server and learn what you have.

Don't discuss hands in play During World War II the Allies used to say, "Loose lips sink ships," and that's good advice at the poker table too. Discussing your hand with others at the table, even if you have released it and are no longer contesting that particular pot, may yield information that provides an opponent with an edge. If you're playing online and sending instant messages to a buddy who's also in the game, or colluding via telephone, you're not just stepping outside the bounds of etiquette, you're cheating, plain and simple. Although it may be easier to chat about hands online, the sophisticated game software and hand histories stored in game servers make it much easier for online casinos to spot any irregularities that may be going on.

Toking Tipping the dealer—it's called "toking" in poker parlance—is customary when you win a pot. If you're unsure of how much to toke, just take your cues from others at the table. There's no toking online, which is one advantage of playing on the Internet.

Be honest Don't try to shortchange the pot or otherwise cheat. In a casino, cheating can get you barred or arrested; in a home game, the punishment might be much worse.

Play quickly Everyone wants a speedy, efficient game.

Be a good winner and a courteous loser Don't gloat. Don't make fun of other players, and don't whine when you lose. You won't be the first player to lose to an impossible draw against long odds. Bad bets happen to everyone, and no one really wants to hear about it.

Don't give lessons at the table Poker's defining rule is this: One player per hand. Don't give an active player advice during the play of a hand, and don't advise him after the hand's conclusion, either. You'll anger that player or possibly others at the table.

Don't look at another player's hand He won't like it and neither will anyone else at the table. Some things are still private in this world and poker hands are among them.

Demeanor at the table Patterns of culture vary from society to society and what's acceptable table demeanor in one country might be considered downright rude in another. In the U.S. poker players can be a loud, unruly lot, given to comments and snide remarks at the table, but as long as they are not providing information to others actively involved in a hand, "talking trash" is just part and parcel of the way the game is played. But some behavioral manifestations that are acceptable in Las Vegas, California, or Atlantic City would probably get you bounced from an overseas poker room in a New York minute. Conversation at the poker table there is often sparse by American standards, and much more civilized. Dress and bearing are much the same. Players dress better in the U.K. and much of the European continent than they do in the states. Attire and demeanor are part of the cultural norms of whatever country you happen to be playing in, and it pays to know them beforehand. It takes little to tune into the cultural norms of wherever you might find yourself because good etiquette is nothing more than a means to a smooth, well-paced game.

2

The Mechanics
of the Game

TEXAS HOLD'EM **Betting**

In fixed-limit games, betting limits usually double on the turn. If two chips are the wagering limit for the first two rounds of betting, wagering on the turn and river will increase to four-chip increments.

In spread-limit games, players may wager any amount within the limits on every betting round. If the limits are $2 to $10, wagers may be made anywhere within that range, with the proviso that any raise must be at least as large as the bet preceding it.

In pot-limit poker, players may bet any amount from the size of the blind to the size of the pot. Raises can be exponential, because you can count your call as part of the bet you have chosen to raise. If that sounds complicated, a simple example will clarify. Suppose

there are two blind bets of $10 and $5 in the pot, and Player 3 calls for $10. If Player 4 were to make a pot-sized raise, he'd match Player 3's $10 bet—making the total pot $35—then raise that amount. Player 4, in all actuality, is tossing $45 into the pot, which now totals $70. It may sound complex but it really isn't. Here's the math: A pot-sized raise is three times the size of the last raise, plus the prior size of the pot.

In a no-limit betting structure there's very little math involved. Players can bet any amount of the chips in front of them at any time. However, unless it is an all-in situation, a bet must still be at least as large as the big blind, and a raise must be the size of the previous bet or raise.

PLAYER 2 posts a $10 blind before the cards are dealt.
Move 1: Having seen his two hole cards, he must call, reraise, or fold.

PLAYER 3, having seen his hole cards, calls. His call makes the pot $25.

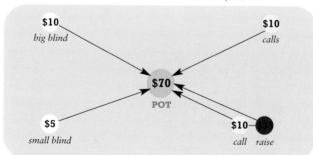

$10
big blind

$10
calls

$70
POT

$5
small blind

$10
call *raise*

PLAYER 1 posts a $5 blind before the cards are dealt.
Move 1: Having seen his hole cards, he must call, reraise, or fold.

D

PLAYER 4, having seen his hole cards, raises the pot. First he puts in $10 to call, bringing the pot to $35, then he matches the $35 in the pot. In other words, he announces a pot-size raise and adds $45 to the pot, making the pot size $70.

Any time a player wishes to call a bet but does not have sufficient chips to cover the bet, he is said to be all-in. At that point he is eligible only to win that portion of the pot covered by his chips, and a side pot is created for those players who still have chips and an interest in wagering.

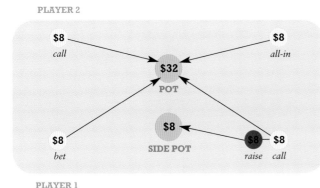

PLAYER 2

$8
call

$8
all-in

$32
POT

$8
SIDE POT

$8
bet

$8 $8
raise call

PLAYER 1

PLAYER 3 calls for $8, which is all the money he has. He is all-in and cannot make any further calls.

PLAYER 4 raises the pot by $8. Player 3 is all-in so Player 4 matches the $8 call, but his $8 raise must go into a side pot. Calls from Players 1, 2, and any further bets will go into the side pot. Player 3 cannot win the side pot.

Opening the betting
BETTING STRUCTURE: FIXED-LIMIT, $4–$8

Two players place blind bets before the cards are dealt. The small blind is placed by the player immediately to the left of the dealer button. The big blind is placed by the player immediately to the small blind's left. The small blind is usually some fraction of the big blind, while the big blind is almost always the size of the first-round bet limit. For example, in a game with $4 and $8 betting limits, the blinds are usually $2 and $4. In a game with betting limits of $15 and $30, blinds are typically $10 and $15.

PLAYER 2

PLAYER 3

$4
big blind

$2
small blind

PLAYER 1

D PLAYER 5

PLAYER 4

Betting round 1 (BEFORE THE FLOP)

Once the deck is shuffled and the blinds posted, two cards are dealt face down to each active player. These are private cards and can only be used by the player to whom they are dealt. All other cards are dealt face up on the table and are the communal property of all players involved in the hand. Each participant, beginning with the player immediately to the left of the big blind, may fold, call the big blind, or raise.

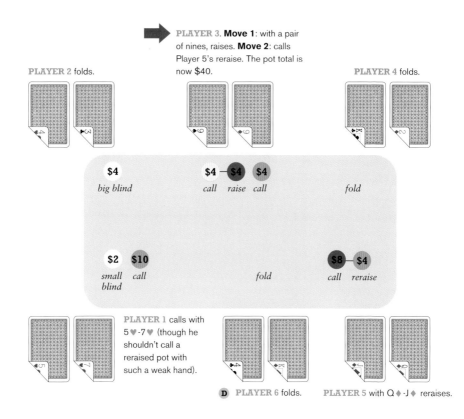

PLAYER 3. **Move 1**: with a pair of nines, raises. **Move 2**: calls Player 5's reraise. The pot total is now $40.

PLAYER 2 folds.

PLAYER 4 folds.

$4 big blind

$4 call $4 raise $4 call

fold

$2 small blind $10 call

fold

$8 call $4 reraise

PLAYER 1 calls with 5♥-7♥ (though he shouldn't call a reraised pot with such a weak hand).

D PLAYER 6 folds.

PLAYER 5 with Q♦-J♦ reraises.

The player posting the small blind has an option to fold, call, or raise, but only after everyone at the table, except the big blind, has acted. The player posting the big blind acts last on this betting round. If no one has raised his blind bet, he may check or raise. If an opponent has raised, he has three options when the action gets back around to him: fold, call, or reraise. In most games a bet and either three or four raises are permitted in each betting round.

Betting round 2 (THE FLOP)

On the second, third, and last round of betting, the small blind acts first and may check or bet. Once a player bets, the others may either relinquish their interest in the pot by folding, or they may call, or raise. The player with the dealer button acts last on the final three betting rounds. If the dealer folds, the player to his right acts last.

When the first betting round is complete, the three community cards, the flop, are turned face-up on the center of the table. The second round of betting proceeds.

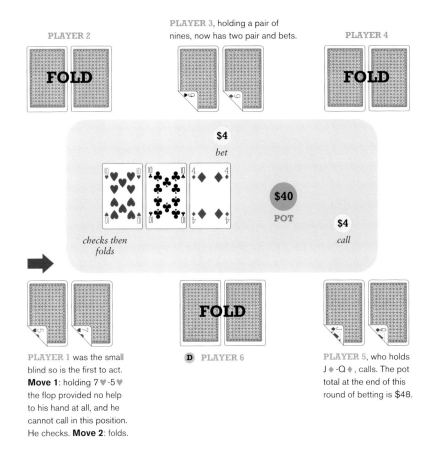

PLAYER 2

FOLD

PLAYER 3, holding a pair of nines, now has two pair and bets.

PLAYER 4

FOLD

$4
bet

$40
POT

$4
call

checks then folds

PLAYER 1 was the small blind so is the first to act.
Move 1: holding 7♥-5♥ the flop provided no help to his hand at all, and he cannot call in this position. He checks. **Move 2**: folds.

D PLAYER 6

FOLD

PLAYER 5, who holds J♦-Q♦, calls. The pot total at the end of this round of betting is $48.

Betting round 3 (THE TURN)

A fourth community card, known as the turn card, is dealt face up and followed by another round of betting.

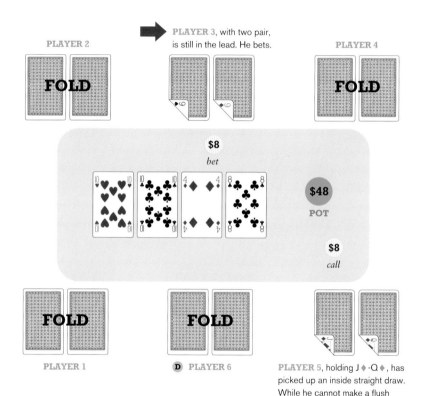

PLAYER 2

FOLD

PLAYER 3, with two pair, is still in the lead. He bets.

PLAYER 4

FOLD

$8
bet

$48
POT

$8
call

FOLD

PLAYER 1

FOLD

D PLAYER 6

PLAYER 5, holding J♦-Q♦, has picked up an inside straight draw. While he cannot make a flush regardless of the next card, if a nine comes on the river, he will have made a straight. Moreover, if a jack or a queen falls, he will have made two pair. He calls, making the pot total at the end of this round of betting $64.

Betting round 4 (THE RIVER)

Finally, a fifth community card, the river card, is placed face up on the table and the last round of betting commences. If at least two players remain at the end of the betting, the hole cards are revealed in a showdown. The player who can make the best hand using any combination of private and community cards wins the pot.

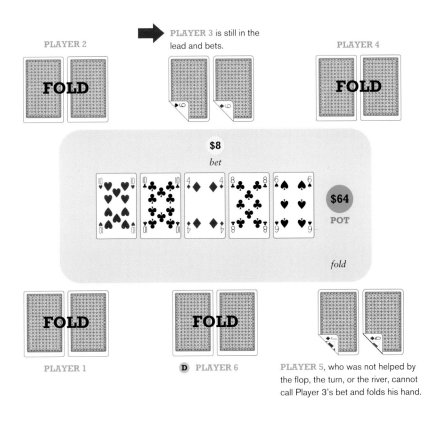

PLAYER 2

PLAYER 3 is still in the lead and bets.

PLAYER 4

FOLD

FOLD

$8

bet

$64

POT

fold

FOLD

FOLD

PLAYER 1

Ⓓ PLAYER 6

PLAYER 5, who was not helped by the flop, the turn, or the river, cannot call Player 3's bet and folds his hand.

The last card helped neither player. Player 3 wins with two pair: T♥-T♣-9♠-9♦-8♣. Player 5's hand is T♥-T♣-Q♦-J♦-8♣, only a single pair that is also usable by Player 3, and he folds, knowing his hand cannot win.

That's all there is to it. Yet within this simplicity lies an elegance and sophistication that makes Texas hold'em the world's most popular form of poker.

How to win

Because those exposed communal cards in the center of the table belong to all the players in the hand, it's more difficult for opponents to draw out on you (beat your hand by catching the card they need) in hold'em than it is in games like seven-card stud, where players only use the cards dealt to them specifically. If your private cards are a pair of jacks and your opponent has a pair of nines, the presence of a pair of fives among the communal cards gives each of you two pair. But you still have the best hand. Unless one of the fives allows an opponent to complete a straight, the only player helped by that pair is one fortunate enough to have one or both of the remaining fives in his hand.

Texas hold'em is a first-come, first-served game because you get to see five-sevenths of your hand after the flop. That's another major difference between hold'em and seven-card stud, where you only see four-sevenths of your hand after the first round of betting. Because you've seen a full 71 percent of your hold'em hand on the flop after the first betting round, staying for the turn and river demands that you have a strong hand, a draw to a potentially winning hand, or good reason to believe that betting on a future round will cause opponents to fold.

Another difference between stud and hold'em is that the betting order in hold'em is fixed for the entire hand, whereas in stud the exposed cards in each round determine who acts first. Acting last in any form of poker is a big advantage, since opponents have to make decisions (and thereby reveal something about their hands) before you do.

Take this advice to heart: Don't invest in mediocre cards before opponents reveal something about the real—or purported—strength of their hands. Fold marginal hands from early position. When you're most vulnerable, you should play only the very best starting hands. Success at hold'em demands patience. But no matter how sweet your first two cards look, an unfavorable flop can render them worthless. If your hand doesn't improve on the flop or provide you with a draw to a very strong hand, you should usually let it go—unless you were fortunate enough to begin with a big pocket pair. Tell yourself this: If I miss the flop, I have to stop.

HOLE CARDS   BOARD CARDS

As a rule of thumb, don't continue beyond the flop without a strong pair coupled with a decent side card, or kicker. Two pair is better still, or if you're really lucky you'll make three-of-a-kind, which is a very strong hand.

Without one of those hands, you'll need a straight or flush draw to continue. With a drawing hand, you'll need at least two opponents for the pot to offset the cost of your investment.

HOLE CARDS

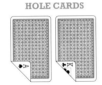

THE FLOP

Here the player is helped by the flop. He has a pair of aces with the very best possible side card, a king.

HOLE CARDS

THE FLOP

From the flop, the player has a straight draw.

HOLE CARDS

THE FLOP

Here the player has a flush draw.

ADVICE FOR GOOD PLAY ON THE FLOP

Here are six tips to help you play successfully on the flop:
- The flop defines your hand. If it doesn't fit your hand, most of the time you're better off cutting your losses early.
- When you flop a big hand, give your opponents an opportunity to make the second-best hand, but avoid giving them a free card that could beat you.
- If you're new to hold'em, err on the side of caution. It costs less.
- Be aggressive with a hand that has multiple possibilities, such as top pair with a good kicker and a flush draw.
- Be selective about hands you play before the flop, and be aggressive when the hand you hold seems to be the best hand because it hits the flop.
- If you flop a draw, stick with it as long as the pot promises a greater payoff than the odds against making your hand. You can find out more about odds on page 161.

OMAHA **Betting**

The dealer shuffles and cuts the cards. The big and small blinds are placed by the appropriate players. Beginning with the player to the left of the rotating dealer button, each player is dealt four cards face down. The four cards belong only to the player to whom they are dealt, and are referred to as that player's hole cards. The remaining cards will be dealt face up on the table and are community cards that belong to each of the players active in the hand.

In Omaha a player must use two and only two of his hole cards, plus any three community cards, to make a hand. This is very different from hold'em and can be the source of much embarrassment—not to mention loss of cash.

Opening the betting
BETTING STRUCTURE: POT-LIMIT,
BLINDS $1–$2

Omaha is most commonly played pot-limit in tournaments and cash games, although it can be played as a fixed-limit or no-limit game as well. Two blind bets are first made to seed the pot. The blinds are placed by the two players immediately to the left of the rotating dealer button. The blinds and the dealer button move clockwise around the table with each new hand, so all players pay their fair share of blinds. We'll assume in this example that the blinds are $1 and $2. In the opening round of betting, the player to the immediate left of the big blind acts first and can either call the big blind's $2, fold his hand, or raise.

NOTE: *A raise does not always have to be pot size. Smaller raises are also allowed.*

In pot-limit poker, a player who raises must first call his opponent's bet and then calculate his raise. For example, at the start of the hand only the two blind bets are in the pot. Someone wishing to raise the maximum must first call the $2 blind bet, making the pot's total $5, then match the $5 already in the pot, resulting in the pot now totaling $10.

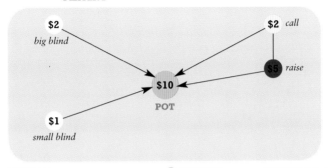

 PLAYER 3, having seen his four hole cards, wants to make a pot-size raise, so he must call the $2 big blind, making the pot total $5, then match the pot, making a pot total of $10.

PLAYER 2

$2
big blind

$2 *call*

$5 *raise*

$10
POT

$1
small blind

PLAYER 1

Ⓓ PLAYER 5

PLAYER 4, having seen his hole cards, must decide if he wants to call for $5.

Each player has the same option, and may call, fold, or raise. There is no limit to the number of raises in pot-limit games, so the exponentially escalating pot size can get a player all-in very quickly.

Because of the potential for large raises, you'll generally find fewer players involved in each pot than you do in fixed-limit games. Moreover, a bet or raise stands a much better chance of winning the pot by making others fold. Good position—and with it the fear of an enormous bet or raise—is far more important too.

Betting round 1

The following hands are dealt to the players in this example:

PLAYER 2 who is already in the pot for $2, has a draw to a very small straight along with the best possible club draw. He calls for an additional $2. At the end of this betting round, there is $16 in the pot.

PLAYER 3, to the left of the big blind, is first to act this round. He has a pair of aces, one of which is suited to the 7♠, along with some straight possibilities. He makes the bet $4—first calling the $2 big blind, then raising by $2—making the pot a total of $7.

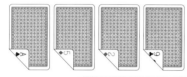

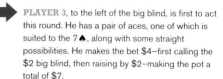

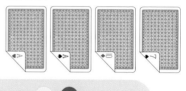

$2
big
blind

$2
call

$2
call

$2
raise

$1
small
blind

$3
call

fold

$4
call

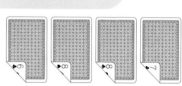

PLAYER 1 is already in the pot for the $1 small blind. He has a hand that's double suited and has straight possibilities, so calls for an additional $3.

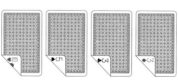

D PLAYER 5, with a pair of treys, a 5, and a 10, folds.

PLAYER 4, who with a pair of 8's, a 6, and a 7 has the possibility to make trip or quad eights, a mid-range straight, or a mid-range club draw, calls the $4.

Player 5, who folded, has relinquished all claims to the pot.

Those who remain will continue to contest the pot until only one player is left, or the betting is concluded and the best hand wins at the showdown.

NOTE: *The player to the left of the big blind always opens the betting in the first round.*

Betting round 2 (THE FLOP)

The flop is dealt face up in the center of the table. It is 9♦ 8♦ 2♣.

The player immediately to the left of the dealer button is the first to act from this betting round on. Here he is identified as Player 1.

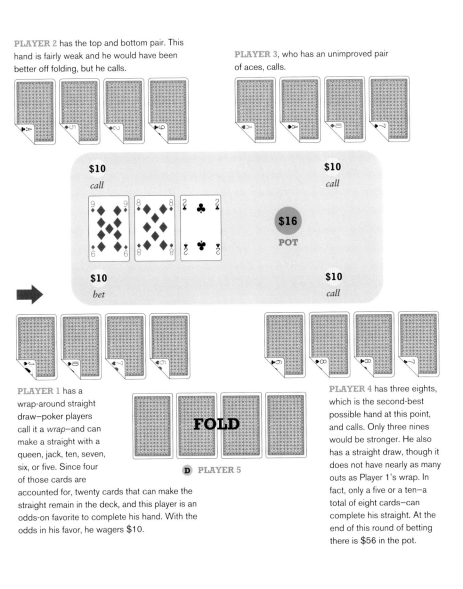

PLAYER 2 has the top and bottom pair. This hand is fairly weak and he would have been better off folding, but he calls.

PLAYER 3, who has an unimproved pair of aces, calls.

$10
call

$10
call

$16
POT

$10
bet

$10
call

PLAYER 1 has a wrap-around straight draw—poker players call it a *wrap*—and can make a straight with a queen, jack, ten, seven, six, or five. Since four of those cards are accounted for, twenty cards that can make the straight remain in the deck, and this player is an odds-on favorite to complete his hand. With the odds in his favor, he wagers $10.

FOLD

Ⓓ PLAYER 5

PLAYER 4 has three eights, which is the second-best possible hand at this point, and calls. Only three nines would be stronger. He also has a straight draw, though it does not have nearly as many outs as Player 1's wrap. In fact, only a five or a ten—a total of eight cards—can complete his straight. At the end of this round of betting there is $56 in the pot.

Betting round 3 (THE TURN)

NOTE: *In pot-limit poker you can force players to fold because the bets get very large.*

PLAYER 2 folds. He knows that two pair will not win this pot.

PLAYER 3 folds his unimproved pair of aces.

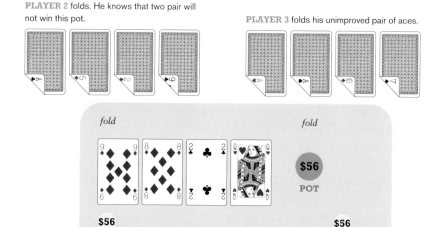

fold

fold

$56

POT

$56

bet

$56

call

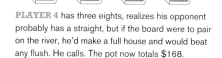

PLAYER 1 has made the highest possible straight. He bets $56, the size of the pot, because he wants to discourage calls from any players who might have draws to a diamond flush.

PLAYER 4 has three eights, realizes his opponent probably has a straight, but if the board were to pair on the river, he'd make a full house and would beat any flush. He calls. The pot now totals $168.

FOLD

D PLAYER 5

Betting round 4 (THE RIVER)

The river card is the 4♠. The player in seat 1 has the best possible hand and cannot be beaten. He bets the pot, hoping for a call from Player 4. However, his opponent, who still has only three-of-a-kind, reluctantly folds.

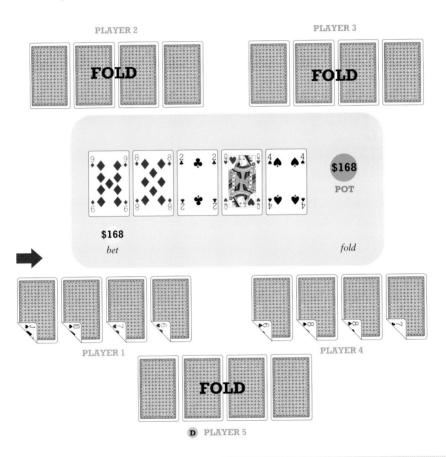

Showdown

There will be no showdown in this hand. Although it is difficult to fold three-of-a-kind, sometimes that's just what you have to do. In Omaha, big hands are the rule rather than the exception, particularly when the betting escalates as rapidly as it does in pot-limit poker.

OMAHA EIGHT OR BETTER, HI/LO SPLIT **Betting**

In Omaha eight or better, hi/lo split ("Omaha/8"), the dealer shuffles and cuts the cards. The small and big blinds are placed by the player to the left of the dealer, and the player to his left, respectively. Beginning with the player to the left of the rotating dealer button, each player is dealt four cards face down. The four cards belong only to the player to whom they are dealt, and are referred to as that player's hole cards. The remaining cards will be dealt face up on the table and are community cards, meaning they belong to each player active in the hand.

In Omaha/8 you may use different hole cards and different community cards to form your high and low hands.

Just as in Omaha, you must use two hole cards plus three community cards to make any hand, whether it is high or low.

Opening the betting
BETTING STRUCTURE: FIXED-LIMIT, $2–$4

NOTE: *A lot of players will stay to see the flop in limit Omaha or Omaha/8.*

Two bets are already in the pot. These are the blinds placed by the two players immediately to the left of the rotating dealer button. The blinds and the dealer button move clockwise around the table with each new hand, so that each player is fairly assessed. In a game with betting limits of $2 and $4 the blinds are $1 and $2. As with hold'em and Omaha, the betting doubles on the turn, so there are two rounds of small bets and two rounds of double bets. In this opening round of betting, the player to the immediate left of the big blind acts first and must either call the big blind's $2 bet, fold his hand, or raise.

Each player, including the blinds, has the same option and may call, fold, or raise. The small blind can either call the big blind, call any raises, fold, or raise. If he were to call, his small blind would be subtracted from the cost of the call. The big blind may raise his own blind bet, reraise another's raise, or simply check (because he has already contributed $2 to the pot) if no one has raised. One bet and three raises per round are usually permitted.

The following hands are dealt to the six players in this pot:

Betting round 1

PLAYER 3 is first to act this round. With an A–4 for low, an A♦–J♦ for high, and the best possible diamond flush draw, he calls the blind for $2.

PLAYER 2 hasn't much of a hand, but there was no raise. He is the big blind, so he gets to see the flop for no extra cost. The pot at the end of this round of betting is $12.

PLAYER 4, with a pair of eights, a six, and a seven, has possibilities of a mid-range straight, trip, or quad eights, and a mid-range club flush draw. He calls.

$2	$2	$2
big blind	call	call

$1	$1	$2	$2
small blind	call	call	call

PLAYER 1 is the small blind so already has $1 in the pot. He cannot make a qualifying low hand—he would need to hold at least two cards eight or lower—but he could make trips or quads with his pair of kings for a big high hand. He calls for $1 more.

PLAYER 5, with an A–5 for low, a nut spade draw, and a large straight draw, calls.

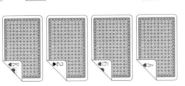

D **PLAYER 6**, with the best possible low draw (an ace with a deuce), the nut heart flush draw A♥–K♥ for high, and a third low card—albeit only a six—calls.

Betting round 2 (THE FLOP)

The flop is dealt face up in the center of the table. It is 8♥ 2♦ 10♦.
This time, and on each succeeding round of betting, the player
immediately to the left of the dealer button (the small blind) acts first.

PLAYER 3. Move 1: calls. This player has a draw to the best possible flush as well
as four low cards. A deuce has already flopped, so A–4 is a draw to the second-best
low hand at this point. Only a player with an A–3 in his hand could make a better low,
and would do so if a third low card that is neither an ace nor a trey came on the turn
or the river. **Move 2**: calls. The pot total at the end of this betting round is $28.

PLAYER 4 raises. He has
three eights, the best high
hand at this point. He also
has two other low cards, a
seven and a six, but a low
draw this weak seldom
holds up.

PLAYER 2. Move 1: calls
Player 1's bet. He has an inside
straight draw, which is a fairly
weak hand. **Move 2**: calls.

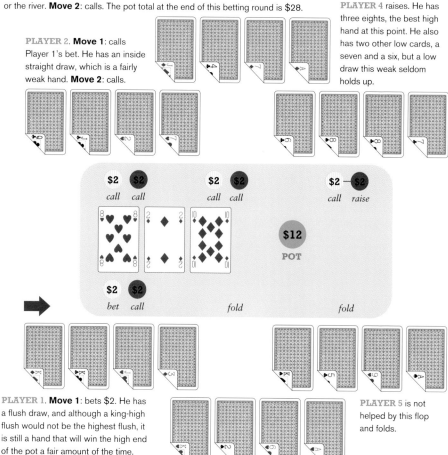

PLAYER 1. Move 1: bets $2. He has
a flush draw, and although a king-high
flush would not be the highest flush, it
is still a hand that will win the high end
of the pot a fair amount of the time.
Move 2: he calls Player 4's raise.

PLAYER 5 is not
helped by this flop
and folds.

D **PLAYER 6** has had the deuce in his hand counterfeited by the one
on the board. His best low possibility now is an A–6, which is not a
good low hand. He has no chance for the best high hand. He folds.

Betting round 3 (THE TURN)

The turn card is the Q ♦. The betting doubles to $4.

NOTE: *Player 1 calls Player 3's raise. Consider your outs and pot odds when deciding whether or not to call.*

PLAYER 3 has made the highest possible flush, called the nut flush, in diamonds. He raises $4. He also has an A–4 for a draw to the second-best low hand. He will make a qualifying low hand if a card lower than a nine that does not pair either his ace or four appears on the river.

PLAYER 4, with three eights, realizes he may be losing to a flush at this point, but he calls. If the board pairs on the river, his three-of-a-kind will be elevated to a full house, which would beat any flush—except a straight flush—for the high end of the pot. He calls. He must call the original bet and the raise, making his call $8.

PLAYER 2 folds.

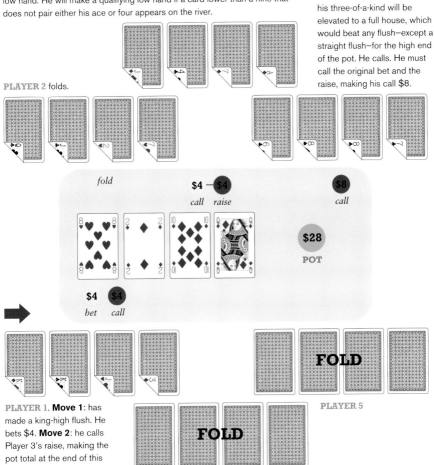

PLAYER 1. **Move 1**: has made a king-high flush. He bets $4. **Move 2**: he calls Player 3's raise, making the pot total at the end of this round of betting $52.

PLAYER 5

D PLAYER 6

Betting round 4 (THE RIVER)

The river card is the 6♠.

PLAYER 3 now has the nut flush along with the second-best possible low hand. He is assured of winning half the pot with his ace-high flush and has a chance to scoop the pot if no one has either tied or bested his low hand. He bets.

PLAYER 4 did not improve his hand, and is sure he is beaten, but he makes a crying call to stay in the game.

PLAYER 2

FOLD

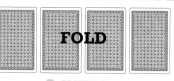

$4
bet

$4
call

$4
call

$52
POT

PLAYER 1. **Move 1**: checks with the king-high diamond flush. His concern is that he may be facing a better flush, because his bet on fourth street was raised. **Move 2**: like Player 4, he too makes a crying call.

FOLD

D PLAYER 6

FOLD

PLAYER 5

Showdown

PLAYER 3, with an ace-high diamond flush and 8–6–4–2–A for low, wins both the low and the high ends of the pot.

HIGH HAND

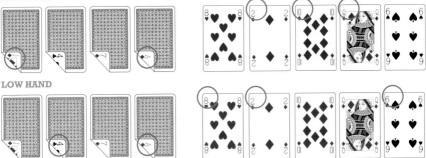

LOW HAND

PLAYER 1 does not have a low hand, because a player must use exactly two—no more, no fewer—of his hole cards to make a hand.

HIGH HAND

PLAYER 4 does not have a low hand, because his low was counterfeited by two of the cards on the board.

HIGH HAND

If the notion of a counterfeited low hand seems confusing to you, try this: Using exactly two cards from Player 4's hand of 8♠-8♣-7♣-6♣, try to form a five-card low hand with three of the low communal cards of 8♥-2♦-6♠. Remember, a low hand must have five unpaired cards all of rank 8 or below. Try as you might, you just can't do it.

> **NOTE:** *Learn to recognize when the board has counterfeited your low hand.*

SEVEN-CARD STUD **Betting**

Each player posts an *ante*, a mandatory bet made before any cards are dealt. The dealer shuffles, cuts the cards, and—beginning with the player on the left—deals clockwise until each player has three cards. The first two cards are dealt face down, the third face up. The two cards dealt face down are yours alone to look at and are referred to as your *hole cards*. Hence the expression: "an ace in the hole." The card that is dealt face up is called your *door card*.

Opening the betting
BETTING STRUCTURE: FIXED-LIMIT, $2–$4

The player with the lowest-ranking door card must make a token bet called the *bring-in bet* or simply the *bring-in*. In the $2–$4 game we're discussing, the bring-in would be $1. If two or more door cards are of the same rank, the low card by suit brings it in. The lowest suit

NOTE: *Each player posts an ante of $1 to seed the pot before any cards are dealt.*

is clubs, followed by diamonds, hearts, and spades—alphabetical order makes it easy to learn—and this is one of the very few times that suit matters in poker.

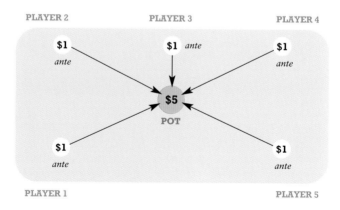

Betting round 1 (THIRD STREET)

This first betting round is known as third street, as three cards have been dealt. If you bet or raise and your opponents all surrender the pot by folding, you win. If two or more players remain after the first betting round, the dealer will give each remaining player another card face up.

Player 5 has the lowest door card and so must make the bring-in bet.

Once the bring-in bet has been made, each player (commencing with the player to the left of the bring-in) must do one of the following:
• Relinquish any claim to the pot by folding.
• Call the amount of the bring-in.
• Complete the bet to the $2 limit.

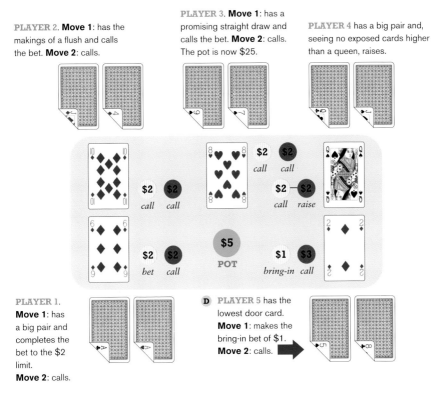

PLAYER 2. **Move 1**: has the makings of a flush and calls the bet. **Move 2**: calls.

PLAYER 3. **Move 1**: has a promising straight draw and calls the bet. **Move 2**: calls. The pot is now $25.

PLAYER 4 has a big pair and, seeing no exposed cards higher than a queen, raises.

PLAYER 1.
Move 1: has a big pair and completes the bet to the $2 limit.
Move 2: calls.

D PLAYER 5 has the lowest door card.
Move 1: makes the bring-in bet of $1.
Move 2: calls.

Player 4 raised the bet, so all other players must either call the raise for an additional $2 ($3 for Player 5) or fold, or they may reraise by another $2. Generally, rules permit either three or four raises per betting round.

To be eligible to win a pot or a portion of a pot, a player must either match the highest bet made that round or be all-in.

Betting round 2 (FOURTH STREET)

Players refer to this second round of betting as fourth street.

In this and all subsequent betting rounds, the holder of the highest hand *on board* now acts first. He may either check, which means make no bet, or wager the $2 limit. Then, starting with the player to his immediate left,

the remaining players must call, fold, or raise.

If any player in the fourth street betting round has an exposed pair on board, then any player has the option of making either the standard bet of $2 or a double bet of $4.

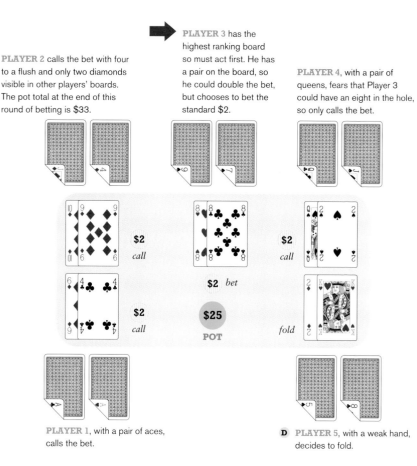

PLAYER 3 has the highest ranking board so must act first. He has a pair on the board, so he could double the bet, but chooses to bet the standard $2.

PLAYER 2 calls the bet with four to a flush and only two diamonds visible in other players' boards. The pot total at the end of this round of betting is $33.

PLAYER 4, with a pair of queens, fears that Player 3 could have an eight in the hole, so only calls the bet.

$2 call

$2 bet

$2 call

$2 call

$25 POT

fold

PLAYER 1, with a pair of aces, calls the bet.

D PLAYER 5, with a weak hand, decides to fold.

Betting round 3 (FIFTH STREET)

If two or more players remain after fourth street, each player receives another card face up, and another betting round—you guessed it, it's called fifth street—begins. But now the bets double, and in our example the betting limit escalates from $2 to $4.

The highest ranking hand still acts first and may check or bet. Action proceeds as before.

NOTE: *On fifth street the bet limit doubles for this and all subsequent rounds. Bets and raises are now in increments of $4.*

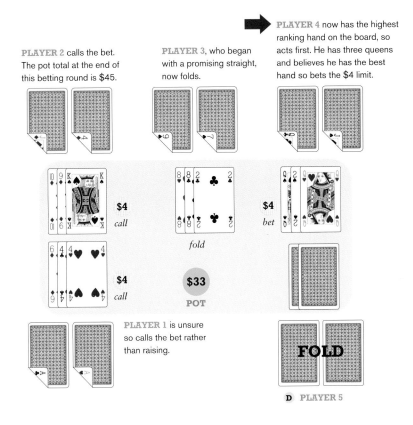

PLAYER 2 calls the bet. The pot total at the end of this betting round is $45.

PLAYER 3, who began with a promising straight, now folds.

PLAYER 4 now has the highest ranking hand on the board, so acts first. He has three queens and believes he has the best hand so bets the $4 limit.

$4
call

$4
bet

fold

$4
call

$33
POT

$4
call

PLAYER 1 is unsure so calls the bet rather than raising.

FOLD

D PLAYER 5

Betting round 4 (SIXTH STREET)

Sixth street is a mirror of fifth street. The dealer gives each player another card face up and another round of betting begins. If several players are still active, there's a nice pot by now.

NOTE: *Even after folding, never reveal your cards while the hand is still being played as it can give an advantage to someone still contending for the pot.*

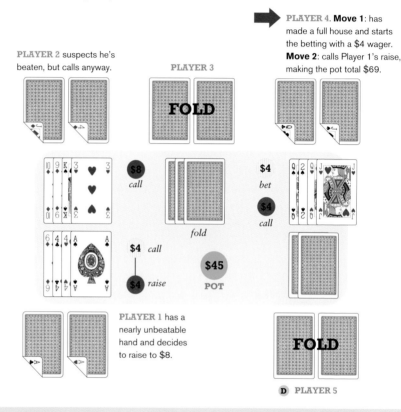

PLAYER 4. **Move 1**: has made a full house and starts the betting with a $4 wager. **Move 2**: calls Player 1's raise, making the pot total $69.

PLAYER 2 suspects he's beaten, but calls anyway.

PLAYER 3

FOLD

$8 call

$4 bet

$4 call

fold

$45 POT

$4 call

$4 raise

PLAYER 1 has a nearly unbeatable hand and decides to raise to $8.

FOLD

D PLAYER 5

Showdown

The player who makes the final bet or raise is the first to reveal all his cards. The remaining players then each show their cards in turn, starting with the player to the immediate left of the first player to show.

$93 FINAL POT

NOT USED

PLAYER 1 was the last to raise so shows his hand first. Full house: aces full of fours. He wins with a higher full house than Player 4.

Betting round 5 (SEVENTH STREET OR THE RIVER)

On seventh street, also known as the river, each remaining player gets a final card dealt face down. If two or more players are still vying for the pot when the betting concludes, the player with the best five-card poker hand that can be made from his own seven cards is the winner.

Because the final card is dealt face down, the player who was first to act on sixth street will always be the first to act on the river too.

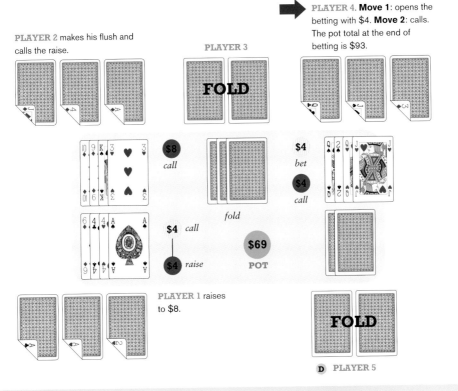

PLAYER 2 makes his flush and calls the raise.

PLAYER 3 FOLD

PLAYER 4. **Move 1**: opens the betting with $4. **Move 2**: calls. The pot total at the end of betting is $93.

$8 call

$4 bet
$4 call

fold

$4 call
$4 raise

$69 POT

PLAYER 1 raises to $8.

FOLD

D PLAYER 5

PLAYER 2 Flush: ace-high, diamonds.

PLAYER 4 Full house: queens full of jacks.

SEVEN-CARD STUD EIGHT OR BETTER, HI-LO SPLIT **Betting**

Seven-card stud eight or better, hi-lo split (seven-stud/8) begins in the same way as seven-card stud, with each player posting an *ante* before cards are dealt. The dealer shuffles, cuts the cards, and—beginning with the player on the left—deals clockwise until each player has three cards. The first two cards, the hole cards, are dealt face down and the third card, the door card, is dealt face up.

Opening the betting

BETTING STRUCTURE: FIXED-LIMIT, $20-$40

> NOTE: *Each player posts an ante of $3 to seed the pot before any cards are dealt.*

The player with the lowest-ranking door card starts the betting in round 1. This player must make a fixed token bet called the *bring-in* or *forced bet*. In the $20–$40 game structure we're discussing, each player will have anted $3 before the initial deal, and the bring-in is $5.

If two or more door cards are tied for the lowest rank, the lowest card by suit brings it in. The lowest suit is clubs, followed by diamonds, hearts, and spades.

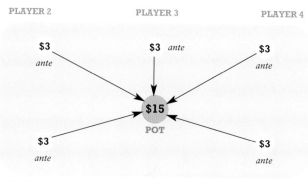

PLAYER 2   PLAYER 3   PLAYER 4

$3 ante $3 ante $3 ante

$15 POT

$3 ante $3 ante

PLAYER 1   PLAYER 5

Betting round 1 (THIRD STREET)

Once the bring-in bet has been made, commencing with the player to the left of the bring-in, each player may either:
- Fold and relinquish any claim to the pot.
- Call the amount of the bring-in.

- Complete the bet to the $20 limit.
- Raise a completed bet or the previous raise by $20.

Generally, once the bet has been completed, only three raises are permitted in a betting round.

PLAYER 2 has the lowest ranking door card, so he is the bring-in and must wager at least $5 or complete the bet to $20. He bets the minimum.

PLAYER 3 has three spades, plus a draw to both a flush and a straight. He calls.

PLAYER 4 has a pair of jacks and two hearts on third street, but the presence of three other hearts visible on the table diminishes his chance of making a flush. He folds.

$5
bring-in

$5
call

fold

$18
POT

$5
call

$5
call

fold

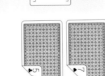

PLAYER 1 has only two hearts to a flush and only two cards to a low. He should fold but wants to see a fourth card. He calls. The pot total is now $38.

D PLAYER 6 has a pair of fives as well as two good low cards. He calls.

PLAYER 5 has two diamonds and two cards in sequence. It's not enough to keep playing. He folds.

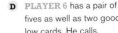

NOTE: *If a player had raised to the $20 limit, all other players would have to call $20.*

If two or more players remain after the first betting round, each player is dealt another card face up, and a second round of betting ensues.

Betting round 2 (FOURTH STREET)

From this point on, the holder of the lowest card is spared, because the player whose open cards, or board, shows the highest card or combination of cards must act first. The player with the highest board may either check, which in essence is a bet of nothing, or wager $20. Players in turn may call, fold, or raise.

Unlike "regular" seven-card stud, the presence of a pair on the board of any player on fourth street does not provide an option for a player to wager either $20 or $40. In seven-stud/8, betting limits don't double until fifth street.

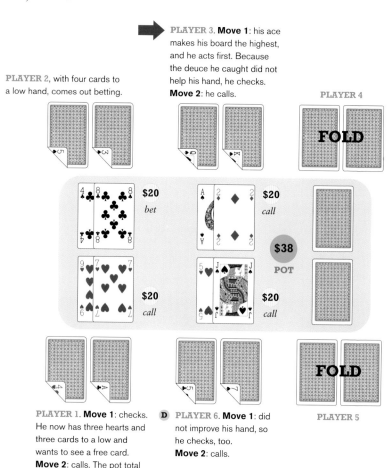

PLAYER 3. **Move 1**: his ace makes his board the highest, and he acts first. Because the deuce he caught did not help his hand, he checks. **Move 2**: he calls.

PLAYER 2, with four cards to a low hand, comes out betting.

PLAYER 4

FOLD

$20 bet

$20 call

$38 POT

$20 call

$20 call

FOLD

PLAYER 1. **Move 1**: checks. He now has three hearts and three cards to a low and wants to see a free card. **Move 2**: calls. The pot total at the end of this round of betting is $118.

D PLAYER 6. **Move 1**: did not improve his hand, so he checks, too. **Move 2**: calls.

PLAYER 5

Betting round 3 (FIFTH STREET)

Each remaining player receives another card face up, and another betting round begins. Now, the bet limit doubles, and from fifth street through to the end of the hand all bets will be in increments of $40.

NOTE: *The highest board acts first, and may check or bet. Action proceeds as before.*

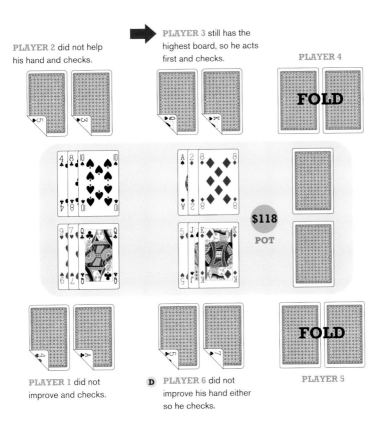

PLAYER 2 did not help his hand and checks.

PLAYER 3 still has the highest board, so he acts first and checks.

PLAYER 4 FOLD

PLAYER 1 did not improve and checks.

D PLAYER 6 did not improve his hand either so he checks.

$118 POT

PLAYER 5 FOLD

Although Player 2 has the only low hand draw, he cannot be sure about Player 3, who is showing three low cards that suggest a better low hand than his. If he were aware, as we are, that Player 3 has two big cards in the hole, Player 2 would have come out betting.

Betting round 4 (SIXTH STREET)

Sixth street is a mirror of fifth street. The dealer gives each player another card face up, and a round of betting begins. With some players trying to make the best high hand and others the best low hand, there's usually a good-sized pot by now.

On sixth street things often change dramatically.

PLAYER 3 has a threatening looking low board, but has two big cards in the hole. He does not have a strong high hand or a qualifying low hand (five unpaired cards, ranked eight or lower), but his draw to a low hand is strong. He calls, making the pot total $278.

PLAYER 2 now believes his low hand is probably the best, so he calls.

PLAYER 4

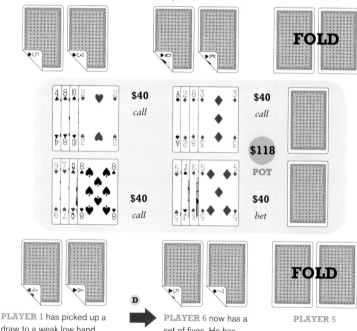

PLAYER 1 has picked up a draw to a weak low hand. He should fold but calls.

PLAYER 6 now has a set of fives. He has paired his door card, and because he now has the highest exposed hand, he must act first. He comes out betting.

PLAYER 5

Betting round 5 (SEVENTH STREET; THE RIVER)

On seventh street, also known as *the river*, each player receives a final card dealt face down. If two or more players are still vying for the pot, there's a final round of wagering. The player who acted first on sixth street has that honor again on the river.

PLAYER 2 has caught a miracle card, an ace, giving him a five-high straight, also called a *wheel* or a *bicycle*. He has a straight for his high hand and the very best possible low hand of 5-4-3-2-1. He raises.

PLAYER 3 has caught what is known as a brick and has failed to make a qualifying low hand. Moreover, his high hand cannot even beat the exposed pair of fives on Player 6's board. He folds.

PLAYER 4

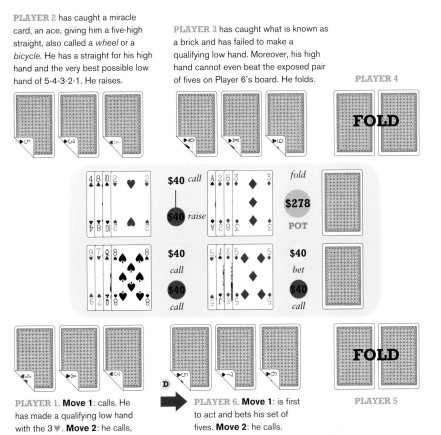

PLAYER 1. **Move 1**: calls. He has made a qualifying low hand with the 3♥. **Move 2**: he calls, making the pot total $518.

PLAYER 6. **Move 1**: is first to act and bets his set of fives. **Move 2**: he calls.

PLAYER 5

> **NOTE:** *A qualifying low hand consists of five unpaired cards with a rank of eight or lower.*

Showdown

Player 6 and Player 1 both called the raise by Player 2. Player 6 hoped his set of fives would win the high hand and Player 1 hoped his qualifying low would be low enough to win half the pot. But Player 6's set of fives loses to Player 2's straight (for high) and

Player 1's 8-7-4-3-A is not good enough to beat Player 2's 5-4-3-2-A (for low). Player 2 has scooped the pot and wins the entire $518.

$518

FINAL POT

PLAYER 2 has 5-4-3-2-A, the best possible low hand. It is also a five-high straight. Any combination of three cards from your hand and two community cards can be used to form the best high and low hands, and the same cards could be used to form both your low and your high hands.

HIGH HAND

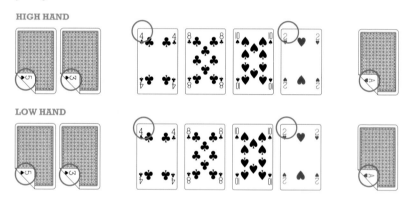

LOW HAND

PLAYER 1
HIGH HAND

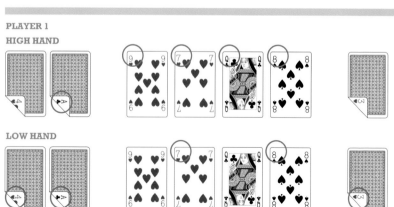

LOW HAND

PLAYER 6
HIGH HAND

LOW HAND There is no qualifying low hand

When the dust clears, the best high hand wins half the pot and the
best qualifying low hand wins the other half.

3

Starting Hands

TEXAS HOLD'EM

Poker is a game of decisions. Although you cannot control the way the cards fall or your opponents' actions, the decisions you make are how you exercise your skills in a poker game.

Decisions separate winners from losers. When the cards have evened out in the long run, the true measure of any player's skill is the quality of that person's decision-making. The better your decisions, the more you can expect to win.

Whether or not to see the flop with your first two cards is generally the most important decision you'll make playing hold'em. Choosing to play or toss your cards away is really about choosing to invest money in a pot with hopes of winning it back plus a substantial return. It's a decision you have to make each time you're dealt a hand.

Starting Hands

With only 169 different two-card starting combinations, as shown on the chart opposite, learning to play them is not as tough as you might think. Pairs of the same rank have equal value before the flop. So do similarly suited cards. For example, prior to the flop, 9s-9h is equal to 9d-9c, and Kc-Qc is just as worthy as Kd-Qd. But if the flop contains three diamonds, then the Kd-Qd might be priceless, and the Kc-Qc unplayable.

Sometimes you'll need to deviate from the chart's guidance. Consider a hand like Th-9h. Just because it may be a playable early position hand in a normal game doesn't mean you must play it. In a game with frequent raises or shorthanded pots, it is unplayable. It is a very speculative hand—one best played inexpensively, from late position. Ideally, this kind of hand plays best on the button with five or more callers ahead of you in a pot that hasn't been raised—then it's worth a call. You can always toss your hand away whenever the flop is unfavorable.

Playable hands in early position begin with big pairs and big connectors, which fan out from the chart's upper left-hand corner. Middle and late position playable hands are tucked under the curve formed by the early position hands, and unplayable two-card holdings are located toward the right-hand side of the charts. With a little work you should be able to commit this to memory or visualize it and be able to recall it at will.

Notice that you'll play far fewer hands in early position. You'll also find that suited cards have a lot more value than unsuited cards of equal rank. Please understand that the strategic plan embodied in this chart is not a formula to blindly follow. If the pot has been raised, you'll need to tighten up significantly on the hands you play, particularly those that are played from early position.

PAIRS AND SUITED CARDS

A-A	A-K	K-Q	Q-J	J-T	T-9	9-8	9-7	7-6	6-5	5-4	4-3	3-2
K-K	A-Q	K-J	Q-T	J-9	T-8	9-7	8-6	7-5	6-4	5-3	4-2	
Q-Q	A-J	K-T	Q-9	J-8	T-7	9-6	8-5	7-4	6-3	5-2		
J-J	A-T	K-9	Q-8	J-7	T-6	9-5	8-4	7-3	6-2			
T-T	A-9	K-8	Q-7	J-6	T-5	9-4	8-3	7-2				
9-9	A-8	K-7	Q-6	J-5	T-4	9-3	8-2					
8-8	A-7	K-6	Q-5	J-4	T-3	9-2						
7-7	A-6	K-5	Q-4	J-3	T-2							
6-6	A-5	K-4	Q-3	J-2								
5-5	A-4	K-3	Q-2									
4-4	A-3	K-2										
3-3	A-2											
2-2												

KEY

- Play in any position
- Play in mid/late position
- Play in late position only
- Unplayable hands

UNSUITED CARDS

A-K	K-Q	Q-J	J-T	T-9	9-8	9-7	7-6	6-5	5-4	4-3	3-2
A-Q	K-J	Q-T	J-9	T-8	9-7	8-6	7-5	6-4	5-3	4-2	
A-J	K-T	Q-9	J-8	T-7	9-6	8-5	7-4	6-3	5-2		
A-T	K-9	Q-8	J-7	T-6	9-5	8-4	7-3	6-2			
A-9	K-8	Q-7	J-6	T-5	9-4	8-3	7-2				
A-8	K-7	Q-6	J-5	T-4	9-3	8-2					
A-7	K-6	Q-5	J-4	T-3	9-2						
A-6	K-5	Q-4	J-3	T-2							
A-5	K-4	Q-3	J-2								
A-4	K-3	Q-2									
A-3	K-2										
A-2											

Starting hands categorized

Each one of the 169 unique starting combinations you might be dealt fits into one of only five categories: pairs, connecting cards, gapped cards, suited connectors, or suited gapped cards. That's it. Five categories. That's all you have to worry about.

If you're not dealt a pair, your cards will either be suited or unsuited. Both suited and unsuited cards can be connected or gapped. Examples of connectors are K-Q, 8-7, and 4-3.

Unconnected cards might be one-, two-, three-gapped or more and would include holdings such as: K-J, 9-6, 6-2, or 9-3. While you can improve to a straight with one-, two-, or three-gapped cards, the general rule is: The smaller the gap, the easier it is to make a straight.

Suppose you hold 10-6. Your only straight possibility using both your cards is 9-8-7. But if you hold 10-9, you can make a straight with K-Q-J, Q-J-8, J-8-7, and 8-7-6.

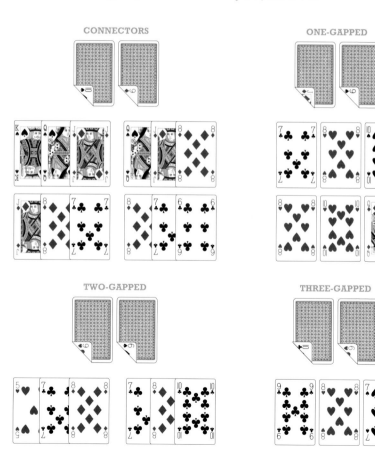

With every rule, however, there are certain exceptions. A hand like A-K is technically a connector, but can make only one straight. It needs to marry a Q-J-T. An A-2 is in the same boat. It needs to cozy up to a 5-4-3. Although they are connectors and not gapped, each holding can make only one straight because they lie at the end of the spectrum.

There are other exceptions, too. K-Q and 3-2 are also limited. K-Q can make a straight only two ways, by connecting with A-J-T or J-T-9, and 3-2 is in a similar fix. The only other limited connectors are Q-J and 4-3. These two holdings can each make three straights. The Q-J needs A-K-T, K-T-9, or T-9-8. It can't make that fourth straight because there is no room above an ace. The 4-3 is similarly constrained because there is no room below the ace. But any other connectors can make straights four ways, which is a big advantage over one-, two-, or three-gapped cards.

ADVICE FOR BEGINNERS
Here are four guidelines to follow while you're learning hold'em:
- Cards that are neither suited nor paired, unconnected, and four-gapped or larger should never be played under normal circumstances.
- Play few hands in early position.
- Suited cards are more valuable than unsuited cards of equal rank.
- Gapped cards are usually not as valuable as connectors because of their difficulty in completing straights.

The importance of position

Since acting later in a hand is more advantageous than acting early, you can afford to see the flop with weaker hands in late position. In fact, if you're last to act, you'll have the advantage of seeing how each of your opponents acts on the current round of betting. That's a big edge, since some starting hands play better against a large number of opponents, while others play better heads-up. In late position you'll also know who's representing strength, because you'll see which players have checked or bet, folded, called, or raised. The later you act, the more information you'll have at your disposal. The later your position, the less limited your starting hand requirements.

Pairs You Can Play in Any Position

A strong starting hand gives you the flexibility to play in any position—early, middle, or late— and there's no stronger starting hand than a big pair, as the extreme left column of the chart on page 85 shows.

Aces

Aces are the very best two-card holding you can be dealt before the flop. When you're dealt a pair of aces, with the flop yet to come, no one has a stronger hand than you. If someone bets, go ahead and raise. If there's a bet and a raise in front of you, feel free to reraise. There's not a hand out there right now that's better than yours—and you can bet on it.

Kings

If you've been dealt a pair of kings before the flop, you are favored against any hand except a pair of aces. "How often," you might ask, "will I be dealt kings when an opponent is dealt aces?"

It happens so rarely that you really don't have much to worry about if you raise with kings and someone else makes it three bets. As long as an ace doesn't flop, you're probably still in the lead.

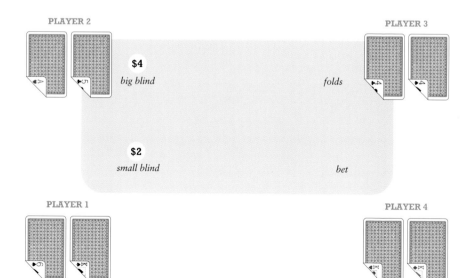

PLAYER 2

PLAYER 3

$4
big blind

folds

$2
small blind

bet

PLAYER 1

PLAYER 4

One key to playing kings is to be conscious of the flop. Many of your opponents will see the flop with any hand that contains an ace. As a result, you have to be a bit wary whenever an ace hits the board. That doesn't mean you have to surrender your kings every time an ace falls—and you'd almost never do so if you were heads-up—but against a relatively large number of opponents, or if there is a bet and raise before it's your turn to act, you might quickly determine that your kings are doomed.

Queens and jacks

Whenever you're dealt a pair of queens or jacks before the flop, you probably have the best two-card holding, and your concern is usually with the flop. Anyone who calls with an ace or king in their hand will be in the lead if the flop contains overcards. Of course, you could be fortunate enough to catch one of the most profitable flops of all—one that makes top pair or two pair for your opponent, but makes a set for you.

While queens or jacks are powerful hands, unlike aces and kings, you do have to think about playing defense. It is now critically important to narrow the field. When it's your turn to act, you must raise. If there's a raise, you must reraise. This is mandatory.

Make it too expensive for anyone holding an ace or a king with a weak kicker to see the flop.

If you can eliminate an opponent who holds one of these two cards, you have significantly increased your chances of winning.

Middle pairs (TENS, NINES, EIGHTS, SEVENS)

When dealt one of these mid-range pairs before the flop, you'll encounter the same kinds of problems you had with jacks and queens. Only the magnitude differs. The smaller the pair, the bigger the problem.

Even with the best of these holdings—a pair of tens—there are 16 cards that could give one of your opponents a higher pair.

When you have a pair of sevens or eights and the flop contains three smaller cards, you have an additional worry: The cards will be so tightly clustered that one of your opponents might make a straight.

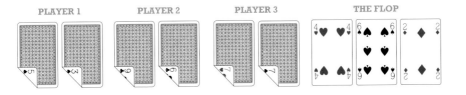

PLAYER 1   PLAYER 2   PLAYER 3   THE FLOP

Early Position Hands

Assuming you don't start with a big pair, a playable early-position hand must have two characteristics: strength and potential. High-value cards are always nice to have, of course, but in the absence of pairings you're relying on a favorable flop to maximize the potential of your hand and turn it into a winner.

Big suited cards (A-K, A-Q, A-J, A-T, K-Q, K-J, K-T, Q-J, Q-T)

While these ace/big-kicker holdings can grow into powerful hands, bear two important considerations in mind:

First, understand that they are *premium drawing hands*, not premium hands in themselves—they have to match the board to win.

Second, although many players treat these hands—A-K suited in particular— as though they were as valuable as a pair of aces or kings, nothing could be further from the truth. With a pair, your hand has immediate value. With a drawing hand, it has none. Before the flop all you have is potential—and it won't always be realized. In fact, if you're dealt A-K, you'll flop an ace or a king only about one-third of the time. Keep this in mind and you'll be able to release them when warranted. That's a big edge over many of your opponents, specifically those players who seldom fold these hands regardless of the flop and subsequent betting action.

Big unsuited cards (A-K, A-Q, A-J, A-T, K-Q, K-J)

What's the difference between big connectors and big suited connectors? Other than the fact that one is suited and the other isn't, nothing: The pair of aces you make with Ad-Ks is identical to the pair you'll make with Ah-Kh, and an ace-high straight is an ace-high straight regardless of suit. But in practice, the fact that one of these starting hands is suited does make a difference, and that difference is flush potential.

While you won't make a flush that often, the nut flush is almost always the winning hand in an unpaired board. Because you can expect to rake in a nice pot with the nut flush, the earning potential of these suited holdings makes them much more valuable than their unsuited cousins. Even if you don't make a flush, consider the following.

Suppose you raise with a hand like Ad-Kd, and the flop is Td-3d-2h. Although it doesn't provide immediate assistance, the fact that you've flopped a flush draw allows you to continue contesting the pot. Now suppose the turn card is the Kc. You've turned top pair, which may well be the best hand. Even if it's not, you still have a flush draw. If one of the remaining nine diamonds falls on the river, you'll improve from top pair to the nut flush.

If you make the nut flush on the river, with a board that has no pair or straight-flush potential, you can raise with impunity.

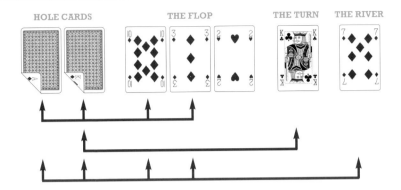

Middle Position Hands

Middle position is a tricky seat to occupy: Because it offers some cover it may tempt inexperienced players holding a middle pair or suited ace to rashness. Exercise careful judgement and avoid overplaying a mediocre hand.

Pairs

In middle position you can add sixes and fives to your list of playable pairs. However, if the game you're in features frequent raises, especially from players who act after you, consider changing games or seats. If not, you'll have to constrict the range of hands you play,

because pairs such as sevens or eights—never mind sixes or fives—just don't fare very well in raised pots.

With sixes and fives, as with other small and middling pairs, your objective is to get in cheaply and either flop a set or get out.

HOLE CARDS

NOTE: *Any of these 27 cards on the flop could mean a higher pair for another player.*

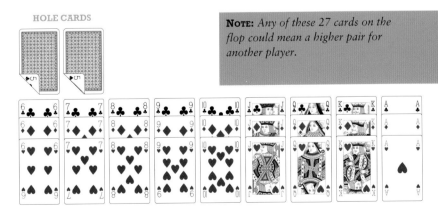

Suited cards (A-9s A-8s, A-7s, A-6s, K-9s, Q-9s, Q-8s, J-8s, T-8s, 9-8s)

NOTE: *Player 1's hand A♠-A♥-Jc-9♠-7♠ beats Player 2's hand A♦-A♥-J♣-7♠-6♦.*

PLAYER 1   PLAYER 2

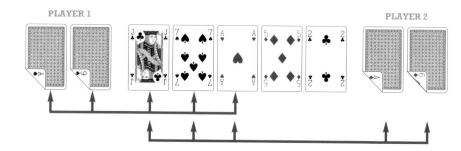

If you are in the kind of game where your opponents routinely play any suited ace, you can extend your playable repertoire and add A-9s through A-6s. In these games your A-9 will usually be the best ace if there was no pre-flop raise, since most low-limit players raise with an A-Ts or better.

But A-8s, A-7s, and A-6s are not as strong as A-9s, and are still dangerous hands in middle position, no matter what kind of game you're in. The danger lies in flopping an ace and finding yourself outkicked.

Hands like K-9s, Q-9s, Q-8s, J-8s, T-8s, 9-8s may look good, but with the exception of 9-8s they are all gapped and therefore offer fewer straight possibilities than connectors.

One danger with this group of starting hands is that they can look good, especially to the uninitiated.

Unsuited cards like K-T, Q-J, Q-T, J-T are the last group of hands to consider adding to your playing repertoire from middle position.

King-ten can be dangerous whenever there's a raised pot and a king flops.

Most players raise with hands like A-K, K-Q, and often K-J. If the pot was raised and you call with K-T, you'll have no idea whether yours is the best hand. When you play K-T and the pot is raised, chances are you'll wind up on the defensive for the remainder of the hand—and that's not a position most players are comfortable with.

Queen-ten has all of the same problems associated with K-T, plus it is a weaker hand. Q-J and J-T are both marginal hands. Ideally, you'd like to flop at least a straight draw. Flop a pair and you have to worry about an overcard falling on the turn or river. If you make top pair with either of these hands, you may as well bet or raise right on the flop to thin the field and get some idea about the strength of your hand.

Late Position Hands

In late position you've had the advantage of seeing how most if not all of your opponents have played their hands. If you are faced with cold-calling a raise, release the marginal holdings you'd play only in unraised pots.

You also know with certainty whether you are taking the flop with a large or small number of opponents. Some hands, like smaller suited connectors, can only be profitably played in unraised pots with a large number of opponents. Others, like large pairs, play better when you can reduce your opponents to a few.

In poker, as in life itself, knowledge is power. Acting last affords a major strategic edge simply because of the information at your disposal. Play small

suited connectors in early position and you're forced to guess the number of opponents who will see the flop with you and whether or not you'll be raised. In late position you'll have this information at your disposal.

> **ADVICE**
> Use the extra information that acting late provides to make better informed decisions.

Pairs

When you're on or near the button, you can play any pair—providing the pot has not been raised before it's your turn to act. Go ahead and play twos, threes, and fours. If you're up against a large

number of opponents, there's no chance you'll have top pair on the flop, and your strategy at this point is to flop a set, an open-ended straight draw, or release the hand.

Ace suited (A-5s - A-2s)

In late position with little fear of a raise you can play hands as weak as A-5s through A-2s. You'd love to flop a flush with this hand, since it would be the nut flush. But if you don't flop a flush or a flush draw, what then? If an ace flops you may be in deep kicker trouble. Play these hands carefully. Be willing to release them whenever you suspect your ace might be bested because of your poor kicker.

HOLE CARDS

THE FLOP

NOTE:
Anyone playing an ace with a three kicker or higher is now beating you.

King suited (K-8s - K-2s)

These are similar in character to the small ace suited hands. You are hoping to flop a flush or a flush draw, and are in danger with any other flop. Your kicker is weak, and if there is any appreciable action, you are likely to be up against another king with a bigger side card. These are bargain-basement hands only to be played against many opponents in unraised pots.

Gapped and suited jacks, tens, and nines (J-7s, T-7s, 9-7s, 9-6s)

These are very ragged hands. Avoid them under all circumstances and you won't be leaving much money on the table.

Connectors and one-gappers, eights, sevens, sixes, and fives (8-7s, 8-6s, 7-6s, 7-5s, 6-5s, 5-4s)

These are classic fit or fold hands. If you don't flop a big hand or a big draw, you'll simply have to release your hand. Eights and sevens seldom hold up as top pair, and when they do you've always got to worry about a straight draw. Play these hands cheaply, if at all. Make sure you've got lots of opponents who will presumably pay you off on the few occasions when you find yourself the recipient of a miracle on the flop.

Other unsuited cards (A-9 - A-7, K-9, Q-9, J-9, J-8, T-9, T-8, 9-8, 9-7, 8-7)

These hands are much more dangerous than their suited cousins. The reason? You can't make a flush that uses both of your cards. As a consequence, the upside potential with these holdings is severely limited. What's more, you still run the risk of losing a large pot if you flop what appears to be a reasonable hand, only to learn too late that you're on the down-side of kicker trouble.

Complex Situations

Sometimes you face a situation that doesn't fit the requirements shown on the starting hands chart. What should you do, for example, when you're dealt a medium to big pair in early position and someone raises before it's your turn to act?

If your big pair is aces, kings, or queens, you ought to raise or reraise. If you're the first one in, raise with a pair of tens or higher. To add deception to your game, raise on occasion with a pair of sevens or higher. With a small pair,

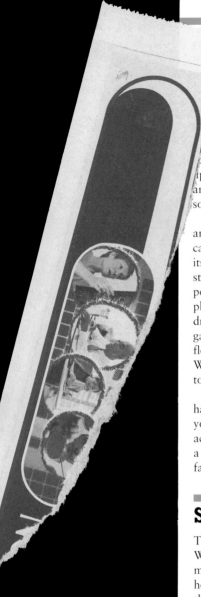

off either heads up—in ... you're hoping your opponent ... big cards—or against a large ... you're playing a small pair ... a large field you'll have to flop a ... justify continuing. Here you're ... ting your small pair like a drawing ... nd. It will have to improve to keep ... ou in the game, because when you're ... p against a large number of opponents ... and overcards appear on the board, ... someone is likely to have a better hand.

If you hold a pair of sevens or eights, and they are higher than any of the cards appearing on the flop, the board itself will be so tightly clustered that a straight or straight draw is usually a real possibility. In higher-limit games, tricky players may seize these opportunities to drive you off the pot. In lower-limit games, where many opponents take the flop, the need for trickery is minimized. With so many callers, you generally have to show down the best hand to win.

With a medium pair you might have to flop a set to win the pot. If you're holding a pair of kings, only an ace on the flop may give another player a bigger pair. But if you hold tens, every face card on the board creates a

potential pair bigger than yours. If you don't flop a set or overpair, it is difficult to justify continuing with your hand, particularly when two or three bigger cards fall on the flop and there are a number of callers.

Suppose you're dealt a pair of tens in early position and there are four callers. The flop is A-J-6, of mixed suits. Because players tend to play big cards, chances are one of them has paired an ace or a jack, especially if there is a bet and call before it's your turn to act. If you ride your pair of tens to the end of the track, you'll throw off a bundle of money along the way.

With smaller pairs, unless you are up against only one other player, you almost have to flop a set to make it worth playing on. If you don't flop a set when dealt a pair of deuces, for example, every subsequent card is an overcard. The only way to win under these circumstances is for the board to miss everyone, and with multiway action, that's unlikely. Expert players routinely throw away small pairs unless they can play them against many opponents for just one bet.

Selectivity—The Key to Winning Play

The secret of winning is to put yourself in situations that offer favorable pot odds. When you're in a favorable situation, you need to be aggressive, either to get more money in the pot when you have a big hand or to eliminate competition when you're holding the kind of hand that plays best against fewer opponents. Underlying all these strategic ideas is the need to be a selective, aggressive, and disciplined player. All the theory you'll need to become a skilled hold'em player is right here in this book; the discipline is not. You'll have to find that for yourself. If you're able to exercise discipline 100 percent of the time, you can look forward to a bright future at the tables.

OMAHA

If you're learning Omaha after first playing Texas hold'em, you'll have to make some adjustments in selecting starting hands. After all, one good hold'em hand embedded within a four-card Omaha hand may not be a good hand at all.

For example, a hand like Q-Q-7-3 of mixed suits is not nearly the equivalent of a pair of queens in hold'em. Pocket queens are a premium starting hand in hold'em, but in Omaha, your pair of queens is only one of six possible combinations you can make from your four starting cards. In this example, the five other combinations are pretty worthless when you consider each of them individually.

While it's easy to look at this kind of hand and say to yourself, "Wow, I've got queens, the third-best possible pair," you need to assess all six two-card combinations before becoming ecstatic. In this case, five of the six combinations aren't worth playing. Plus, in the case of your queens, in Omaha it's more likely than in hold'em that one of your opponents will have been dealt a pocket pair of kings or aces.

Even a hand like Ad-Jh-8s-8c—four cards that combine to make two pretty good hold'em hands—is not worth much in Omaha.

While two of the hands are okay, the other four combinations don't work well together. The ace isn't suited, and

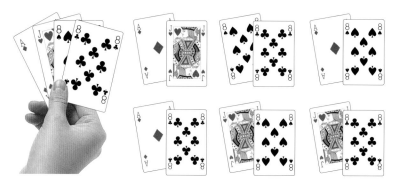

neither are any of the other combos. Were you to flop a set of eights, it still might not be the best possible set. Even if it were, sets are much more vulnerable in Omaha than in hold'em, because winning hands tend to be a lot bigger in Omaha. And why not? You're making a five-card Omaha hand from a selection of nine cards—four in your hand and five on the board. It stands to reason that the winning combination will be bigger on average than in hold'em, where you're making the best five-card hand from seven cards.

Another thing to consider is the number of starting card combinations.

In a nine-handed hold'em game, there are a total of nine, two-card combinations seeking help from the flop. In Omaha, where each player can combine his four starting cards into six two-card combinations, you have a total of 54 two-card combinations looking at the flop. When there are 54 two-card combinations out there, the flop is usually going to help someone. If that someone isn't you, it's generally a long way to the end. With 54 two-card combinations, the more your starting cards work with each other, the better your chances of hitting the flop.

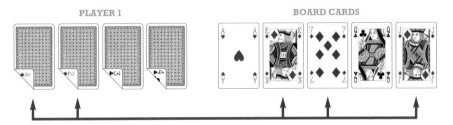

PLAYER 1   BOARD CARDS

Learning Omaha's rules

In terms of hand selection, Omaha played for high is a very different game from Omaha/8, in which a high hand and a qualifying low hand will split the pot. Those very desirable Omaha/8 low hands, such as A-2-3-4 or 2-3-5-6, are not desirable in this version of Omaha.

A low straight like A-2-3-4 is often beaten by a bigger straight. In fact, the only guaranteed way to make the best hand with A-2-3-4 is when the ace is suited to any of your other cards, the board never pairs, there is no straight flush possible, and you make your ace-high flush.

But if that were the case, you'd only be using one of your six-card starting hand combinations, and that's not the way to win in the long run. If your ace and deuce were suited, you'd be looking toward the flop with your suited ace-deuce combination, but ignoring A-3 and A-4—both of which are offsuit—as well as 4-3, 4-2, and 3-2. Even if some of the latter three-card combinations were suited, each makes a paltry flush, and any straights could easily be beaten.

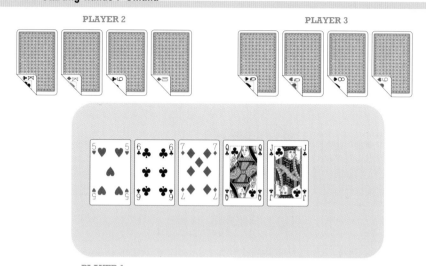

PLAYER 2   PLAYER 3

PLAYER 1

NOTE: *Player 1 flopped a straight with his 3♣-4♣, but Player 3 flopped a bigger straight. On the river Player 1 made a flush with his 3♣-4♣ to beat Player 3, but Player 2 easily made a bigger flush with his K♣-9♣ to win the hand.*

Another major difference between Omaha/8 and Omaha high-only is that Omaha/8 is generally played at fixed limits, whereas Omaha is more typically played pot-limit. In North America you'll find Omaha played as a tournament game in casinos and card rooms, but infrequently as a cash game. Omaha/8, however, is a staple cash game in many North American casinos. In the U.K., Ireland, and many other European casinos, Omaha is usually played high only, pot-limit. Why are things this way? There's no reason why you couldn't play Omaha/8 as a pot-limit game and Omaha high-only at fixed limits, but things just didn't work out that way. However, if you play online, where you might be playing against opponents from all over the world, you'll find both games available in limit and pot-limit versions, depending on which Internet site you decide to visit.

As in Omaha/8 the most important decision you'll make in Omaha is whether to play or fold after you are dealt your four face-down cards. Every other tactical choice during the play of a hand stems from this initial decision, and it's a decision you'll face each and every hand. To become a winning Omaha player you'll have to be right about playing or folding the vast majority of the time.

Omaha versus Omaha/8

If you're learning Omaha after playing Omaha/8, you might want to consider the following differences in strategy.

Dump Your Low Hands Making the best low hand won't win anything in this game, unless it's the best high hand too, and that won't happen often. If you're dealt A-2-3-4—a real powerhouse in Omaha/8 because it can easily make the best low hand and capture at least half the pot—feel free to mutter under your breath about holding the right hand in the wrong game, but ditch it; it's a dog.

Mid Ranging In Omaha/8 you'd seldom play a hand like 9-8-7-6, because if you make a straight you'll probably have to give half of it to an opponent with a better low hand. In Omaha high, however, you never have to worry about someone snatching half the pot from under your nose.

Omaha versus hold'em

If you're coming to Omaha from hold'em, here's something else to think about.

Wrap It Up Omaha can often be a game of straights and flushes, and they are not the rarity they are in hold'em. Whenever a possible straight exists in the array of community cards on the board, someone is much more likely in Omaha to have the right two-card combination in his or her hand. Likewise, whenever the board is paired someone is more likely to have a full house or four-of-a-kind, but beyond those possibilities, straights and flushes are the name of the game. If the board contains three cards of the same suit, chances are pretty good that someone has made a flush. If the board does not contain three cards of the same suit, a flush cannot possibly be made by you or your opponents.

That's where wraps come into play: If you have four sequenced cards or four cards with small gaps, you can make a straight in any number of ways. In hold'em the maximum number of cards you can have that will complete a straight is eight. Not in Omaha. You can have straight draws with 13, 17, and even as many as 20 outs to complete a straight. In fact, if you flop a straight draw with 20 outs, you will be an odds-on favorite to make it. If you have a 20-out wrap hand, you'll make your hand 70 percent of the time.

Here's how it works. Suppose you begin with T-8-6-5 and the flop is 9-7-4. You can make a straight with any one of four jacks, three tens, three eights, three sixes, three fives, or four treys.

Although you'll complete your straight an astonishing 70 percent of the time, don't get carried away. You may still lose, since 20 outs to a straight does not mean 20 outs to the best hand, and sometimes a bigger straight is possible. Moreover, if you make even the biggest possible straight, but the board either pairs or comes up three-suited in the process, your hand might lose to a flush, full house, or quads.

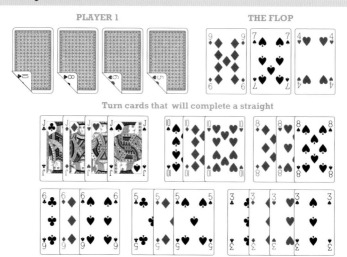

But all of this is for future consideration. For the time being, just be aware of the incredible possibilities that sequenced cards can offer you when you're looking at your four starting Omaha cards.

Your choice of starting hands depends on your position in the betting order and how competently your opponents play. The starting hands we'll discuss do not constitute a restrictive list of hands you may play, nor does it exclude all other hands. They are guidelines that you can adjust as you gain experience. If you're new to the game, you might want to follow these guidelines to the letter, but with experience you should feel free to adjust for changing conditions.

You'll be dealt four starting cards that should work in concert with one another. Card "A" plays with "B." "A" also plays with "C" and "D." "B" plays with "C" as well as with "D." Card "C" plays with card "D." Add up the possibilities and you'll find that six

unique two-card combinations can be made from these four cards.

If one of your starting cards doesn't relate to the other three, your possibilities for forming a hand have been greatly reduced, and along with it your chances for winning. Suppose you have three coordinated cards and a fourth card that doesn't fit—it's called a dangler—such as: king, queen, jack, and an offsuit deuce. That deuce doesn't coordinate with any of your other three cards.

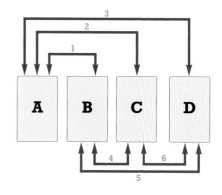

Danglers sorely reduce the number of outs to a straight because you are essentially wrapping only three cards around a board rather than four.

If you insist on playing danglers, you're going to be up against four of your opponent's cards with only three of your own. That means your opponent can combine his four starting cards into six effective two-card combinations, whereas the best you can manage with three cards that work together is three two-card combos. Three versus six represents long odds that you'll have to avoid much of the time to become a good Omaha player. While a hand with only three coordinated cards can be worth playing sometimes, it ought to

contain at least a medium pair in combination with a draw to the best possible flush, such as Ac-3c-8h-8d. The ideal flop for this hand would be two clubs that included the eight of clubs, but even if you flop the nut flush draw or a set of eights you'll be okay.

Before discussing specific starting hands, we'll take a broader, more conceptual look at things, with an eye to determining the kinds of hands you'd like to make when playing Omaha.

HOLE CARDS   ALL SIX-CARD COMBINATIONS

Dangler

Big hands are bigger in Omaha

Full House The bigger the better. There's nothing that's going to cost you more money than making a full house and losing to a bigger one—unless you make the biggest full house and run up against four-of-a-kind, but that's a rarity. If you've set your sights on a flush or a straight, remember that whenever a pair appears among the

communal board cards a full house usually grabs the pot. But if the board is Q-J-5 and a jack falls on the turn, the player who makes a full house with a pair of fives in his hand can easily lose to queens full, jacks full, or even quad jacks. As in other forms of poker, high cards are much more valuable than lower-ranked holdings, and winding up

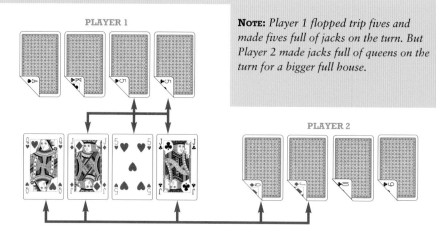

PLAYER 1

NOTE: *Player 1 flopped trip fives and made fives full of jacks on the turn. But Player 2 made jacks full of queens on the turn for a bigger full house.*

PLAYER 2

second-best in any hand is a lot more costly than missing the flop altogether and tossing your hand away.

Nut Flush It's worth remembering that a suited ace can make the best possible flush and any other flush can be beaten. Unless you have a clear-cut reason to play lower-ranking flush draws, as you would if you also had a draw to a straight or a set, you're better off avoiding any situation where you might make the hand you're hoping for and lose with it.

Nut Straight One reason that low cards are troublesome in this game is that low straights are often beaten by higher ones. If you are fortunate enough to flop a big wrap hand, one that gives you 13, 17, or even 20 outs to a straight, remember that outs to your hand is not the same as outs to the nuts. As a general rule, the more wrap cards you hold that are higher than the cards on the board, the more likely that you'll make the highest possible straight. In fact, if you're very lucky, you'll flop the

highest possible straight with a redraw to an even higher one. If that's the case, and you and an opponent both make a straight on the turn, you might get lucky and make a bigger one on the river.

Poker players call this "freerolling" and you're in a situation where you will either win the entire pot or split it, whereas your opponent will either win half the pot or lose all of it. It's wonderful to be able to bet and raise with impunity, knowing you're in a no-lose situation.

While we've considered straights and flushes separately, it's important to realize that some of your better starting hands contain both straight and flush draws and offer a variety of ways to win the pot. This allows you to play aggressively, because you can bet and raise without fear of one of the other hands coming to fruition with the turn of another communal card.

PLAYER 1 makes a straight on the flop with J♣-8♥-7♠
from the board and T♠-9♠ from his hole cards.

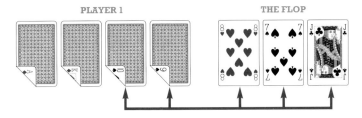

PLAYER 1 has the straight that he made on the flop.

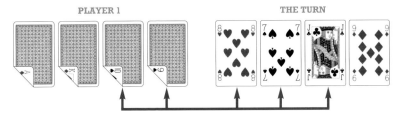

PLAYER 2 makes a straight on the turn with J♣-9♦-7♠
from the board and T♣-8♠ from his hole cards.

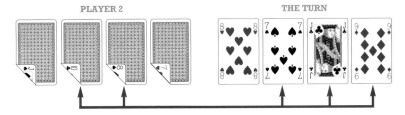

PLAYER 1 makes a higher straight on the river with Q♥-J♣-9♦
from the board and K♦-T♠ from his hole cards.

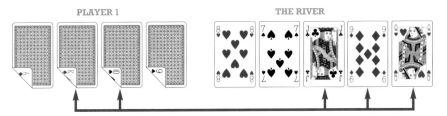

PLAYER 2 has the same straight on the river as he did on the turn.

Recommended Starting Hands

If you follow the advice given in this list of starting hands, you'll seldom get into trouble or find yourself confused about whether you ought to continue to play or fold. Please bear in mind that these starting hands differ greatly from the suggested starting hands for Omaha/8. Although the mechanics of the games are identical, the games themselves are quite different, as are the strategies required to win.

Ace-ace combinations

Any hand containing a pair of aces is a terrific starting hand, though some are stronger than others. Obviously a hand like As-Ad-Ks-Kd is about as good as it gets. You're starting with the two best pairs and if you flop a set it will be the highest possible set. Any full house that may be derived from this holding would also be the highest possible full house.

Consider the difference in quality between the above hand and a pair of "dry aces," such as As-Ad-9h-5c. It lacks flush and straight potential, can only flop one set rather than two, and can easily be run down by a group of opponents. Nevertheless, this hand would be favored against any other opponent who does not hold a pair of aces in his hand. It's as important to raise with this hand in hopes of reducing the field as it is to raise with a higher quality hand containing a pair of aces—perhaps even more important.

Other good hands involving a pair of aces would include such holdings as A-A-Q-Q, A-A-J-J, A-A-T-T, A-A-9-9, and any pair along with a pair of aces. If one of the aces is suited to another of your cards so much the better, and if both aces are suited that's better yet.

Aces are valuable even if they're not accompanied by another pair. Hands like

NOTE: *This player has flopped a set of kings. The added presence of two aces in his hand means that it won't be possible for any other player to make a bigger set. If the board does not pair, and no three cards of the same suit appear, his kings will win the pot.*

PLAYER 1

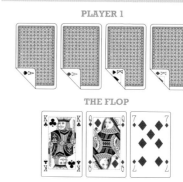

THE FLOP

A-A-J-T, A-A-K-Q, A-A-Q-J, A-A-K-T, and A-A-K-J are all terrific starting hand combinations and can be played very aggressively before the flop. After all, no one can have a bigger hand before the flop than one containing a pair of aces. The difference between an incredibly good hand such as A-A-K-K double suited and A-A-8-4 is that the former has so much more potential for making big hands over and above its pair of aces that it is a far superior holding.

King-king and queen-queen combinations

Just as any hand containing a pair of aces is a good starting hand, so are hands containing a pair of kings and a pair of queens. The quality of each particular holding that includes either a pair of kings or queens is similar to that of hands containing a pair of aces.

In the best of these hands the big pair is supported by another big pair and is double suited. Thus Kd-Ks-Qd-Qs is a better hand than Kd-Ks-9d-9s. Although the flushes will only be king-high, the first hand can make bigger sets and therefore bigger full houses than the second. K-K-Q-Q can make bigger straights too.

Next in desirability are hands that are single suited. Once again, a hand like Kd-Ks-Qd-Qh is a better hand than Kd-Ks-9d-9h, for the same reasons.

A single pair of kings or queens supported by potential straight cards is also very desirable. A hand such as Kd-Ks-Qd-Js offers a big pair, a draw to a very big set and full house, the second-best possible flush draw in two suits, and a variety of very big straights.

Wrap hands

Wrap hands can be incredibly strong, with the strongest of them all being J-T-9-8 double suited. Double-suited hands are better than similar hands that are only single suited, and a single-suited hand is more desirable than one that's unsuited. The strength of these hands lies not so much in their flush potential—they can easily be beaten by queen-high, king-high, or ace-high flushes—but in all the straights that can be made with these cards.

Wrap hands need not be as tightly bound as the above holding. A hand with a gap in it can also provide a draw to a straight that can be completed by any of 20 outs. Since bigger is better, the higher the starting cards, the more likely yours will be the nut straight. So what's the difference between this hand and one like A-K-Q-J, which is also a terrific holding? With the jack-high grouping you can make more straights, because it

can meld with cards above as well as below in ranking. On the other hand, although you won't make as many straights with the ace-high grouping, all of them will be the nut straight.

FOLDING WRAP HANDS
Small wrap hands can cost you most or all of your chips in pot-limit games, and quite a few chips in limit poker games as well. Good Omaha players have the discipline to release these weaker wrap hands and save their time, chips, and energy for bigger holdings.

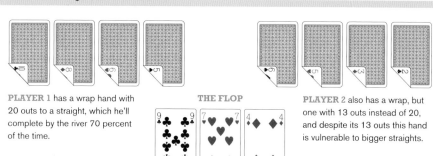

PLAYER 1 has a wrap hand with 20 outs to a straight, which he'll complete by the river 70 percent of the time.

THE FLOP

PLAYER 2 also has a wrap, but one with 13 outs instead of 20, and despite its 13 outs this hand is vulnerable to bigger straights.

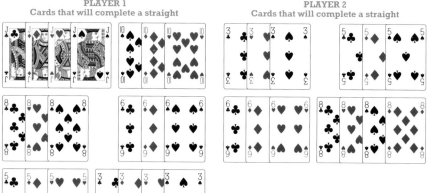

PLAYER 1
Cards that will complete a straight

PLAYER 2
Cards that will complete a straight

Because higher hands are generally better than lower ones, small wraps such as 6-5-4-3 are much worse than they might first appear. Yes, everything we've said about making straights with this hand and others like it are just as true as that for J-T-9-8. The big difference lies in the quality of the straight you make when the flop hits you. If you make a straight with 6-5-4-3, one of your opponents might have made a bigger straight. Even if he hasn't there may be one or more opponents lurking in the weeds with a draw to a bigger straight.

NOTE: *Notice that some of Player 1's hole cards are in Player 2's outs, and some of Player 2's hole cards are in Player 1's outs. Players do not know what hole cards their opponents hold, so those cards are counted among the possible cards that comprise each person's outs.*

The Very Best Omaha Hands

Here are the best starting hands you might expect to be dealt in an Omaha game. In all cases, double-suited hands are superior to those that are single suited, and single-suited hands are superior to those that are unsuited. All of these selections support the construction of big full houses and big straights. When suited or double suited they also support building big flushes too—the kinds of hands that usually win pots in Omaha games.

A A K K	K K Q Q	Q Q J J	A K Q J
A A Q Q	K K J J	Q Q T T	A K Q T
A A J J	K K T T	Q Q 9 9	A K J T
A A T T	K K 9 9	Q Q A K	A Q J T
A A 9 9	K K A Q	Q Q A J	A J T 9
A A K Q	K K A J	Q Q A T	K Q J T
A A K J	K K A T	Q Q K J	K Q J 9
A A K T	K K Q J	Q Q K T	K J T 9
A A Q J	K K Q T	Q Q J T	Q J T 9
A A Q T	K K J T	Q Q J 9	
A A J T	K K J 9		

Very Good Hands

The hands that follow are emblematic of good starting hands for Omaha. They are not nearly as good as those hands based on pairs of aces, kings, or queens; nor are they as strong as big-suited connectors such as K-Q-J-T. But they are playable. This list is certainly not exclusive, but these hands provide examples of entire groups of analogous hands that are playable.

All of the very good hands are playable, because they offer numerous possibilities such as sets, straights, and flushes. The time to play hands of this type is when the pot has not been raised before it's your turn to act. These hands have difficulty growing into the nuts, and having to call a raised pot is a strong indication that the raiser is starting out with a bigger hand than yours. This puts the double-whammy on you: Not only are you an underdog to the better hand, but it will cost you two bets instead of one just to see the flop.

Call. You can flop a flush and straight draws with this hand.

Call if the pot has not been raised. With a hand like this you want to either flop a set of queens, a straight draw, or get packing.

This hand is significantly weaker than the very best hands, but it has high-card potential for a straight and can be played if the pot has not been raised before it's your turn to act. If the pot has been raised, someone probably has a bigger hand than yours and you ought to save your money for a better opportunity.

Call if the pot has not been raised. You've got some draws that are possible with this holding, though it's unlikely you'll ever make the best possible hand.

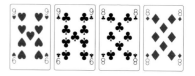

You have potential to build a straight or a flush, and you might flop a set too. This is a playable hand.

Unplayable Hands

The following are examples of hands you probably shouldn't play, even at the cost of a bet. These hands are either weak or tend to lead you into costly traps.

   The recommended hands are not the only ones you can play before the flop, but if you are learning the game and stick to these and others like them, you should be able to avoid the flaw of playing too many hands. Follow these suggestions and you'll seldom find yourself trapped in hands that are confusing. Releasing hands that do not catch part of the flop will be easy and less costly too. And when you do play, the quality of your hands will be quite high. Since most people play Omaha because it offers an easy rationale for playing more hands, our recommendations will allow you to take advantage of that propensity and profit from it.

Two straight possibilities with nothing else is another example of two nice looking hold'em hands adding up to a lot less than one good Omaha hand. Save your money.

Many hold'em players gravitate to hands like this: Two fair hold'em hands that are completely uncoordinated for Omaha. Neither the five nor the six work in any way with the queen or jack, and two playable hold'em hands don't always add up to a playable Omaha hand. There are lots of hands that fit into this category. Examples are A♠-T♥-5♣-5♦, J♥-8♥-5♣-4♣, and A♥-K♥-3♣-3♥. You should be able to think of a few others with some practice.

Although you'd raise with this hand in Omaha/8, you shouldn't even call with it in Omaha high. Any straight you make can be bested by a bigger one, and winning the pot with a three-high flush qualifies as a modern miracle. If an ace falls, your pair of aces will lose to any other ace because your kicker is so low.

Low sets and baby straights can doom you to a second-best hand that costs a lot more than you are apt to win if you get lucky. Just dig up the discipline to say "no" to hands like this.

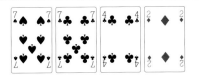

All of your possibilities are weak. A set of sevens is no guarantee of winning the pot. Making a seven-high flush or a straight using either your four-deuce or seven-four combination will produce hands that can easily be bested by others.

Fit or Fold

If your cards don't fit the flop, you should release your hand most of the time. Regardless of how many cards you start with, once the flop is dealt your hand needs to coordinate with it. If you begin an Omaha game with K♠-Q♠-J♣-T♣ but by the turn the board is 7♥-6♥-5♦-4♦, your hand has lost all of its value. Any red card probably gives at least one of your opponent's a flush and any one of them might already have a straight or two pair. Your hand, which admittedly was pretty imposing before the flop, is now worthless. Just toss them as soon as there's a bet and it's your turn to act.

HOLE CARDS

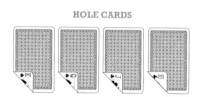

BOARD CARDS

Hand selection

Every form of poker requires a blend of skills, but in Omaha, as in Omaha/8, hand selection outweighs all else. Any hand that is possible is also probable in Omaha. You need not be as skilled at reading your opponents as in other forms of poker. Just reading the community cards to ascertain the best possible hand is usually enough. Bluffing too, particularly in lower limit games, is not nearly as important in Omaha as in other forms of poker. However, when you graduate to big-money, pot-limit play, bluffing and the ability to detect a bluff becomes a critically important skill.

Because many players will start with almost any four cards, if you can exert the discipline to wait for good starting cards—hands that are coordinated with cards that support each other in some discernable way—you will have an edge over most of your opponents in low-limit Omaha games.

Since acting later in a hand is a big advantage, you can afford to see the flop with weaker hands from late position. The later you act, the more information at your disposal, and poker is a game of information—incomplete information to be sure, but information nevertheless.

Before you decide to call with the four cards you've been dealt, ask yourself what kind of flop would be ideal for your hand. When you see the flop, determine which hand would be a perfect fit for it. This kind of analysis will help you ascertain how well the flop fits your hand.

Omaha Flops

Here are the convenient ways to characterize Omaha flops.

Paired When a pair flops, the best possible high hand is four-of-a-kind. Although flopping quads is a rarity, a full house is a distinct possibility.

Ideally, if you make a full house it will be a big one, and that's a good reason to play big pairs and avoid small ones.

Flush or Flush Draw Three or two cards of the same suit. The bigger the better.

Straight or Straight Draw Three or two cards in sequence, or gapped closely enough so that a straight is possible. You can flop straight draws with 8, 13, 17, and even 20 outs. Not every straight you make will ensure your winning the pot. Be careful of cards that might give an opponent a higher straight than yours, a card that completes your straight but results in three suited cards on the board, or a paired board. Either one is dangerous to your straight regardless of how big it might be.

These groupings are not mutually exclusive. Some of these attributes can appear in combination. For example, if the flop were A♣-A♦-Q♣ it would be paired and contain both a flush draw and a straight draw.

It's important to recognize when a flop has multiple possibilities and to understand how your hand stacks up in the pecking order of possibilities.

Suppose you called on the first round of betting with A♦-T♦-3♣-K♠, and the flop is Q♦-9♦-4♠. You don't have a completed hand at this point, but you do have draws to the nut flush and the highest straight. Any diamond on the turn gives you the best possible flush and a jack would complete your straight. Of course, if the 4♦ happens to fall you'd make your flush, but someone else would make a full house if they held a pair of queens or a pair of nines. They would even make four-of-a-kind if they had a pair of fours.

As a general rule you shouldn't continue beyond the flop without the best possible hand or a draw to the best possible hand. With each player holding six two-card combinations a lot of hands are possible. Make certain that you'll have the best hand if you catch the card you need.

HOLE CARDS

THE FLOP

HELPFUL TURN CARDS Any diamond except the 4♦, any jack

DANGEROUS TURN CARD 4♦, any queen, nine, or other card that pairs the board

DANGEROUS RIVER CARDS Any queen, nine, or other card that pairs the board

Should I continue beyond the flop?

DRAW QUALITY
If I make my hand, will it be the nuts?

Suppose you have Q♠-J♠ among your starting cards and the flop contains two spades. Although you do have a flush draw, two higher flushes are also possible. This is a dangerous hand. Drawing to the second- or third-best straight or flush or thinking you have this pot won because you've flopped the third- or second-best set are common variations on this theme. Omaha is a game of drawing to the best possible hand.

OPPONENTS
Do I have the right number and mix of opponents to justify drawing to my hand?

Some hands play better against large fields; others play better short handed. With a *flush draw* or *straight draw* you'd like more opponents in the pot with you if you make the nuts. However, with a starting hand like A-A-K-K unsuited, you need to raise or reraise to play the pot against as few opponents as possible. If you can accomplish this, your big pair may win without improving.

HOLE CARDS

THE FLOP

PLAYER 1

OR

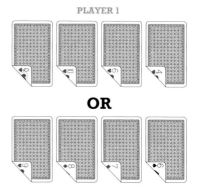

PLAYER 1 With a hand like one of these, you want to keep your opponents in the pot with you, because with fewer opponents the size of the pot will probably be too small to offset the odds against making your hand.

PLAYER 2

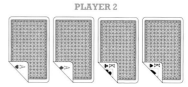

PLAYER 2 With a hand like this you should play against as few opponents as possible.

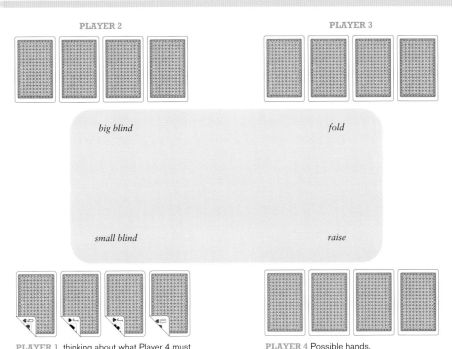

PLAYER 2

PLAYER 3

big blind

fold

small blind

raise

PLAYER 1, thinking about what Player 4 must hold in his hand in order to raise before the flop, decides to fold his good, but not great, pair.

PLAYER 4 Possible hands.

Pair of aces

Pair of kings or 2 high pairs

Draw to the nut straight

WAS IT RAISED?

Is my opponent the kind who usually raises only with big pairs, and if he is, how can I take advantage of the fact that he is essentially playing with his cards exposed, while mine are hidden?

When the pot is raised before the flop in Omaha, the raiser usually has at least a pair of aces in his hand, something like K-K-Q-Q, or a draw to the nut straight with a hand like K-Q-J-T. If you have big cards too, but not as big as the raiser, you'll probably be better off releasing your hand and awaiting a better opportunity.

OMAHA/8

Of all the decisions to be made playing Omaha/8, the most important is whether to play or fold after you are dealt four face-down cards before the flop. Every other tactical choice during the play of a hand stems from your initial decision about whether to fold or play, and it's a decision you'll face each and every hand. To become a winning Omaha player you'll have to be right about playing or passing the vast majority of the time.

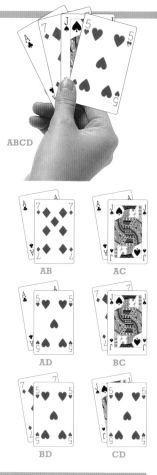

ABCD

Your choice of starting hands depends on your position in the betting order as well as how well your opponents play. The suggested starting hands here do not comprise a restrictive list of hands you may play, nor does it exclude all other hands. These hands form guidelines that you can adjust as you gain experience. If you're new to the game, you might want to follow these guidelines to the letter, but with experience you should feel free to adjust for changing conditions.

Omaha/8 provides four starting cards ("A," "B," "C," and "D") that should work in concert with one another as illustrated (right). Add up the possibilities and you'll find that six unique two-card combinations can be composed from these four cards.

AB

AC

AD

BC

BD

CD

Making comparisons

In some casinos you'll find five-card Omaha/8. With five private cards you can make ten two-card combinations instead of six. Compare that to hold'em, where you're dealt only two cards. That's a major difference between the two games.

How many two-card combinations can be made with two starting cards in hold'em? The answer is simple: one. It's one hand and one hand only. If each two-

card combination is considered unique, there are 1,326 of them in hold'em (multiply 52 by 51 and divide by 2—half the hands will be the same, for example 9s-6c is the same hand as 6c-9s), but with two cards you can make just a single two-card starting hand. In Omaha you will have six unique two-card combinations among your four cards or ten combinations among your five cards.

If you're beginning to get the

impression that four-card Omaha is a game where you should either have or be drawing to the best possible hand most of the time, in five-card Omaha having the best hand is an absolute imperative. In this game, if you don't have the nuts or a draw to the nuts, you have an unplayable hand and must fold. In five-card Omaha you should play even fewer starting hands than you would in the four-card variety. But that's not what most people do. And that's a trap that skilled Omaha/8 players spring on their opponents in a five-card game.

This should tell you something about the complexity of Omaha/8 compared to hold'em. If one of your starting cards doesn't relate to the other three, your possibilities of forming a hand have been reduced, and along with it your chances for winning. Suppose you have three coordinated cards and a card that doesn't fit—it's called a dangler—such as: king, queen, jack, and an offsuit

deuce. That deuce doesn't coordinate with any of your other three cards. Even if you make a full house with two kings and a deuce on the board, it can be good news and bad news. That full house is the good news; the bad news is when an opponent also makes kings full, but with a higher card than your deuce. Other than miracles where you have an absolutely perfect fit, such as making a full house that involves a dangler, your dangler won't play. The very first thing you should know about starting hands is that most of the time you should avoid playing hands with danglers, or three-legged dogs as they're sometimes called.

If you insist on playing danglers, it's almost like you're playing three cards against four of your opponent's. Three versus four represents long odds, and you'll have to avoid that to become a good Omaha player.

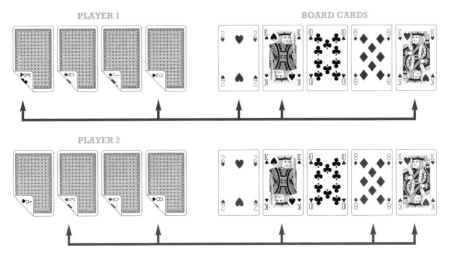

Recommended Starting Hands

If you follow this list of recommended starting hands, you'll rarely get into trouble or find yourself confused about whether you ought to continue playing or fold your hand.

Play any hand with an ace-deuce in it.

Here's an exception to the dangler rule. Play any hand containing ace-trey, as long as the ace is suited to one of your other starting cards. If you have the ace of spades, one of your other three cards must be a spade. It doesn't need to be the three of spades, any spade will do.

Double-suited hand

Trey suited with one other card

Play any ace-trey where your other two cards are tens, jacks, queens, and kings, sometimes referred to as "ten-point" cards. If you have ace-trey and your ace is not suited, but your other two cards are ten-point cards—K-Q, Q-T, J-T, K-T, K-K, Q-Q, J-J, or T-T— go ahead and play. If your trey is suited with any of your other cards, so much the better. If your hand is *double-suited*, that's better yet. For example, if you have A♠-3♦-T♠-Q♦, that's much better than having A♠-3♦-T♥-K♣, where all four suits are different. Nevertheless, any ace-trey accompanied by two ten-point cards is playable.

Ace with two unpaired prime cards

Ace with two paired prime cards

Play any ace plus two prime cards. Prime cards are aces, deuces, treys, fours, and fives. You can play an ace with any two other prime cards. So you could have A-3-5, A-4-5, and even A-5-5, because those paired fives are prime cards. Logic suggests, however, that A-5-5 is a pretty weak hand. Unpaired prime cards are what you are really looking for, because they give you three-wheel cards. If one of your wheel cards is counterfeited—a counterfeited card means that one of the community cards matches a card in your hand—you still have two other low cards that play.

Play any suited ace if your other two cards are ten-point cards. You may play a suited ace if two other cards in your hand total 20. So you can have A-7-K-T with either the seven, king, or ten suited to your ace.

Play any four prime cards, even four prime cards without an ace in your hand, as long as there has been no raise in front of you. The best hand in this situation would be 5-4-3-2 double suited. The worst would be 5-5-4-4 of mixed suits. When playing four prime cards without a raise in front of you, the closer you are to the button, the more valuable the hand becomes. Omaha/8 is no different from Texas hold'em in this regard.

PLAYER 3 If you are in first position, immediately to the left of the blinds, you probably should not play this hand even though it meets our suggested requirements. But if you feel you must, make sure you are in a very loose passive game with plenty of callers before the flop and very little raising regardless of what your opponents might be holding.

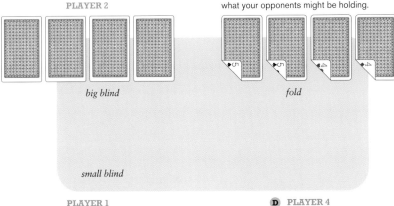

PLAYER 2

big blind

small blind

fold

PLAYER 1

PLAYER 4

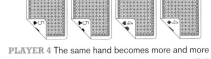

PLAYER 4 The same hand becomes more and more playable as you move closer to the dealer button, if the pot has not been raised.

When to play

Many of your opponents will look for any excuse to play a hand. They aren't on the lookout for reasons to fold. If you're aspiring to become a winning player, you'll have to develop the discipline required to release marginal hands. Take time to think before you play some of these borderline hands—even though they are on the list—and use logic as well as judgment.

So far every hand we've recommended has had an ace in it, with the exception of four prime cards without an ace. Now we'll add another cluster for you to play.

• Play any hand that totals 40 points. Count aces as eleven points. Take deuces through nines at face value.

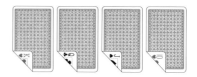

Tens and picture cards are ten-point cards. You can play any 40-point hand. Hands like K-Q-J-T or Q-Q-J-T play very well in situations where a lot of people have come in before you.

Look out for the aces

Many players will play any hand with an ace in it, especially if that ace is suited. The presence of many opponents can be an indication that they hold low cards. In fact, low hands dominate our recommended list of starting hands, and it is this penchant for low hands that makes 40-point hands so playable. With a lot of callers in front of you, most of the low cards are probably in your opponents' hands, and the deck should be rich in high cards.

A deck contains 20 high cards, including the 11- and 10-point face cards, along with 32 cards comprising deuces through nines. If you eliminate the nines—because nines can't be used to make a low hand—then there are 28 remaining low cards to go along with 20 high cards, plus four worthless nines.

If five players have already come into the pot and the blinds haven't had an opportunity to act, that's an indication that most players hold low cards. If you're holding high cards, your hand is very valuable. You can raise in this situation, even without an ace, because your chances of hitting the flop are quite good. If the flop misses you, it's a very easy hand to get away from. If you catch a big hand, you stand a very good chance of scooping the entire pot.

If you're on the button or in the *cutoff* seat immediately to the right of the button, and there are four or more players in the pot and it's been raised, you can even reraise with a 40-point hand. After all, when most players raise, it's as though they are announcing they have an ace in combination with another ace or other low cards. Three of the aces are probably accounted for in situations like this and if somebody cold-calls that raise, all four aces are probably out.

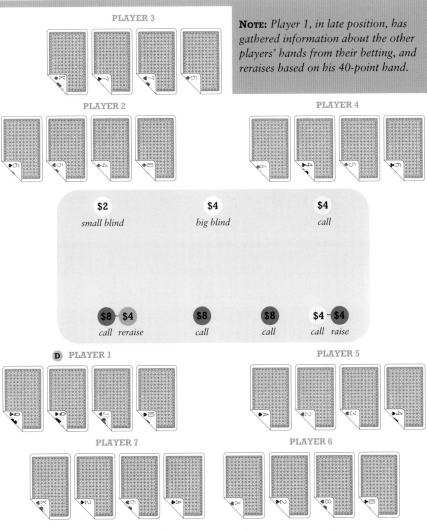

NOTE: *Player 1, in late position, has gathered information about the other players' hands from their betting, and reraises based on his 40-point hand.*

PLAYER 3

PLAYER 2

PLAYER 4

$2
small blind

$4
big blind

$4
call

$8 — $4
call   reraise

$8
call

$8
call

$4 — $4
call   raise

D PLAYER 1

PLAYER 5

PLAYER 7

PLAYER 6

Under these circumstances your high hand may scoop a big pot. It's unlikely to be a split pot, because so many players already hold low cards. This means there are fewer low cards left in the deck to hit the board and complete anyone's low hand. In any event, it's worth a raise or even a reraise. If the flop misses you entirely, you'll never be in jeopardy because this hand is very easy to release when confronted with a low flop.

These recommended hands are not the only hands you can play before the flop, but if you are learning the game there is safety in knowing that you won't be seduced into playing too many hands, as this is the downfall of many Omaha/8 players.

Fit or Fold

If your cards don't fit the flop, you should release your hand most of the time. Regardless of how many cards you start with, once the flop is dealt your hand needs to coordinate with it. If you begin an Omaha/8 game with A-A-2-3 with both aces suited—a hand most players consider the very best Omaha/8 starting hand—but the flop is K-Q-J of different suits than those you're holding, your precious gems have been turned into fool's gold. They're worthless. While they may be difficult to throw away, that's precisely what you'll have to do with them.

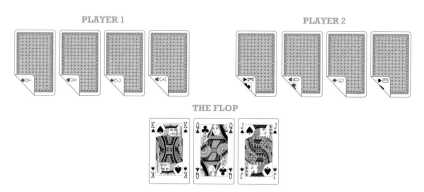

The worst hand to play might be 9-9-8-8, because it looks playable but generally leads down that old primrose path. If you never play this hand—and you won't get this combination of cards very often—you won't miss a thing, and your bankroll will be the better for it.

The biggest trap in Omaha/8 is 6-5-4-3 double suited. Although you'll occasionally win with this hand, you'll also lose much of the time, and your losses will exceed your wins. It's one of those "win a little, lose a lot" hands. When you make a hand with this holding, you won't be able to be very aggressive. And when you lose—flush over flush is a good example—you're likely to be hammered by someone holding a much bigger hand.

If all of this sounds a little like Mom telling you to look both ways when crossing the street, remember that with

Omaha/8 starting hands it's better to be safe than sorry. Start slowly. Err on the side of caution and stick with these recommendations. They won't lead you astray, you'll seldom find yourself in a confusing situation when you see the flop, and any down time can be spent getting a fix on your opponents.

This is not an exclusive list, but on the next page are some specific hands that give you an idea of how these suggestions translate into a strategy for playing an Omaha/8 game.

Very Best Omaha/8 Hands

Each of the following offers several possibilities, so they make ideal starting hands for Omaha/8.

A suited ace with three low cards can make the nut low as well as a straight and the nut flush. By having four sequenced low cards, you have protection against being counterfeited if one or even two of your low cards hit the board.

Ace-king double suited offers two flush combinations, two straight combinations, a draw to a very good low hand, and protection against making a low and having it counterfeited.

A pair of aces, two nut flush draws, a low hand with counterfeit protection, and a draw to the nut low are the features of this hand.

No low possibilities here, but a double-suited ace-king is a very powerful hand. You can make a straight, two flushes, and sets of aces or kings that can become a full house if the board pairs. If big cards flop that help your hand, they reduce the chances of any opponent making a low hand and splitting the pot with you.

Only three of the cards coordinated, but with a large number of players in the pot you have a draw to the nut flush and to the nut low with counterfeit protection.

Very Good Hands

Here is a selection of the next best
starting hands, definitely worth
persevering with.

A flush draw, nut low draw, and a straight draw are
some of the possibilities from this hand. You might
also flop a set of fives, and the presence of a five on
the board helps opponents who are drawing for the
low end of the pot. Ace-deuce suited with any pair
can be counterfeited for low, and is not as strong as
the very best hands, but it is a good one all the same.

You'd like to see either all picture cards or three
clubs on the flop, in hopes of making the best
possible straight or flush. If you flop a flush and two
small cards are present, you must bet or raise at
every opportunity to make it as costly as possible for
low hands to draw against you. If a low hand is made,
you've lost half your equity in this pot.

You're hoping an ace falls along with two other low
cards. If it does, you've made the nut low and
probably have a straight draw for high too.

While this is a good low draw along with nut flush
possibilities, you won't make the best possible low
hand unless the community cards include a deuce.
But you can easily make the second-best low hand,
which often spells trouble.

Flush draw, difficult straight draws with the A-K,
A-4, and 8-4, a draw to a marginal low hand
unless a deuce and trey miraculously appear on
the flop, make this hand look a lot better to new
Omaha/8 players than it really is.

Playable Hands

Here are several playable hands that aren't ready for the prime time.

This hand offers a draw to a flush, but not the nut flush, and a draw to a low hand that won't be the best low unless an ace hits the board. Nevertheless, it is playable in late position—though it's the kind of hand that often must be released if the flop doesn't fit it precisely.

This is a good-looking hand that's somewhat troublesome. On the plus side, it's double suited and makes possible two flush draws, two straight draws, and a low hand. The down side is that neither flush draw contains an ace, nor can you make the best possible low hand unless an ace appears among the communal cards. This hand and many others like it are what poker players call "trouble hands." They're seductive and even when you catch what appears to be a good hand, it might be more trouble than it's worth. Hands like this are always treacherous and often disastrous.

This is a straight draw with no flush possibilities. If you make a 5-6-7-8-9 straight, any low hand will take half of this pot. If you make a big straight, you run the risk of losing the entire pot to a bigger straight. Mid-range cards are dicey holdings in Omaha/8 and this is another of those hands that looks a lot better than it is. You'd be quite happy to be dealt this starting hand if you were playing Omaha high-only, but it's a mixed blessing in Omaha/8.

Mid-range cards spell trouble—even double suited as in this example. With mid-range cards you stand very little chance of scooping a pot. You, on the other hand, can be scooped, particularly when you make a straight and your opponent makes a bigger one.

Here's a hand that can make a straight with some difficulty and a flush that is not the best flush. The hand can improve to a set or a full house too. It's playable, but it's the kind of hand that looks a lot stronger than it really is.

Reading the cards

Every form of poker requires a blend of skills, but in Omaha/8, hand selection carries the most weight by far. Any hand that is possible is also probable in Omaha/8, so your ability to read opponents is not as important as in other forms of poker. Just reading the community cards to ascertain the best possible hand is usually enough. Bluffing too, particularly in lower-limit games, is not nearly as important in Omaha/8 as in other forms of poker.

For example, if you are playing Texas hold'em and all the cards are out, you might be successful at bluffing one or

> **NOTE:** *An Omaha/8 board combined with a dozen or more two-card combinations makes possible so many big hands that a bluff by Player 1 is practically futile.*

two opponents. Not so in Omaha/8. With four starting hole cards, each player has six starting combinations, so trying to bluff two players is like trying to run a bluff against a dozen starting hand combinations. It just won't work most of the time.

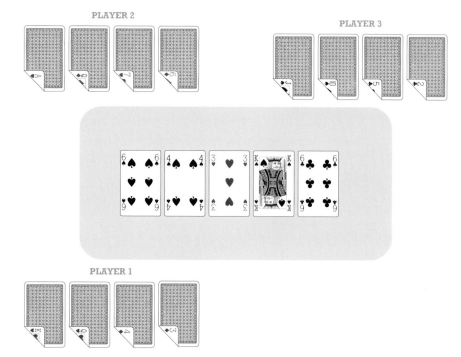

Judging Your Hand

The single most important skill required to win at Omaha/8 is hand selection. Because many players will start with almost any four cards, if you can exert the discipline to wait for good starting cards—hands that are coordinated, with cards that support each other in some discernable way—you will have an edge over most of your opponents.

Because acting later in a hand is a big advantage, you can afford to see the flop with weaker hands from late position. The later your position in the betting order, the more information you will have at your disposal. Before making the decision to call with the four cards you've been dealt, ask yourself: What kind of flop would be ideal for this hand? And when you see the flop, determine which hand would best fit it. This kind of analysis will help you ascertain how well the flop fits your hand.

Omaha/8 Flops

Here are five convenient ways to characterize Omaha/8 flops.

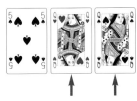

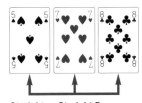

Paired When a pair flops, the best possible high hand is four-of-a-kind. Although flopping quads is a rarity, a full house is a distinct possibility.

Flush or Flush Draw Three or two cards of the same suit.

Straight or Straight Draw Three or two cards in sequence, or gapped closely enough so that a straight is possible.

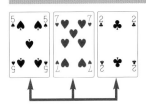

Low or Low Draw Three or two cards with the rank eight or lower.

High Three or two cards above an eight. If three cards higher in rank than an eight flop, no low is possible with this hand.

Multiple options

These groupings are not mutually exclusive. Some of these attributes can appear in combination. For example, if the flop were A♣-2♣-2♦ it would be paired and contain a low draw, flush draw, and straight draw.

It's important to recognize when a flop has multiple possibilities and to understand how your hand stacks up.

Suppose you called on the first round of betting with A♦-2♦-3♣-K♠ and the flop is Q♦-5♦-4♠. You don't have a completed hand at this point, but you do have a draw to the best flush and the best low hand. In poker parlance, you have a draw to the nut flush and the nut low, both powerful hands.

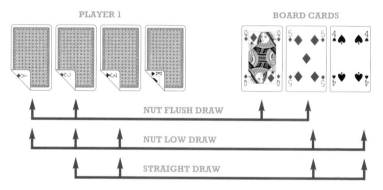

THE TURN

Any diamond on the turn will give you the best possible flush. Of course, if that card happens to be the 4♦ someone else might have made a full house if he held a pair of queens or

fives, or four-of-a-kind if he held a pair of fours. If any card with a rank of eight or lower falls and does not pair either the 5 or 4 on the board, you will have made the best possible low hand and have a straight draw too.

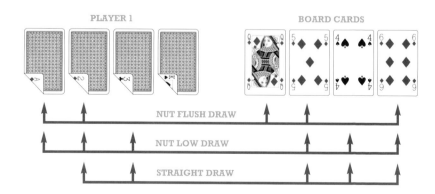

Counterfeits

If a deuce falls on the turn or river, then the deuce in your hand and in Player 2's is said to be *counterfeited*. That deuce on the board belongs to everyone. You'd still have the best possible low hand, even though you might have to share the low end of the pot now. The third low card in your hand provides insurance against counterfeits.

NOTE: *Both players had the same low draw on the flop. The 2♣ on the turn has counterfeited both players' low hands. However, Player 1 can still use his 3♣ to make the nut low hand and a straight to the five for high. Player 2 can only make two pair for a losing high: tens and twos.*

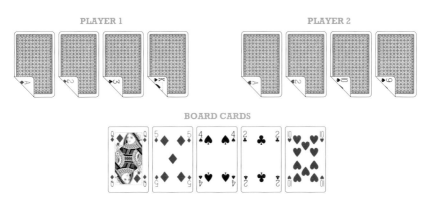

PLAYER 1

PLAYER 2

BOARD CARDS

Playing low draws

If there are only three players contesting a hand and two of them tie for low, each of the low hands will lose money—even though they each win one-fourth of the pot. Here's how to figure it. Suppose each of you has put $40 in the pot for a total of $120. The high hand wins half, in this case $60. The remaining $60 is then divided between the winning low hands, each receiving $30. Because each of you contributed $40, the return on your investment is only 75 cents on the dollar. You can't afford to keep winning pots like that!

With four players in the pot, you can be quartered—that's where you win only one-fourth of the pot—and still break even. With five or more players, you'll come out a bit ahead if you are quartered. Nevertheless, being quartered is anything but a journey lined with roses.

Worse than being quartered is playing hands which don't stand much of a chance to make the best hand in either direction. If you play mid-range cards like 9-8-7-6 you might make a straight, but wind up splitting the pot with a low hand. If you make the bottom end of a straight with Q-J-10

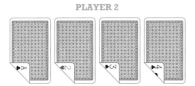

PLAYER 2

NOTE: *Player 1 wins half the pot ($60) with a full house, jacks full of tens. Players 2 and 3 split the other half of the pot ($60) with identical nut lows, A-2-3-4-5. Each player contributed $40 to the pot, so Player 1 wins $20 while Players 2 and 3 each lose $10.*

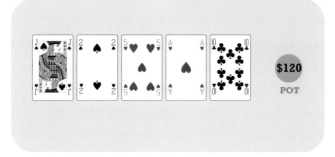

$120 POT

PLAYER 1

PLAYER 3

you won't have to worry about a low hand taking half the pot, but you will have to worry about losing the entire pot to a bigger straight.

Playing low draws that do not contain an ace and deuce is an invitation to make the second-best low hand. This is how many Omaha/8 players lose money. They play hands that look good, but are not good enough to become the best hand in their direction.

As a general rule, you shouldn't continue beyond the flop without the nuts or a draw to the nuts in one or both directions. With six two-card combinations in each player's hand a lot

of hands are possible, so make certain that you'll have the best hand if you catch the cards you need.

Here's an example. Suppose the flop is K-8-7 of mixed suits and you hold deuce-trey among your four cards. If a four, five, or six hits the board, you'll make a low hand, but so will your opponent who was drawing to an ace-deuce.

Once you see the flop, here are some questions to ask yourself before deciding whether to keep playing.

Should I continue beyond the flop?

If I make my hand, will it be the nuts?

Suppose you have Qs-Js among your starting cards and the flop contains two other spades. While you do have a flush draw, two higher flushes are also possible. This is a dangerous hand. Drawing to the second- or third-best straight, drawing to the second- or third-best low hand, or thinking you have this pot won because you've flopped the third-best or second-best set are common variations on this theme. Omaha/8 is a game of drawing to the nuts.

WAS IT RAISED?
Is my opponent the kind who usually raises only with good low cards, and if he is, how can I take advantage of the fact that he is essentially playing with his cards exposed, while mine are hidden?

When the pot is raised before the flop in Omaha/8, the raiser usually has a superb low draw, such as A-2-3-4, or A-2-3-5, with the ace suited to another of his cards. If the flop contains all big cards, you probably have nothing more to fear from this raiser.

POT SIZE
How much money will I win if I scoop the pot, take half of it, or only make a low hand and it's quartered?

Just drawing to hit a hand isn't enough. The prize has got to be worth the game,

and sometimes winning only part of the pot is a pyrrhic victory. For a draw to be viable the size of the pot compared to your cost to call bets has to exceed the odds against making your hand. For example, if it will cost you $10 to call a bet, and you figure to win $30 if you make your hand, then the odds against making your hand must be less than 3-to-1 for this call to be worthwhile.

POT PERCENTAGE
How much of the pot am I hoping to win?

Do you have a hand that might scoop the pot if you make it, or are you drawing for only half of the pot? More than one player can have a draw to the best low hand, and unless there are at least four opponents, you'll lose money whenever you are quartered.

OPPONENTS
Do I have the right number and mix of opponents to justify drawing to my hand?

Some hands, such as straight or flush draws, play better against large fields; others play better short handed. With a flush draw or straight draw you need five or six opponents to make it worthwhile to split the pot. If you have fewer opponents, the size of the pot will probably be too small to offset the odds against making your hand.

SEVEN-CARD STUD

Patience is a virtue in every form of poker, but nowhere is it more of a virtue than in seven-card stud. Unlike games with communal cards, seven-card stud starting hands must be assessed with an eye to your opponents' visible cards. In hold'em, for example, a pocket pair of queens is always a strong starting hand. But in seven-card stud, a pair of queens can be a very strong hand if you see no exposed cards higher than yours, or it might be a candidate for the discard pile if you see an ace or a king among your opponents' cards.

Because you get to see exposed cards in seven-card stud, you'll know something about the real or purported strength of your opponents' hands, as well as the availability of the cards you need to improve your own hand. After all, if you have three clubs in your hand to start out with, you're hoping to catch two more of them and make a flush. But if you see three more clubs staring out at you from your opponent's hands, those exposed cards are unavailable to you and have reduced your chances of making a flush to such an extent that your hand is virtually unplayable.

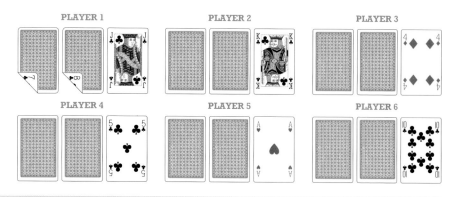

Very Good Hands

Seven-card stud is a game of live cards, and there's a big advantage to being able to see your opponents' cards because their presence or absence significantly affects the chances of improving your own hand.

The key to winning at seven-card stud is to start with the best three-card hand. The strength of your starting hand must be assessed against the cards in your opponent's hands. For example, if you begin with J-9 / J—where J-9 are your hole cards and the last jack is your door card—and see that the highest exposed card other than yours is a ten, you should raise. But if you see an ace, king, and queen, you probably only want to call and wait to see whether any of your opponents seem to have a strong hand.

If you play seven-card stud correctly, you won't find yourself entering too many pots.

Trips

Three-of-a-kind is the best you can do when you receive your three starting cards. A hand composed of three aces is the very best of the best. The odds against being dealt trips are 424-to-1, which means you can expect to find it about once every ten hours. In other words, if you go out to your local casino to play seven-card stud, you can't expect to be dealt three-of-a-kind during your entire session unless you sit there for a long time.

Trips is such a powerful starting hand that you figure to win the majority of times you're dealt it. But when you lose with trips, you'll probably lose a couple of stacks of chips in the process.

Your opponent will have to make either a flush or a straight to win, and that's only if your hand doesn't improve to either four-of-a-kind or a full house. And if your hand improves, your opponent needs at least a full house of his own in order to beat you. One big hand confronting another usually means lots of chips in the pot—which means a nice win for someone and a bad loss for someone else.

Although few poker hands are invulnerable, trips are strong enough to win without improvement much of the

time, and the odds are only 2-to-1 against making a full house or quads.

Question: Should you raise if you're dealt three-of-a-kind, hoping to knock out opponents who might draw against you? Or are you better off deceiving them by quietly calling in order to lure them along to the more expensive betting rounds?

Like most poker questions, the answer is a resounding, "It depends." And what it depends upon is the opposition. If you're at a table with players who generally call the first raise, you should raise to get more money in the pot because you're favored to win it. On the other hand, if your opponents are tight players who tend to fold much of the time, lure them in by playing slowly, as though you have a much weaker hand. If my trips were premium—tens through aces—I'd be more prone to give my opponents a chance to catch up than if I had a smaller set.

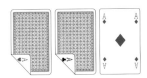

PLAYER 1 The best possible starting hand.

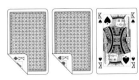

PLAYER 2 Premium trips are strong enough to be played slow or fast, depending on your opponents' nature.

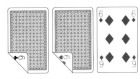

PLAYER 3 Smaller trips are better played fast to protect your hand.

Regardless of the table's style of play, you should raise if a number of players have already called the bring-in bet by the time it's your turn to act. Most of these players, with one bet already invested in the pot, will automatically call your raise. And they might keep calling with weak hands simply because of their investment in the pot.

If one of your opponents has raised before it's your turn to act, you should reraise. If your trips are higher than his exposed door card, you know you have the best hand at that juncture and are favored to win a heads-up confrontation. If he has a higher exposed door card, go ahead and raise anyway; the chance that he holds a higher set of trips is miniscule and you're still favored to have the best hand.

Reraising the initial raiser will probably eliminate most other opponents. They won't be there to keep contributing to your expected winnings, but you won't lose to someone who stuck it out with a long-shot draw to a straight or flush and got lucky. Besides, you're likely to win nearly as much money from a lone opponent who had a hand good enough to raise with as you'd win from a greater number of opponents who were just calling one bet at a time.

> **TRIP STRATEGY**
> In summary, here is your playing strategy for trips:
> - Always play trips.
> - Raise if your opponents are loose players and likely to call.
> - Call and lure your opponents along to a more expensive betting round if they are tight players who frequently fold.
> - Raise if a number of players have already called when it's your turn to act.
> - Reraise if any opponent has raised before it's your turn to act.

Premium pairs

Next to trips, the strongest starting cards you can be dealt to begin a hand are pairs. However, whereas even a lowly set of deuces can become a powerful holding if it improves, pairs differ dramatically in value. Aces are incredibly powerful, because as long as none of your opponents are holding three-of-a-kind or the other pair of aces with a larger side card, you'll have the biggest hand possible. A pair of deuces, on the other hand, is not much of a hand, because anytime one of your opponents pairs one of his cards, it will be larger than yours.

A pair of tens through a pair of aces is called a "premium pair" by many seven-card stud players, and it's a raising hand for a number of reasons. First and foremost, you'll want to raise with premium pairs because they play better against one or two opponents than against a large field. A big pair is favored over a lone straight draw or flush draw, but if you're up against several draws you are an underdog.

The biggest plus about a premium pair is that they are favored against almost any lone opponent, even an

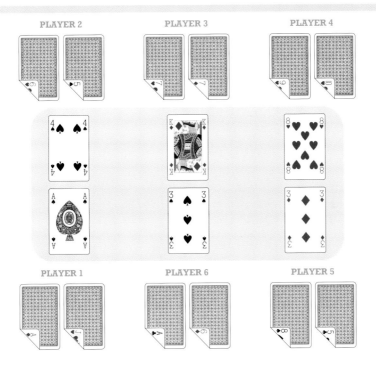

PLAYER 2   PLAYER 3   PLAYER 4

PLAYER 1   PLAYER 6   PLAYER 5

opponent with a big drawing hand. But premium pairs have a downside too. They don't usually improve to very big hands. Most of the times that there is improvement, you'll pair again and wind up with two pair. That's good enough to win a lot of seven-card stud pots, but it won't beat a straight or a flush. If your raise knocks out marginal straight or flush draws that might otherwise get lucky and beat you, you'll be the one dragging the pot.

When you have a big premium pair, don't try to lure others into the pot by quietly calling. Raise instead. The only time you might want to *slow-play* a big pair is when it's hidden. Suppose you have a hidden pair of aces and a player raises with a jack showing. If it appears as though the two of you are going to be

NOTE: *Player 1's aces are the best hand now, but they could lose to the combined opposition of Player 2's straight draw, Player 3's potential trip sevens, and Player 4's flush and straight draws if those players are not driven out of the pot.*

the only ones involved in this pot, you can call and then check-raise on a later betting round—as long as his board doesn't appear to have improved and yours has. But if the player with the exposed jack raises and there are players who called his raise prior to the action getting around to you, or others who called the bring-in before the jack raised, then you should reraise.

Not all premium pairs are created equal. If you are planning on raising with a pair of tens or jacks, and sometimes even queens, take a look around. If you see a number of bigger cards behind you poised to act, you might want to call instead of raise.

NOTE: *Player 1 has a pair of queens. Normally he would raise, but because the betting starts with Player 4 (the low card brings it in) Player 1 has to consider that Players 2 and 3 might have kings or aces.*

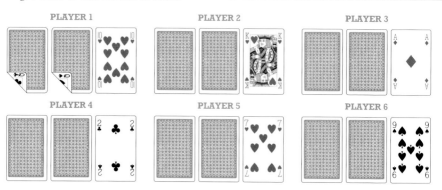

If one of the players holding a card bigger than your pair raises, you can call if your cards are live and your pair is hidden. With your pair hidden, your opponents won't be suspicious if you make trips. Then you can trap them for several bets.

You can also call if you have a pair and your third card is live and bigger than your opponent's exposed card. If you believe one of your opponents holds a premium pair bigger than yours and you don't have a live side card bigger than the suspected pair, fold your hand.

If a card the same rank as your premium pair is showing in an opponent's hand, you should call instead of raising; your chances of making trips are significantly reduced.

The best you can realistically hope for is to make two pair. If both remaining cards are dead you should probably fold, unless you have a very big, live side card to support your hand.

NOTE: *Player 1 knows his chance of making trip queens is much lower because of Player 5's queen. If Player 2 or 3 has a pair, his hand could be way behind.*

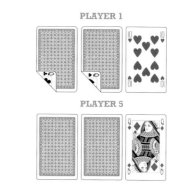

Even though you hate to release a big pair, there's no reward for second place, and second-best hands can be costly.

Here's a summary for playing premium pairs:
- Raise whenever the opportunity presents itself in order to limit the field.
- If an opponent raises before it's your turn to act, and your premium pair is bigger than the hand he's representing, always reraise.
- Don't slow-play a premium pair; bet, raise, or reraise to reduce the field.
- Premium pairs play best against a small field, but not particularly well against a large number of opponents.
- A big pocket pair is favored over a straight draw or a flush draw individually, but is a collective underdog against multiple drawing hands.
- Always try to knock out drawing hands by making it too expensive for them to call.
- Call, don't raise, if another player is showing a card the same rank as your premium pair, unless you intend to narrow the field.
- Fold usually if both remaining cards the same rank as your premium pair are dead, unless you can get it heads-up, which is often enough.

Other pairs

Middle pairs, such as sevens, eights, and nines, as well as all other low pairs, should generally be played conservatively. You can raise with a pair of nines if you don't see a board card higher than yours, but that's not going to be the case most of the time.

When you play smaller pairs, your side card, or kicker, should be bigger than any of the exposed cards showing in your opponents' hands. That way, if you are fortunate enough to pair your kicker, you'll make two pair bigger than your opponent. If your side card is an ace and it's completely live, so much the better, because aces up is the best version of two pair you can muster.

Do you see what's happening here? Start with a premium pair and any second pair you make will give you two pair under the leadership of your big, premium pair. But if you begin with a smaller pair, you're really hoping to pair your big side card instead of any lower cards you hold. A hand of two pair where the highest pair is a pair of eights or sevens is frequently bested by two bigger pair, and because two pair is a difficult hand to fold it can cost you some chips.

Small and medium pairs are much more valuable when both cards are hidden and not split, meaning one of the pair is showing and the other is hidden. Buried pairs are naturally deceptive. If you started off with a hand like 7-7 / Q and catch a seven on a successive betting round, not one of your opponents

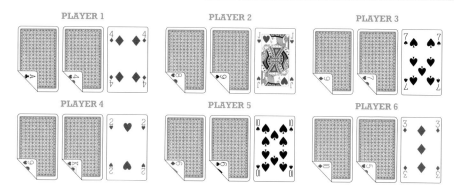

NOTE: *Player 1 only has a pair of fours. Player 3 has a pair of sevens and Player 5 a pair of sixes. If no player makes trips, and Player 1 pairs his kicker, he will have the best two pair hand even if Players 3 and 5 pair their kickers.*

would suspect you of having trip sevens. But if you began with 7-Q / 7 and paired your door card by catching another seven, your aggressive play would lead opponents to suspect that you now have three-of-a-kind.

When smallish and medium pairs are involved, seven-card stud is not only a game of live cards, it is a game of big kickers too. After all, if you begin with a smallish pair, you can't make a big two pair unless you have a big, live side card to accompany it. Big kickers are frequently the cards that either render smallish and medium pairs playable or consign them to the trash can.

Regardless of the size of your kicker, if you have a small or medium pair and an opponent has raised before it's your turn to act, you're usually much better off releasing this hand. Two bets is just too high a price to pay for a hand that's almost assuredly in second place. The cost is high and there's no guarantee you'll make a better hand than your opponent. Even if you do improve to two pair or trips, your opponent might also improve and still beat you. Finally, as long as he's in the lead, he's going to be driving the betting and you'll be calling unless you catch a miracle card.

Calling is not nearly as desirable as being able to bet and raise, force the action, and build a big pot, all because you have the best of it.

Position is another consideration when you have anything less than a premium pair. If you are in late position or, best of all, last to act, you'll have the advantage of knowing how many opponents you'll have to beat to win the pot, and how aggressively the hand is being played.

If you hold a hand like 6-6 / K it's nice to know that all of your opponents have called, that your king is live and higher than any of the board cards, and the cost to try to catch one of the two remaining sixes or three remaining kings is only one bet. It's a different kettle of fish entirely if you're second to act and call, only to find the pot raised and

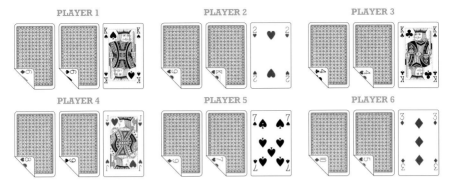

reraised by opponents who act after you. When that happens, you're torn between desperately hoping to catch one of the cards you need—seldom knowing whether you have the best hand—and desperately hoping you don't, so you can easily throw your hand away on the next betting round.

Premium pairs often play themselves, but smaller pairs require judgment, as well as an ability to deduce whether you have the best hand or a good draw to a hand that could be the best hand if you make it. Smaller pairs often befuddle inexperienced seven-card stud players. If you fall into this category, just pay

NOTE: *Player 1 and Player 3 have similar hands. However, because Player 2 is first to act, Player 1 has the advantage of knowing who is in the pot and if anybody raised before deciding whether or not to play. Player 3 can only guess.*

attention to our advice: Play these hands conservatively and realize that there's no harm in folding anytime you suspect you're beaten.

ADVICE FOR PLAYING SMALL AND MEDIUM PAIRS
Here's a summary of playing tips for smallish and medium pairs:
- Play conservatively most of the time.
- When you play smallish pairs, be sure your side card is big and live.
- A small pair that's hidden is far better than a split pair of the same rank. With the former, your opponent will never suspect it if you catch a third card of your pair's rank.
- Don't play smallish or medium pairs for more than one bet. The bring-in is often less than a full bet, so you won't lose much.
- Less-than-premium pairs are more easily played from late position.

Three to a straight flush

If you're not dealt trips or a pair as your starting hand, the next best array is three cards to a straight flush, such as J♥-T♥ / 9♥. But don't expect miracles. If you start with this combination you'll make a straight flush only 1.5 percent of the time. The good news is that a hand like this is full of possibilities. How you play these starting cards is frequently dependent on how they stack up against the cards exposed in your opponents' hands.

If two of your cards are live—if all three are live, that's better yet—and bigger than any exposed cards, you can raise. If raising eliminates opponents who already called a single bet, you now stand a better chance of winning, and the pot is full of dead money too. Even

NOTE: *Player 1 and Player 6 both have straight flush draws, but Player 1 has a much stronger hand, because:*
- *His cards are higher than his opponents' exposed cards.*
- *His cards are live, meaning his opponents' hands are not showing a jack, ten or nine.*
- *There are no other hearts visible.*

if you never make your straight flush—or a garden variety flush or straight, for that matter—but you happen to pair one or two of your big cards, you can always play the pot that way.

Although three to a straight flush is a draw and probably an underdog to a

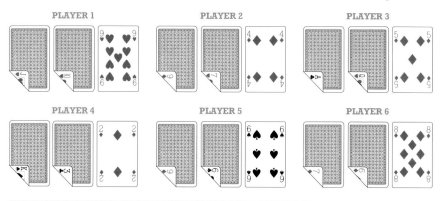

ADVICE FOR PLAYING STRAIGHT-FLUSH DRAWS

Here's a summary for straight flush draws:
- Straight flush draws offer myriad opportunities to win. You can make a straight, a flush, pair your cards, and occasionally make a straight flush.
- Big straight flush draws are far superior to smaller ones.
- Small straight flush draws will build weak straights and pair weakly.
- You can usually raise with big straight flush draws, but play smallish draws conservatively.

premium hand right now, it's about as good a draw as you can start with. As long as your cards are live, any one of ten suited cards or nine unsuited cards that support your straight will improve your hand and advance your draw.

There are some downsides to certain straight flush draws. If your cards are smallish, you'll seldom make two big pair, and there's just no way a small straight can morph into a big one. At least with three small flush cards you can make a big flush by catching big cards of your suit.

When you begin with a straight flush draw, you have three possibilities for improving. You can make a straight. You can make a flush. You can pair your starting cards and wind up with one or two pair. But if your starting cards are small, your straight and pairing possibilities are extremely vulnerable. You'll also have to catch at least one big card of your suit to build a high flush. If you begin with three premium cards, your straights and flushes will be high, and if you make two pair, they'll be super-sized instead of smallish.

Flush draws

By now you ought to be able to figure out the ground rules for playing flush draws. In an ideal world, you'll be dealt three cards of one suit and you won't see a single card of that suit exposed in any of your opponent's hands. When this happens, your hand is completely live and your chances for building a flush are as good as can be.

But you can continue playing even if one or two of the cards you need aren't available, if at least one of your cards is an ace, or a king that's higher than any

NOTE: *Player 1's chances of making a flush are limited because of the exposed hearts in other players' hands. However, going by the cards he can see, his ace and king can still pair and make a fairly big hand.*

other exposed card. Even if three of your cards are exposed, you can play on if you hold big, premium cards. But when this happens you're looking to win the pot by pairing as much as by flushing.

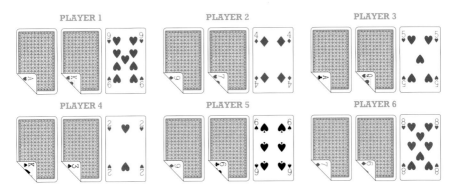

If you have lower flush cards, the quality of your hand is compromised. You'll seldom win by pairing your cards. If three or more of your suit are dead to you, just release your hand and save your money for a better opportunity.

Small flush draws are also vulnerable from early position whenever you have aggressive players acting after you who show big cards in their hands. You can anticipate a raise from one or more of them, and drawing hands such as flushes are better played inexpensively. Not only that, a raise or two from aggressive opponents might cause most other players to fold their hands. Now you're in the unenviable position of having to play a flush draw against a big premium pair or two. Because you figure to win a confrontation like this only about one time in five, you're usually better off releasing a small flush draw from early position whenever you're confronting aggressive players holding big cards. To play your flush draw in circumstances where you're forced to act before your aggressive opponents, you'll need at least one of your cards to be bigger than any pair an opponent represents, and that big card has to be live.

Suppose you start with 8♣-5♣ / 2♣. You really don't have much of a chance to win unless you complete your flush. But if you begin with a hand like A♦-K♦-5♦ you'll improve if you catch another diamond or an ace or king of another suit. Now you have six additional cards to go along with the ten diamonds that will help you, and that's a sizeable improvement. Also, with an ace and a king in your flush, it will probably be bigger than any flush made by an opponent.

Flush draws can grow into very big hands, so you'd prefer to play them against more opponents rather than a few. Playing a flush draw heads-up is a losing proposition, because the odds against making a flush won't be offset by the size of the pot. With three or four opponents, the pot's size will make up for the relatively long odds of drawing to a flush. The only time to consider playing a flush draw heads-up is when you have some very big cards in your hand and figure you can win if you make one or two big pair. When that's the case, your flush draw is added equity, and just another way to win.

ADVICE FOR PLAYING FLUSH DRAWS
Here's a summary to guide you in playing flush draws:
- Make sure your draw is live, unless you have bigger cards than your opponents.
- If one or two of your cards are dead to you, you can still play if you have an ace or king—or both—and cards of those ranks are completely live.
- Lower flush draws win by completing a draw; they won't win by pairing.
- Be prepared to release most flush draws if you are confronting aggressive opponents with bigger cards than yours.
- Flush draws play better against a larger field than a smaller one.
- Don't play a flush draw heads-up without other possible ways to win.

Straight draws

Playing a straight draw composed of three sequenced cards is a lot like playing a flush draw and many of the concerns are the same:

- Are your cards big enough to make a good hand if a subsequent card pairs you?

- Are your cards live?
- Are your cards bigger than any of the cards that are exposed?
- What is your position in the betting sequence?

Drawing for a straight is a bit dicier than starting with three big cards to a

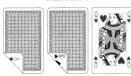

PLAYER 1

Cards that will complete the straight

AND

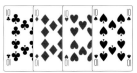

NOTE: *Any pair Player 1 makes will be bigger or equal to any pair made by Player 2.*

Cards that will complete the straight

PLAYER 2   SET 1   SET 2

AND

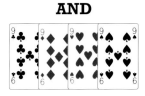

OR

AND

OR

NOTE: *Player 1 seems to have the better cards, but Player 2 has two sets of cards that will make a straight. However, Player 1 has the advantage when it comes to pairing big cards.*

flush. For one thing, if you're drawing to a straight and your opponent is drawing to a flush, you will be the loser if you each make your hand.

Moreover, if an ace and a king are part of your flush draw, you can still make a very high pair and win the pot that way. But you normally wouldn't play A-K-Q as a straight draw because you can only complete that straight in one direction, by catching a jack and a ten. If you began with Q-J-T—the highest possible straight draw offering an opportunity to complete your hand with cards both higher and lower in rank than your starting sequence—there's no guarantee that any pair you'd make would be bigger than an opponent's pair.

Because of these concerns, you'll find many top-notch poker players who never play straight draws. They just ignore them altogether. Other experts recommend playing straight draws, but suggest you play only Q-J / T, J-T / 9, and T-9 / 8. These are the only combinations that can produce open-ended, four-card straights while giving you a chance to make a premium pair as well. When viewed from that perspective, Q-J-T is vastly superior to a hand like T-9-8. The latter can make just one premium pair and it's the lowest of the bunch, but a starting hand of Q-J-T gives you three premium cards to pair.

A straight draw is a hand at odds with itself. The opportunity to make a premium pair is compromised by the need to pick up a fourth card to an open-ended straight draw on the next betting round. What you wind up with is a compromise paid. By backing off from any high pairs you might make, you have a straight draw that provides the maximum latitude for improvement.

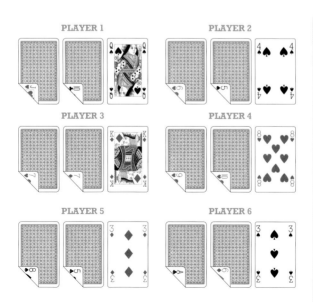

PLAYER 1 PLAYER 2 PLAYER 3 PLAYER 4 PLAYER 5 PLAYER 6

NOTE: *Primary cards are sequential in rank to three sequenced cards held in a player's hand. In this illustration, Player 1 holds Q-J-T, so the primary cards needed are a 9 and a king. Secondary cards can complete a straight only if the correct primary card is in place, and are those adjacent in rank to the primary cards—in this example, an ace or an eight.*

Compare that to a flush draw, where you can make a very high pair if you begin with big suited cards and pair on the next betting round.

Straight draws also require live cards. There's nothing more futile than drawing for cards that aren't available to you. How live does your hand need to be? We'll use the old "Rule of Four Points." If you have Q-J-T, look around you. If you see any of your primary cards already unavailable to you because they've been exposed in your opponents' hands, they'll count as two points each. In this example, your primary cards would be a nine and a king. Secondary cards, which in this case are an ace and an eight, count one point each. If you see a king and an ace exposed, that's three points and your hand is live enough to play. If you see two kings and a nine, that's five points and your hand is unplayable. Any combination of four or fewer points is playable; five or more points is an unplayable hand.

Overcards

If you have been dealt overcards, such as A-K-J with no flush draw and not much chance of making a straight, your hope lies in pairing on the next round. If you pair, you can continue playing, but only if you are either heads-up or against two opponents. If there are more than two opponents and all you've been dealt are three big cards, you're probably better off folding and waiting for another opportunity.

If you pair up against only one or two opponents on the next round, you're in good shape, particularly if you are playing against one drawing hand and a pair smaller than yours. But be careful when playing overcards. You might not make a hand at all, or you might make a marginal hand and lose with it. Remember, the winner in seven-card stud is usually the player who begins with the strongest hand.

Ante Stealing

Ante stealing is very profitable when done correctly, and you ought to try to steal the antes every chance you get. This is usually done from late position after most or all of your opponents have folded.

If you have a reasonably big card and all your opponents have folded, stealing is almost automatic play, especially if your only opponent is the guy forced to bring it in with the lowest card on the board. If you have a premium card showing, go ahead and raise. He might even suspect you of stealing, but what can he call you with? You might even have the best hand at that point, and if your biggest card is higher than his, that's precisely what you're doing.

If you're on a pure ante steal and are reraised, give it up unless you have a chance for real improvement with the next card. You can call if you were ante

> **NOTE:** *Player 1 has time to assess the moves of his opponents. In this case the situation was ideal for ante stealing and Player 1 makes an $8 profit without having to play the full hand.*

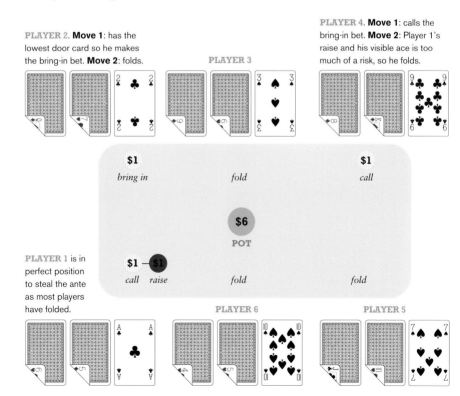

PLAYER 2. Move 1: has the lowest door card so he makes the bring-in bet. **Move 2**: folds.

PLAYER 3

PLAYER 4. Move 1: calls the bring-in bet. **Move 2**: Player 1's raise and his visible ace is too much of a risk, so he folds.

$1
bring in

fold

$1
call

$6
POT

PLAYER 1 is in perfect position to steal the ante as most players have folded.

$1 — $1
call   raise

fold

fold

PLAYER 6

PLAYER 5

stealing with three cards to a flush, but if you are raised when holding 3-7 / A just accept the fact that you've been caught by an opponent who either has a hand or was able to read you for having nothing at all.

Ante stealing works better against tight, predictable players than it does against adversaries who will call with almost anything. Just remember that any time bluffing won't work—and ante stealing is nothing more than a specific form of bluffing—betting your good hands for value is the strategy you should employ.

There's an art to ante stealing, and you should try to steal the antes anytime you think you'll succeed. If you get caught a few times, back off for a while, but as long as this ploy works often enough to show a profit, keep it up. Remember the ante stealer's motto: If the shoe fits, steal it!

> **NOTE:** *Player 1 tried to steal the ante, but Player 4 called his bluff. With three unsuited cards, Player 1 decides it is not worth calling the reraise, so he loses the pot. If Player 1 had had a better hand— three cards to a flush, for example—he would have called to see what happened on fourth street.*

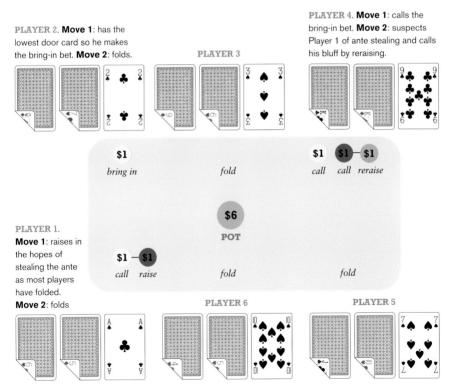

PLAYER 2. **Move 1**: has the lowest door card so he makes the bring-in bet. **Move 2**: folds.

PLAYER 3

PLAYER 4. **Move 1**: calls the bring-in bet. **Move 2**: suspects Player 1 of ante stealing and calls his bluff by reraising.

$1
bring in

fold

$1 $1—$1
call call reraise

$6
POT

PLAYER 1.
Move 1: raises in the hopes of stealing the ante as most players have folded.
Move 2: folds

$1—$1
call raise

fold

fold

PLAYER 6

PLAYER 5

SEVEN-STUD/8

Seven-card stud eight or better, hi/lo split, which we'll call seven-stud/8 for simplicity's sake, is a game that's rapidly growing in popularity as a cash game and a tournament staple. Because players are trying to make low hands as well as high ones, there's more action in seven-stud/8 than in traditional seven-card stud games. The structures of the two games are identical in terms of the use of antes instead of blinds, the number of betting rounds, and the low card bringing it in with a forced bet, but the games' strategies are very different—and so are starting hand values. Certain hands that you'd usually raise within seven-card stud are frequently discarded in this game.

In seven-stud/8 the best high hand wins half the pot and the best qualifying low hand wins the other half. One player can win both halves—scoop the pot—or different players can win separately the high or low hand. The rule of thumb in high-low split games is to play low hands, because they frequently back into high hands too. High hands seldom morph into low ones.

The objective of split-pot games is to scoop the pot, which means playing two-way hands that have a chance of making a high hand along with a low one. Here is where you'll make most of your money. Choosing the right cards to play and learning to recognize those flashy hands that look good but really ought to be folded can put a beginning seven-stud/8 player on the right track in a hurry. Players who don't conceptualize a set of starting standards for seven-stud/8 find themselves at a big disadvantage, because they are invariably interpolating a starting strategy from seven-card stud. And that causes all sorts of problems.

Starting Standards

Before exploring specific hands it is important to realize that in seven-stud/8, just as in seven-card stud, you are playing a game in which the value of your hand is dependent upon the availability of live cards.

If you start with three low straight cards, but many of the cards you need are already exposed in hands belonging to your opponents, the chance of completing your straight is reduced.

If your cards aren't live you'll have a much harder time catching them. That will only add to your frustration and cost you money.

If you hope to start with two-way hands, you can't do much better than 3-4-5. You've got straight potential as well as a chance to make a very good low hand, and any ace, deuce, six, or seven on the next card will significantly improve your hand. If you're fortunate enough to start with 3 ♥-4 ♥-5 ♥, you have a hand that can improve to a straight flush, flush, or straight for high, plus a low hand. Even if you catch a

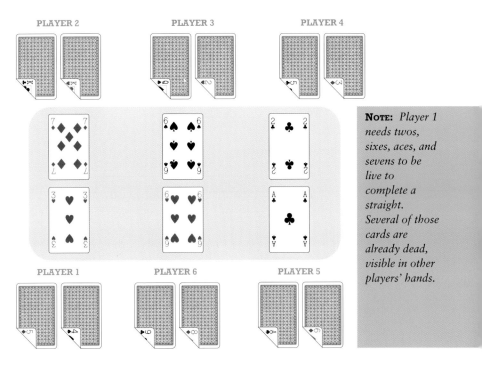

PLAYER 2

PLAYER 3

PLAYER 4

PLAYER 1

PLAYER 6

PLAYER 5

NOTE: *Player 1 needs twos, sixes, aces, and sevens to be live to complete a straight. Several of those cards are already dead, visible in other players' hands.*

card like J♥, you've improved. Now you have four to a flush, and although the jack does nothing to increase your chances of making a low hand, you're not dead either. That fourth heart keeps you in the hunt, and if the next card is, for example, the 7♣, you've got a draw to a low hand to go along with your flush draw—and two chances to get there.

Suppose you catch the Ah on sixth street. What could be better? You've made an ace-high heart flush and a seven-five low and you can raise with impunity. If you've got two or three opponents who look like they're going low, you will probably take the high side and you may even scoop the entire pot. If your opponents all

appear to be going high, you will win the low end and still stand a good chance of scooping.

Although you don't have the absolute nuts in either direction, you should feel very confident with a hand like this. In fact, with two or more opponents, your half of the pot will be quite healthy, particularly if you've been able to continue raising opponents who are contesting the other end of the pot. If you scoop the pot, you'll be stacking chips for the next two hands. If you've got a lock on one end of the pot and are freerolling toward the other, you can really win some money when you're lucky enough to scoop.

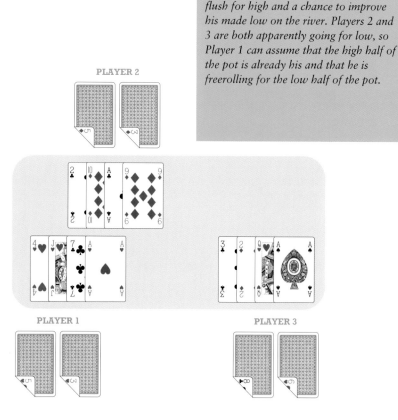

NOTE: *On sixth street, Player 1 has a flush for high and a chance to improve his made low on the river. Players 2 and 3 are both apparently going for low, so Player 1 can assume that the high half of the pot is already his and that he is freerolling for the low half of the pot.*

Big hands in seven-stud/8 are not always big money makers, so playing strategies differ from those for seven-card stud. Suppose you're dealt wired kings and catch the fourth king on the next card against one opponent who is obviously drawing for low. You can bet and raise every chance you get, yet when all the shouting's done, you'll each come away with half the pot and your miniscule profit measured in terms of antes and the forced bring-in bet. In a full game with betting limits of $20–$40 you'll chop $24 in antes, minus the $3 house

drop in a casino, plus a $5 bring-in. That's a profit of $13—not much of a return when you've raised endlessly with four-of-a-kind, is it?

But if you make a two-way hand that figures to have a lock on at least one side, you can and should jam the pot by betting and raising at every opportunity. You'll scoop if you get lucky. Whenever there are multiple opponents, every dollar you bet generates a profit, even if you only split the pot.

The flip side of this is also true. You must avoid situations where you are the one being sliced and diced. You can't duck this entirely. Sometimes you will find yourself against two or three opponents, all of whom are going high while you are going low. There's no guarantee you'll make that low, however, and you may wind up calling all the way to the river only to fold your hand. Most seven-stud/8 players can tell you stories about the occasions when they started out with four cards to a six- or seven-low only to catch three high cards in succession; seven-stud/8 players refer to these useless high cards as *bricks* or *bananas*. They had to throw their hand away on the river, because they failed to make even a pair for high and they had no low hand at all.

Because you need to build a low hand from five unpaired cards with ranks of eight or lower, you can begin with a high-quality draw and catch a fourth low card on the next round, yet fail to catch that fifth low card you so desperately need. There's nothing you can do about it either, because seven-stud/8 is a game in which you're forced to gamble with good low draws.

On the other hand, you can avoid situations where your draw to one side of the pot is not the best. You'll frequently see a player drawing to an eight low against an opponent drawing to a low that's obviously better. When both make their hand, the eight low player suffers for that indiscretion.

What makes a desirable starting hand? Generally it is a hand with two-way possibilities that allows you to scoop a big pot when you get lucky with it. The example we discussed earlier, 3♥-4♥-5♥, is a perfect starting hand. It begins with three cards to a wheel— the very best possible low—yet can easily become a high hand too by making either a straight or a flush. If you get extremely lucky, you might even make a straight flush. Most starting hands are not in that league, not by a long shot. Still, there are many others that are very playable.

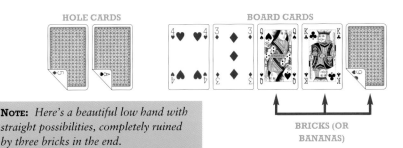

NOTE: *Here's a beautiful low hand with straight possibilities, completely ruined by three bricks in the end.*

BRICKS (OR BANANAS)

Ace hands

Aces are like two cards in one. They're simultaneously the highest and lowest card in the deck. Whenever you have an ace showing as your up-card on third street it's guaranteed to give pause to your opponents. They have no idea whether you have a potential high hand, low hand, or both. If your hole cards are 6-5, you're working on a very good low. If you have another ace in the hole you have the highest hand at that point, unless one of your opponents was dealt three wired cards, which is unlikely.

If you continue to catch low cards, your opponent will assume you are drawing to a low hand. If you catch a high card and continue to contest the pot, your opponent won't know whether you have only a pair of aces, paired one of your hole cards and now have two pair, or simply caught one bad card and are still chasing the field for the low side.

Suppose you start with 6-5/A, catch a trey on fourth street, and then pair your ace on fifth street. Now your opponent must take a very hard look at his own hand. He sees your paired aces. He has to consider the possibility that you're holding three of them or that you've made two pair. He also has to think about four cards to a good low along with a pair of aces as a valid possibility.

Against a lone opponent, this kind of hand stands an excellent chance of scooping the pot. Aces are not only the most potent cards in this game, they are also the most powerful scare cards you can hold.

Another excellent starting hand is two aces with any low card. It's even better whenever the low card is a deuce through five—a wheel card—that's suited to one of your aces. In this case it does not matter too much whether you have an ace or deuce showing, although if you show a deuce, catch a few low cards and then connect with a third ace, your opponents will never suspect that you have a high hand. Now if you pair your board, your opponents will think you've missed your low draw when in reality you've made a huge full house.

The profit potential is huge whenever your opponents think you're going in one direction and you're actually headed the other way, as in the example above. Suppose two other players, one going high and the other obviously holding a low draw, are competing for this same pot. The player going high will think you have a low hand and continue to raise, because he believes he will win half the pot while you and the "other" low will be left to split your half. You will keep reraising, knowing that your aces-full is the best high hand. You will win half of a very large pot for sure, and if your other opponent fails to make his low, you'll scoop a monster.

HOLE CARDS

BOARD CARDS

NOTE: *Aces provide your hand with both power and deception.*

Other low hands

You'll find that most of your opponents will play an ace with any two low cards, even if those low cards are very rough. How playable is a hand like 8-7-A? It depends. And what it depends on is the quality of your opponents' draws. If you have an eight on board with an ace and a seven in the hole and your opponents are all showing high cards other than an ace, it is obvious that you have the only low draw. You can count on winning half the pot if you make your hand. But if other players also hold low cards, you are faced with an entirely different problem. No longer are you concerned only with making a low; the issue now is making the best low. It doesn't do any good to draw against two other opponents who are each drawing to a better low hand than yours. Just as in other forms of poker, the best starting hand is often most likely to wind up as the best hand at the showdown.

One of the problems with four- and five-stretch low hands such as 7-5-2, or 8-4-3 is that they have difficulty making a high hand unless you are fortunate enough to make two pair with an eight low, or a flush as well as a low hand. Although straights are possible with holdings like these, they aren't really probable, and that reduces your chances of scooping the pot. It doesn't necessarily render your hand unplayable, but it does limit you to playing for one end of the pot only. When you set off down that road, be certain that you are either the only one headed in that direction or you have the best of it by far.

Any ace in an opponent's hand on third street is a potential killer when you hold a low draw that can't make a straight. Not only does a hand with an ace look to be a better low draw than yours, it is also a better high hand. That ace has surrounded you, and regardless of which direction you are heading, it's probably uphill. If you are playing against a lone opponent showing an ace, he can scoop or split the pot, while your low draw figures to either split the pot or be scooped.

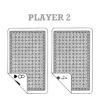

NOTE: *These hands might not look so far apart, but Player 2's ace gives him a huge advantage over Player 1 for either the high or low end of the pot, or both.*

Confrontations like this can cost an enormous amount of money that needn't be lost. You're better off folding one-way hands than you are playing them, unless the pot odds and opponents' exposed cards justify it.

Because the ace is both a low and a high card, holding one is akin to having an extra card. It's almost like playing eight cards against your opponent's seven. But as strong as an ace is, not every hand with an ace is playable. A hand like 9-8-A is utterly worthless. You probably won't win no matter which way you go. You'll find more than enough hands to play in seven-stud/8, so toss your ace away if your other two cards don't support it.

High and two-way hands

The best starting hands are two-way hands. Get lucky with them and you can scoop a big pot. This generally means starting with low cards. Low cards can swing high, but high hands don't swing low very often. If you start with a hand like 6-5-3, you're on your way to a good low, but with a bit of luck you might also make a straight that can take the high side. Three low, suited cards—especially three low, suited cards with an ace—can make a low hand as well as an ace-high flush. On the other hand, if you were dealt Q-J-T you have a straight working, but you can't make a low hand. That doesn't mean you can't ever play high cards. You can. But you have to consider the situation carefully.

Suppose you're high and last to act. The only callers all show low cards and not one of them is an ace. You're probably the only player going high. While low-looking hands can sometimes be deceptive—like starting out with 5-5-5, a hand that looks low but is really high—it's tough for a high hand to disguise itself. After all, if you call with a king showing, you either have the worst possible low hand or you are going high. You could have a pair, a straight draw, or a flush draw. Your opponents won't know which, but they will know the direction you're headed, and that's more important.

> **NOTE:** *You need five cards of rank eight or lower to make a low hand. If you start with three cards all higher than an eight, it is impossible to make a low hand.*

HOLE CARDS   BOARD CARDS   FINAL CARD

PLAYER 2

PLAYER 1

Since you won't generally have any deception built into high hands, when can you safely play them? If all of your opponents are chasing low hands, and you have a good high hand working, go ahead and play it. Unless one of your opponents makes a low straight or a flush, chances are your high hand will hold up. If you both make two pair, yours will take the high side. If you both catch three-of-a-kind, you'll win with ease, unless of course his are aces. But these are rarities.

It is always a good gamble whenever you're the only player going high no matter how many opponents are going low. Against one opponent who looks like he is working on a low hand, if you have a high pair on third street, you are favored. After all, you have a hand. Your opponent is still drawing and there's no guarantee he'll make a low hand.

He might start off with four wheel cards and catch three bananas in a row and never complete his low hand. That's a great situation for the high hand, because it will either take the whole pot or split it. Meanwhile, the guy with the low draw—unless fortunate enough to make a two-way hand or back into a

high hand—will split the pot or lose it all. If you are going to draw for a low hand, you'd ideally like to be up against a bunch of high hands—a guarantee that you'll take half the pot if you make a low. You seldom want to compete with a bunch of low hands for half the pot against a lone high hand.

Another time it pays to go high, regardless of how many opponents you are up against, is when you start with a powerhouse hand. If you were dealt wired jacks, for example, you shouldn't mind any number of opponents who also appear to be going high. You already have three-of-a-kind, along with a strong likelihood of improving to a full house or better. In these situations you are heavily favored. Exploit it for all it's worth by betting and raising at every opportunity, because you want to make it very costly for any opponent with a low draw to stick around and try to capture half of the pot. This is very different from seven-card stud, where you'd probably just call until the bets double on fifth street. In seven-stud/8 you want to raise with big high hands early and often, in order to eliminate any marginal low hands from drawing against you.

Recommended Starting Hands

Let's look at a chart that summarizes the kinds of starting hands you'll want to play.

LOW DRAWS	
Three small cards with an ace	6-4-A and similar hands offer good low draws plus the chance of making a high hand by pairing aces.
Low cards, no ace, no straight draw	Hands like 7-6-3, which have limited straight potential and do not offer a flush draw, are dangerous, unless they are the only low draw, or the only other low draw is to an eight.
Three low cards to an eight	Avoid this hand unless it is: (a) the only low draw (b) has straight or flush possibilities (c) heads up against the bring-in.

TWO-WAY HANDS	
Three to a low straight flush	A hand like 5c-4c-3c is an incredibly powerful starting hand. Any club or low card on the next two rounds keeps you in the hunt. You might make a low hand, a straight, a flush, or a straight flush. You can also make a low hand and a flush.
Three to a low flush	A very strong starting hand, and if you continue to improve you stand a good chance of scooping.
Three wheel cards	5-4-3, 5-4-2, 5-4-A, 5-3-2, 5-3-A, 5-2-A are very strong hands, especially against large fields.
Three small straight cards	6-5-4, 7-6-5 and similar low straight draws do well in multi-way pots. But be careful. Although hands like 8-7-6 can make low straights, you're working only one end of the spectrum. If you catch a nine or ten, you improve your chance of making a straight, but your chances of making a low hand are reduced.

HIGH HANDS

Trips	You won't often be dealt trips, but when you start with three-of-a-kind, you'll be contesting the pot until the bitter end.
Two aces and a low card	A-A-3, A-A-2 and similar hands can go high or low, but aces do better against a small field. Raising with this hand is the preferred course of action.
The best high hand	If you have a pair of kings or queens, and it is the best visible high hand, play if your cards are live. If yours appears to be the second-best high hand, throw it away.
Three to a high straight flush	Play until fifth street if your cards are live and keep playing if you improve.
Small pair, ace kicker	Play if there's no raise and your cards are live.
Three to a high flush	Play against a large field if your cards are big and live.
Three to a high straight	Play against a large field if your cards are big and live. However, this is a marginal hand, and you won't be giving away much if you never play it.

SOME WORDS OF CAUTION

We've discussed how powerful your hand is when it contains an ace, and how an ace as your door card can confuse your opponents, because they won't know whether you have a high or a low hand. But what happens when you see an ace as an opponent's door card? What should you do then?

You shouldn't play many hands when an ace raises; hands that include a pair of kings or a pair of queens should be thrown away. Even if the player with an ace has a low draw, if his aces are live he can easily make a better high hand than yours. The hands you should play against an ace are three cards to a wheel, three cards to a straight flush, three cards to a flush draw and a low draw, and three low straight cards.

Even with hands like these you still have to assess the strength of your hand against the apparent power of your opponent's. Release hands that don't have the potential for scooping the pot. Don't throw good money after bad if it appears your opponent with the ace is continuing to improve and your hand is stymied.

4

Playing Your Hands

TEXAS HOLD'EM

In all forms of poker, position is power. Unlike seven-card stud, where position in the betting order is determined by the exposed cards in players' boards, in Texas hold'em position is fixed for the entire hand.

Your Position in the Betting Order

Acting early is a disadvantage. Acting in late position can be very advantageous. In fact, certain hands that ought to be folded in early position can be raising hands in late position. That's how strong position is, and why each player in a Texas hold'em game yearns for the dealer button.

Some hands play better against fewer players, while others do better against a large field. For example, take a hand like 9-8 suited. If you are fortunate, this hand might grow into a flush or a straight, although that won't happen very frequently. On the other hand, you probably won't have the highest card—and therefore be favored—even against only two opponents with random cards. The implications of this are twofold:

- Because a hand like 9-8 suited will occasionally grow into a very big hand (but most often will result in a weak hand that will have to be folded) it is best played against a large number of opponents. That way you have enough "customers" to pay you off if you get lucky.
- Because this kind of hand is a long shot no matter how you look at it, you'd prefer to play it for one bet and

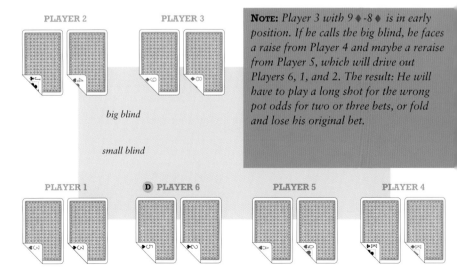

NOTE: *Player 3 with 9♦-8♦ is in early position. If he calls the big blind, he faces a raise from Player 4 and maybe a reraise from Player 5, which will drive out Players 6, 1, and 2. The result: He will have to play a long shot for the wrong pot odds for two or three bets, or fold and lose his original bet.*

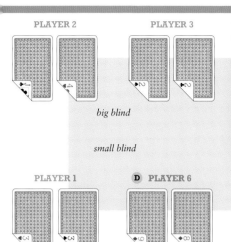

PLAYER 2 PLAYER 3

big blind

small blind

PLAYER 1 **D** PLAYER 6 PLAYER 5 PLAYER 4

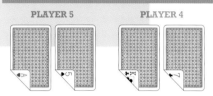

NOTE: *Here, Player 6 has the 9♦-8♦ and he is on the button. If the situation is right, there will be enough callers in front of him to justify his calling too. Then, from the flop on, he will be last to act, which means he will always have a good idea as to the strength of his own hand in relation to the others.*

one bet only. If you are forced to call a raise with this kind of hand, most of the time you'll be wasting your money.

The only way you'll know for sure that you have a sufficient number of opponents in the pot with you, and a reasonable chance you'll be seeing the flop for only one bet, is to play the hand from late position. Barring the occasional raise from one of the blinds, the number of opponents you're facing will be a known quantity, as will the cost to play the hand. If you play a hand like this from early position, you'll be forced to guess about the cost of the hand and the number of opponents you'll be confronting.

A small pair is an example of a hand that plays better against fewer opponents. The flop is very likely to contain cards that are bigger than your small pair. When that happens against a relatively large number of opponents, it's likely that someone will emerge from the flop with a pair that's larger than yours. Against a relatively large field, small pairs either need to flop

three-of-a-kind—and odds against that happening are 7.5-to-1—or the hand needs to be released at the first bet by an opponent, who has presumably been helped by the flop.

On the other hand, if you're in last position and no one has yet called the blinds, even a lowly pair of deuces tends

NOTE: *Even this harmless looking flop is scary to the player holding pocket fours. Calling more than one bet pre-flop could cost you a lot of money over time.*

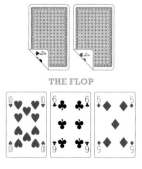

THE FLOP

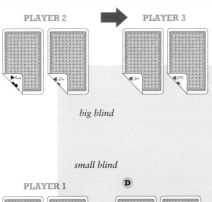

big blind

small blind

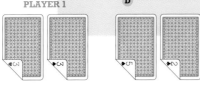

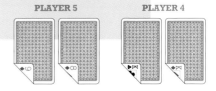

NOTE: *A pre-flop raise with A-K will drive a lot of weaker hands out of the pot. Moreover, if someone has a strong hand, a raise should get you information on that fact too.*

to be better than two random hands. Now you can raise with a hand you would have tossed away.

If you're dealt two big cards like A-K or a big pocket pair in early position, you have a hand that does better against fewer opponents than against a large field. You should raise with hands like these, even from an early position, in an attempt to reduce the field and eliminate hands like 9-8 suited—the very hands we've just discussed—which need a large field and a bargain price to make them worth playing.

If you start with A-K, you'll flop either an ace or a king or a better hand approximately one time in three. But if you raise and eliminate most of your potential opposition and attract only one or two callers, you might have the best hand even if the flop misses you completely. After all, it may miss both of your opponents too. But if you are confronting five or more opponents, you can assume that any flop that misses you will help at least one of them.

Acting last or in late position lets you know for certain:
- How many opponents will be contesting this pot with you
- The real or purported strength of their hands
- The cost to play the hand

Players tend to raise with strong hands, so raises from those who act early on provide a great deal of information about the real or purported strength of their hands. When you have to act early in the betting order, before you have this kind of information at your disposal, you're really flying blind. As a consequence, a raise from early position generally is indicative of a very strong hand—or a very bold bluff—since your opponent's early position raise is essentially telling you:
- I have a very big hand, confront me at your peril.
- I don't care how many opponents call my raise.
- You have to pay to play.

Odds and Outs

Figuring odds in Texas hold'em is easy compared to some other forms of poker. Seven-card stud and similar games like razz and seven-stud/8 are more complicated, because each player's hand has its own exposed cards and therefore its own unique odds calculation.

In Texas hold'em, similar situations arise again and again. It's good to memorize the odds for common situations. That way you're freed from the rigors of having to perform calculations in the heat of battle, something few of us are good at and almost no one enjoys.

Pot odds

Figuring pot odds is a necessary part of any poker player's game. By learning to understand the relationship between the mathematical odds against making your hand and the money you win if you get lucky, you can play skillful, high percentage poker.

This calculation involves comparing the total number of unknown cards with the number of cards that will complete your hand and then doing simple subtraction and division.

Let's say you hold the K♥-J♥ and the board on fourth street shows A♥-8♥-7♣-Q♦. You have four cards to a heart flush: A♥-K♥-J♥-8♥.

NOTE: *Although there are nine hearts that will complete this player's nut flush, the 7h and Qh could give another player a full house. Any non-heart ten will make the player an unbeatable straight.*

OUTS TO A FLUSH

OUTS TO A STRAIGHT

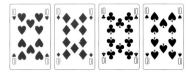

LITTLE OR NO HELP

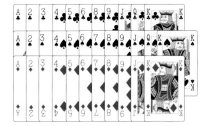

HOLE CARDS

BOARD CARDS

Whenever you hold 4 cards to a flush on the turn in a Texas hold'em game, there are 46 unknown cards. Why 46? Because there are 52 cards total in the deck and you know for certain only the values of your 2 hole cards and the 4 exposed cards on the board. Of the 46 unknowns, 9 cards are potentially the same suit as your flush draw and any one of them will complete your hand. These 9 hearts are called your outs.

To figure the odds of making your flush, you first subtract your outs from the number of unknown cards: 46 − 9 = 37. None of the 37 cards will complete your flush. So now you divide the number of no-help cards by the number of outs: 37 ÷ 9 = 4.1. The odds then are 37-to-9, or roughly 4-to-1, against making your flush draw.

Percentage poker players will call a bet in this situation only if the pot is four times the size of the bet. In a game with betting limits of $20–$40, the pot would need to contain at least $160 for you to call here—or else you'd have to be able to count on winning at least a total of $160 from future calls using implied odds, which is a guesstimate of sorts that we will look at next.

Long shots

If you're the kind of player who's fond of inside straights and other long-shot draws, consider this: You have four outs on the turn. That's all. And it's not much when you consider that 42 of the remaining cards won't help you at all, which means the chance of completing your hand is less than 9 percent. If you'd prefer expressing that figure in odds, here's the bad news. The odds against completing an inside straight draw are 10.5-to-1, and you'd need a pot that's more than ten times the cost of your call in order to make it worthwhile.

If you had two pair and knew for a fact that your opponent had a flush,

NOTE: *This player needs a ten on the river to make his straight, and the odds against him catching a ten are 10.5-to-1. There would have to be at least $400 in the pot to justify calling a $40 bet on the turn.*

you'd be in the same predicament, since only one of four cards will elevate two pair to a full house. When can you play hands like this? On two occasions. The first occurs when you buy a winning lottery ticket, worth $90 million, and playing $20-$40 hold'em becomes the equivalent of playing for matchsticks. The other occasion is in a

HOLE CARDS	BOARD CARDS	OUTS
		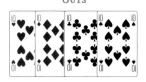

game with complete maniacs whose collective motto is: "All bets called, all the time." You would need to win more than 10 times the amount of your call to justify this kind of draw. But if you figure to win a $450 pot by calling a $40 bet with an inside straight draw, then go for it.

Calculating the odds

The chart provided on the next page makes it easy to learn the odds against all the common draws you're likely to come up against in a hold'em game. If you memorize it, you won't have to waste even a fraction of a second doing arithmetic at the poker table. There are also simplified methods that allow you to approximate the percentage of times you'll make your hand.

An easy method involves multiplying your outs by two, then adding two to that sum. The result is a rough percentage of the chance that you'll make your hand on the next card. Suppose you have a flush draw on the turn. Since there are two suited cards in your hand and two more on the board, and a total of 13 cards of each suit in the deck, you have nine outs. A quick calculation, 9 x 2 = 18, and 18 + 2 = 20, comes pretty close to the 19.6 percent chance you'd come up with if you worked out the answer mathematically.

If you have only four outs, this quick approximate measure—4 outs x 2 + 2 = 10—is very close to the actual figure of 10.5. If you have 15 outs, a quick calculation yields a figure of 32, while the precise figure is 32.6 percent.

The strategic implications of this are: If you have a 10 percent chance of winning, the cost of your call should not be more than 10 percent of the pot's total. With a 32 percent chance, you can call a bet up to one-third the pot's size.

While the "outs times 2 plus 2" method is an easy calculation to make at the poker table, it's even easier to commit the chart to memory. That way you never have to figure a thing. Just tap into your memory banks and pull out the correct figure. And anytime you find yourself fighting a tinge of self-doubt, you can always double-check yourself using the "outs times 2 plus 2" approximation.

If you want to estimate your chances on the flop of making your hand by the river, try this: If you have between one and eight outs, quadruple them. Eight outs multiplied by four yields 32, while the precise answer is 31.5 percent. With four outs, the quadrupling method yields 16 percent, while the accurate answer is 16.5 percent.

With nine outs—a common situation because it represents the number of outs to a four-flush—quadruple the number of outs and subtract one. You'll be right-on when you do, since the arithmetical answer is 35 percent. You can use this method for up to 12 outs, though with 12 outs our shortcut method yields 47 percent, whereas the precise answer is only 45 percent.

For 13 through 16 outs, quadruple the number of outs, subtract 4, and your results won't be any more than 2 percent off. And remember, anytime you find yourself on fourth street with 14 outs or more, you are an odds-on favorite to make your hand so pot odds of any size become worthwhile.

This chart shows odds against making your hand with two cards to come (flop to river), as well as with one card (turn to river) remaining.

DUMP THE UNPROFITABLE DRAWS
Hanging on to unprofitable draws for whatever reason—and many players persist in drawing to long shots even when they really do know better—can be a major weakness in one's game.

ODDS AND OUTS

Outs	Draw	Flop to river		Turn to river	
		Percent	Odds	Percent	Odds
20		67.5	0.48-to-1	43.5	1.30-to-1
19		65.0	0.54-to-1	41.3	1.42-to-1
18		62.4	0.60-to-1	39.1	1.56-to-1
17		59.8	0.67-to-1	37.0	1.71-to-1
16		57.0	0.75-to-1	34.8	1.88-to-1
15	Straight Flush	54.1	0.85-to-1	32.6	2.07-to-1
14		51.2	0.95-to-1	30.4	2.29-to-1
13		48.1	1.08-to-1	28.3	2.54-to-1
12		45.0	1.22-to-1	26.1	2.83-to-1
11		41.7	1.40-to-1	23.9	3.18-to-1
10		38.4	1.60-to-1	21.7	3.60-to-1
9	Flush	35.0	1.86-to-1	19.6	4.11-to-1
8	Straight	31.5	2.17-to-1	17.4	4.75-to-1
7		27.8	2.60-to-1	15.2	5.57-to-1
6		24.1	3.15-to-1	13.0	6.67-to-1
5		20.3	3.93-to-1	10.9	8.20-to-1
4	Two pair	16.5	5.06-to-1	8.7	10.50-to-1
3		12.5	7.00-to-1	6.5	14.33-to-1
2		8.4	10.90-to-1	4.3	22.00-to-1
1		4.3	22.26-to-1	2.2	45.00-to-1

OTHER PROBABILITIES

Wired Pair	Flops a set 11.8 percent of the time
A-K	Flops at least one ace or king 32.4 percent of the time
Two Suited Cards	Makes a flush 6.5 percent of the time
Two Suited Cards	Flops a flush 0.8 percent of the time
Two Suited Cards	Flops four flush 10.9 percent of the time
Two Unmatched Cards	Flops two split pair 2.2 percent of the time

Implied Odds

Sometimes the pot odds seem insufficient to offset the odds against making your hand, but future bets might be substantial enough to justify playing. Implied odds are all about winning money over and above what's in the pot right now. You can't be certain about how many opponents will call your bets or raises if you make your hand, but implied odds is the ratio of your total *expected* win to the current cost of calling a bet.

Let's assume you (Player 5) have a pair of treys and are last to act. You'll have to flop a set to win the pot. If you don't, you'll fold at the first bet.

Suppose there's $40 in the pot and it will cost $10 to see the flop. While those pot odds of 4-to-1 don't offset the 7.5-to-1 odds against flopping a set of treys, you estimate that you might win an additional $80 subsequently if the flop is favorable. Now the pot is offering you

implied odds of 120-to-10 ($40 in the pot now, plus an estimated $80 in future bets), or 12-to-1, which offsets the 7.5-to-1 odds against flopping a set.

Call that $10 bet and see the flop. If you flop a set of treys, you may have the best hand, so you can bet or raise with impunity unless you think someone else might have a better hand. If the flop misses you, just throw your hand away if an opponent bets.

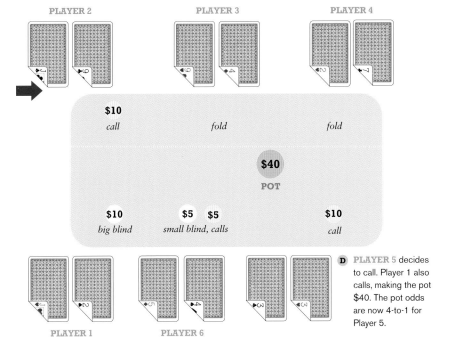

PLAYER 2   PLAYER 3   PLAYER 4

$10   fold   fold
call

$40
POT

$10 $5 $5 $10
big blind   small blind, calls call

PLAYER 1   PLAYER 6

D PLAYER 5 decides to call. Player 1 also calls, making the pot $40. The pot odds are now 4-to-1 for Player 5.

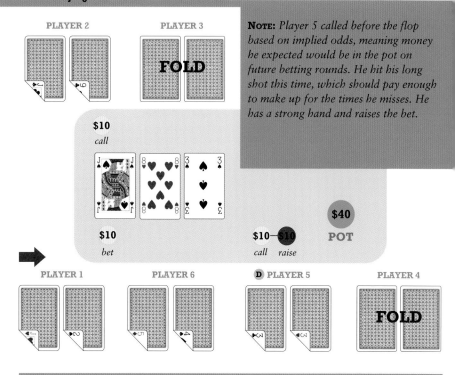

PLAYER 2   PLAYER 3

FOLD

NOTE: *Player 5 called before the flop based on implied odds, meaning money he expected would be in the pot on future betting rounds. He hit his long shot this time, which should pay enough to make up for the times he misses. He has a strong hand and raises the bet.*

$10
call

$40
POT

$10
bet

$10 $10
call raise

PLAYER 1   PLAYER 6   D PLAYER 5   PLAYER 4

FOLD

Implied odds in pot-limit and no-limit games

Implied odds are even more powerful in pot-limit and no-limit games. Let's say you're heads-up at the final table of a tournament. You hold A-6 and flop a gut shot straight when the flop is 4-3-2. Only a five can help you. You are playing in an event where the winner is paid $10,000 and the second-place finisher is rewarded with $5,000. Let's assume the two of you each have $30,000 in tournament chips and there's $500 currently in the pot. Your opponent bets $600 and you know that the pot odds of 11-to-6 ($500 already in the pot plus your opponent's $600 bet, compared to the $600 it would cost you to call) are not sufficient to justify a call.

After all, the odds against making your hand are 10.5-to-1.

Suppose you also knew for a fact that your opponent has two pair. But if you make your hand, you figure you'll be able to take all your opponents' chips and win the tournament. If you consider that your opponent has $30,000 in front of him, your implied odds are now $31,100-to-$600 ($500 in the pot, your opponent's $600 bet, plus an additional $30,000 you figure to win from him if you get lucky, compared to a $600 cost of seeing the next card). Now it's worthwhile to see if you can hit a long shot, win the tournament, and double your prize money in the process.

Deception

Better players will always be more susceptible to your deceptive play than weaker opponents, who are usually unaware of any deceptive "messages" you broadcast their way by virtue of your betting patterns.

In fact, the stronger your opponents appear, the more you'll find yourself playing a hand other than optimally in order to deceive them. Against weak opponents, straightforward play is all that's needed, and too many fancy plays against these opponents will usually cost you money in the long run.

If you've been dealt a pocket pair of aces and the pot has been raised, you might not want to put in the last raise against a skilled player in order to throw him off the scent and lead him to believe your hand is not as strong as it really is.

That way you can lure him into betting and you'll probably be able to trap him on the turn, when the betting limits usually double. But against a weaker player, you might as well raise from the get-go and take advantage of the fact that he isn't paying any attention at all to your actions.

The larger the pot, the less deceptive you'll need to be. When pots are big, most players are getting the correct pot odds to call, and bluffing under these conditions is usually doomed to fail. The same holds true when you're playing

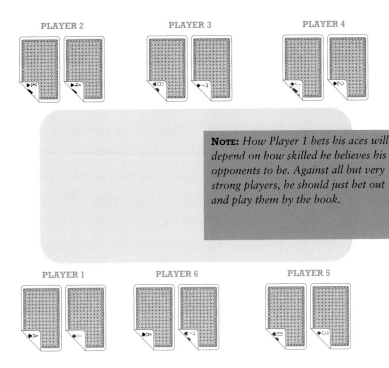

NOTE: *How Player 1 bets his aces will depend on how skilled he believes his opponents to be. Against all but very strong players, he should just bet out and play them by the book.*

against a large field. Since someone is likely to call to keep you honest, straightforward play—betting your good hands and checking weaker holdings—is usually the best course of action.

Most poker players suffer from trying to be too deceptive. Play straightforward poker most of the time and save your fancy play for good opponents, small pots, small fields, and those few occasions when you have a powerhouse hand and can afford to let your opponents improve—just enough to get themselves into trouble.

YOUR HAND	VS SKILLED PLAYER	VS WEAK PLAYER
Strong hand like A-A	Deception can be effective • Do not cap the raise • Trap on the turn	Play straightforward • Cap the raise • Bet out on the flop

Semi-bluffing

Semi-bluffing is a fairly sophisticated strategy, but it's one that every skillful player uses even if he is not aware of the term. The idea of semi-bluffing is based on the fact that the more ways you have to win, the more reason you have to bet. It's a bet made on a hand that's probably not the best hand at the time you bet it, but has a chance to mature into the best hand. If the bet gets everyone to fold, it succeeds as a bluff; if not, the hand might still improve on succeeding cards.

The difference between semi-bluffing and a pure bluff is that a semi-bluff has two ways to win. Players often bet when their hand needs to improve to win, this semi-bluff is known as "on the come." The bettor is hoping to win the pot right there, but if he's called, he can still win if his hand improves. Semi-bluffing also affords players an opportunity to add some deception to their game, and that has value in itself.

Despite its myriad advantages, there are some cautionary measures too. You can't semi-bluff an opponent who calls all the time, because you'll lose one of your two ways to win the pot.

Semi-bluffing is also not all that savvy an idea when you're last to act,

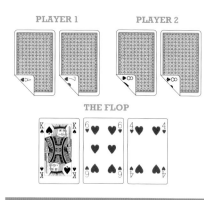

PLAYER 1   **PLAYER 2**

THE FLOP

NOTE: *A typical semi-bluff. With a four-flush, Player 1 bets the flop even though his hand is only an ace-high. It is a bluff, but if a heart falls on the turn or the river, he is likely to win the pot.*

since you might as well take the free card if everyone else has checked.

But when all is said and done, semi-bluffing is a terrific strategy because it gives you two ways to win: Your opponent may fold a better hand or you may catch the card you need and you win the pot. In addition, it allows you to be the bettor instead of the caller, and that's usually a good position to be in. Sometimes you might bet, thinking you're semi-bluffing when you actually have the best hand. When that's the case, your semi-bluff—which in all actuality is a bet with the best hand—prevents your opponent from getting a free card. In fact, your bet may convince him to fold.

Semi-bluffing is a strategy you'll familiarize yourself with as you get more experience playing poker. It's far usually superior to a pure bluff, and is tough to defend against when used in moderation.

> **ADVICE**
> Bluffs are doomed to fail against opponents who call too frequently.

Defending

If a bet saved serves you just as well as a bet you win, then playing defensively is just as critical as playing aggressively when you have the best hand. Defending comes up all the time in poker. Every time you're in the small blind in a hold'em game, you'll have to decide whether to defend your blind by calling. If you're in either blind and someone's raised, you'll have to think about that, too. If you come out betting and are raised, you have to consider whether to play defensively or stay aggressive.

If you're in the small blind and the pot has not been raised, you can usually call with all but the most hopeless of hands. After all, if there are four opponents in the pot with you, and the cost to call is only one-half of a small bet, you are getting 9-to-1 on your money to look at the flop. If the blinds are $2 and $4 and four players have each called, there's now $16 in the pot plus your $2 small blind. That makes a total of $18 and your cost to call is only $2, so you're left with pot odds of 9-to-1. Those odds, plus whatever implied odds you want to assign to the pot based on your best estimates of the pot's size at the end of the hand, usually warrants a call.

But if the pot has been raised and now it will cost you $6 to call, you'll have to throw marginal hands away. Not only have the pot odds been reduced (if everyone calls, you'll be getting pot odds of 34-to-6, or 5.7-to-1) but the raiser probably has a better hand than you do, and so do some of the others who called.

Suppose you called a raise before the flop from the big blind with 8-7. Now the player who raised comes out betting into a 9-8-4 flop of mixed suits. You have second pair, and you're trailing if the raiser had a nine in his hand or any pocket pair bigger than an eight. But he also may have raised with a hand like A-K or K-Q.

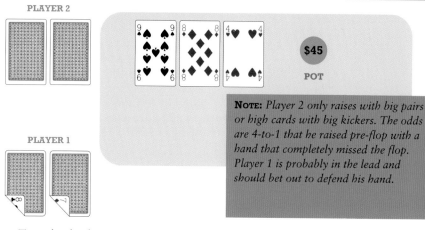

PLAYER 2

PLAYER 1

$45

POT

NOTE: *Player 2 only raises with big pairs or high cards with big kickers. The odds are 4-to-1 that he raised pre-flop with a hand that completely missed the flop. Player 1 is probably in the lead and should bet out to defend his hand.*

To make the decision about whether to defend, you need to know something about your adversary's raising standards. If he is the kind of player who will only raise with a pair of jacks or higher, as well as with A-K, A-Q, A-J, A-T, K-Q and K-J, chances are he missed the flop. There are six ways to make any pair, and sixteen ways to combine two unpaired cards. This produces 96 big card combinations he might have raised with and only 24 paired cards of jacks or higher. As a result, the odds are 96-to-24, or 4-to-1, that he raised with big cards rather than a big pair. If you knew his betting and raising standards for a fact, calling his bet is mandatory, since you'll be in the lead the vast majority of the time.

But deciding to defend is not always based on mathematics. Suppose you have A-K, raised before the flop and

were happy to see a flop of A-J-9 of mixed suits. Now suppose the turn card is something innocuous, like a seven, and you come out betting, thinking all the while that you have the best hand until—surprise—your opponent raises.

The board is not intimidating. No flush is possible, and a straight is remote. Most players will not bluff raise, particularly in lower-limit games. When you're raised on the turn—where the betting limits double—you are usually beaten even when you have a hand as strong as top pair with the very best possible side card. The raise ought to alert you to the possibilities of your opponent having made a straight, or three-of-a-kind, or two pair. Unless you have good reason, you ought to consider folding your hand in this situation.

Poker is always a balance of offense and defense, between being aggressive to win and conserving your chips. Striking the balance is a combination of figuring the odds and understanding your opponents' playing styles. The right decision against an aggressive, loose player can be wrong against a tight, timid opponent.

Raising

Raising can be a dicey proposition. Most of the time when you raise you will not be entirely sure you have the best hand. Moreover, you'll encounter some opponents who take raising so personally that their response to any raise is to raise back—even when their hands don't warrant it. If you're going to be a selectively aggressive player, you can't let the fear of a reraise stop you from raising when proper strategy calls for it. You can't be so selective that you pass on money you would have won but for the fact that you weren't absolutely sure about how your hand stacked up against the opposition.

Here are five good reasons to raise in hold'em. These five reasons often act in concert with one another. While it is logical to raise solely to limit the field, it is seldom worth raising just to define your hand and for no other reason. But if you raise to limit the field, you will always gain some information about how your hand stacks up against the competition.

1. GET MORE MONEY INTO THE POT
This is the most common reason to raise and the most enjoyable. Suppose you've got a powerhouse hand. Someone bets, there are three callers, and now it's your turn to act. What should you do in this situation? You raise.

Of course! You're holding a winner and want to get more money into the pot, since that pot will likely migrate over to your stack of chips once the hand has been concluded.

But here's something that is just as important:

• You don't always need the best hand to raise.

Suppose you're on the button with A ♦ - K ♦ and the flop is J ♦ -9 ♦ -6 ♣.
The blind comes out betting and is called by four others. Now it's your turn

HOLE CARDS

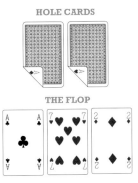

THE FLOP

to act. You're getting 5-to-1 on your money, and with two cards to come the odds against making a flush are better than 2-to-1. Since this bet has a positive expectation, it is worth money in the long run each time you make it, regardless of whether you win this particular confrontation.

2. ELIMINATE OPPONENTS
You have a pair of queens in fifth position and no one has called the blinds. Your pair of queens plays better

against one or two opponents than a whole slew of them. Go ahead and raise. And what if someone else has raised before it's your turn to act? Be bold. Make it three bets. If your opponent is the type who would raise with aces,

NOTE: *Player 6 should raise or reraise if needed to eliminate as many opponents as possible.*

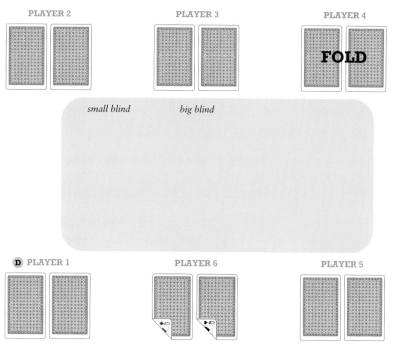

kings, jacks or A-K, A-Q, A-J, K-Q, K-J or maybe even A-10 suited, the odds are against him having a pair bigger than yours; they favor his holding two big cards.

Go ahead and reraise. If a king or an ace doesn't jump out of the deck on the flop, you're the favorite. If two overcards fall, you're probably an underdog and ought to give it up if your opponent bets into you.

But if just one king or ace falls and you're heads-up, it's a judgment call,

and unless you have a terrific read on your opponent, you'll seldom be sure where you stand.

If he's clever, and tries for a check-raise by checking the flop and turn, go ahead and check, too. If he bets the river, you're going to call him anyway, but you've also given him an opportunity to bluff with a hand that is worse than your pair of queens, so calling is not that bad an option.

But if you bet and he check-raises on the turn, you're probably beaten. Fold.

PLAYER 2

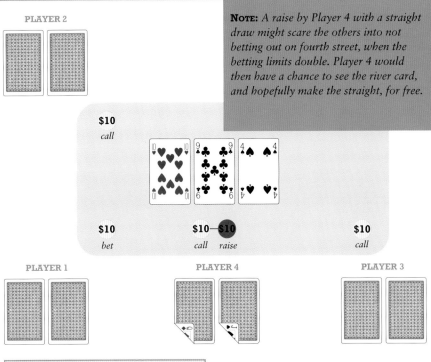

PLAYER 2

NOTE: *A raise by Player 4 with a straight draw might scare the others into not betting out on fourth street, when the betting limits double. Player 4 would then have a chance to see the river card, and hopefully make the straight, for free.*

$10
call

$10 $10—$10 $10
bet   *call* *raise*   *call*

PLAYER 1   PLAYER 4   PLAYER 3

ADVICE
Anytime you have a hand that plays better against fewer rather than more players, raise or reraise to limit the number of opponents.

3. GET A FREE CARD ON A MORE EXPENSIVE STREET

You're last to act with a Q-J. The flop was 10-9-4 of mixed suits and you're facing three opponents. The player who is first to act bets, and is called by the others. Can you raise? Sure! If the turn card is not the king or eight you're looking for, the fact that you raised may enable you to see the river for free—as long as the bettor and subsequent callers each check the turn.

And if you make the nut straight on the turn, well, you've gotten more money into a pot that by all appearances will soon belong to you.

4. DEFINE YOUR HAND

Imagine you are the last to act with a pocket pair of kings and your opponent, a strong player to your right, reraised. The flop was A♣-K♥-4♠. Your opponent bet, you raised, and he reraised. Because you know his play, you are sure he would not raise if he'd flopped a set of aces. He would have checked the flop, called your bet, and check-raised on the turn. So, you figure him for A-K, or possibly a hand like A♥-J♥. The turn card was the 6♥.

He bet and you raised. He called. Now you know for certain that he does not have a set of aces. If he'd had three aces, he would have reraised, because he would have been holding the best possible hand on the turn.

So, you are now sure he has A-K. Since he knows your play very well too, you don't believe he would have called with less than two pair. You are also quite sure your raise told him you had at least two pair, and more likely a set. When the 8♥ fell on the river, however, he bet, you raised, and he reraised. It is here that you learn that your assessment was wrong.

He could not possibly have A-K; he had to have a hand like A-J suited. He had tried to steal the pot with his bet on the turn, because he had top pair with a reasonably good kicker, as well as an opportunity to draw out if another heart fell on the river, which is exactly what happened. He made the nut flush. Although your analysis was correct, you are too late to save yourself any money and he won a big pot.

You can see that by virtue of the bets, raises, and reraises, both players were defining their hands in terms of what they presumed each other to be holding.

Although you defined your set of kings against the possible hands he could have been holding, you incorrectly assumed he had made two pair. This was a costly error in judgment, but you can learn something here about how to raise and reraise to define your own hand against what you suspect your opponent might have.

5. DENY YOUR OPPONENT A FREE CARD
Just as it is correct in certain situations to raise on the flop in order to gain a free card on the turn, it is also correct to raise in order to prevent your opponent

from getting a free or relatively inexpensive card.

Here's an example. You hold A-10 in fifth position. On the flop only three other players are active: the big blind, and seats eight and nine. The flop comes A-9-7. The big blind bets. With no raise before the flop, there's no way to determine what he might be holding. You may be outkicked if he holds A-K, A-Q, or A-J. If he holds A-9 or A-7 or 9-7 you're also beaten. On the other hand, he may be betting with A-6, trying to win the pot right there if no one else holds an ace.

While you have some idea about the players in seats eight and nine, you're not certain you have the best hand. However, it's fair to assume that if either one of those players had A-K, A-Q, or A-J, a raise before the flop was much more likely than a call. While they may have called with a hand like A-5 suited, it's more likely they're holding connectors or a small pair.

What should you do in this position? While calling is not a bad idea, raising is probably better.

If the players in seats eight and nine hold hands like 10-9 or 9-8, they may call a single bet on the flop, in hopes of catching a miracle card on the turn, or perhaps picking up a straight draw. However, if they are reasonably prudent players, they will not call a raised pot with second or third pair and little else to support it.

If your raise forces seats eight and nine to fold, you are heads-up against the blind, and you have the added advantage of acting last on the turn and the river. You may also have the best hand. Unless the blind has flopped a big hand, like two pair or a set, he is

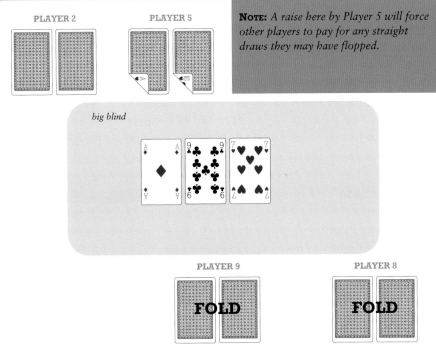

NOTE: *A raise here by Player 5 will force other players to pay for any straight draws they may have flopped.*

PLAYER 2

PLAYER 5

big blind

PLAYER 9

FOLD

PLAYER 8

FOLD

probably not going to bet into you on the turn. This gives you the opportunity to check behind him. If he isn't holding much of a hand, and is an aggressive player, checking behind him may elicit a bluff on the river, which you can easily snap off.

Possible big blind cards

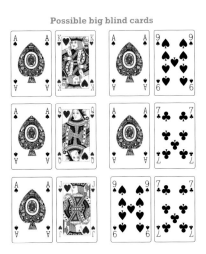

Free Cards

A free card is one that does not cost a bet to receive. The general rule for giving or receiving a free card is very straightforward.

- Most of the time that you have the best hand, you won't want to give your opponents a free shot at catching a card that might snatch the pot right out from under your nose.
- On the other hand, when you're the one holding something less than the best hand, a free card is always desirable.

NOTE: *It might be hard to get action at any point in the hand after a flop like this. But if someone holds a big flush draw or a pair of nines, maybe they will catch up. Four kings is a strong enough hand to give opponents free cards.*

There are some exceptions. Sometimes you have a hand so strong that it's worth giving a free card to your opponents in hopes that they'll catch up a bit and continue calling on future betting rounds. Suppose you flop four-of-a-kind, or a big full house. If you bet, it's unlikely that any of your opponents will have been helped enough by the flop—if they've been helped at all—to call. But if the flop that gave you such a powerhouse hand contained two cards of the same suit, or two cards in ranks that were in close proximity to one another, you can afford to let your opponents catch up a bit. If a flush card comes on the turn, or a card providing one or more of your opponents a straight or a draw to a straight, they are likely to call a bet on the turn.

If the pot is small when you give out that free card, so much the better. There's nothing satisfying anyway about winning a very small pot with a very big hand. You're usually better off trying to win a big pot than a puny one, even if you risk losing the whole thing. Besides, if there's some chance the next card might give an opponent a hand that's

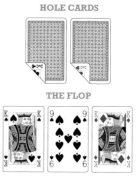

HOLE CARDS

THE FLOP

good enough to bet, you might get a chance to raise or, if you're first to act, try for a check-raise.

If you're the one hoping to make a good hand, then you'll want to get a free card if you can. That's not something that you have total control over, but by betting on the flop you might be able to convince opponents who act before you to check to you on the turn, when betting limits double. It is like raising to get a free card. Once the turn card is exposed, you can always bet if your hand has improved sufficiently, or you can check if your hand was not helped and your opponents checked to you.

Slow-playing

Slow-playing is a form of deception in which you play a very strong hand weakly on an inexpensive round of betting in order to lure your opponents on to the more expensive betting rounds. When you slow-play, you take no action beyond what is required to stay in the pot.

If no one has bet, you check. If someone bets, you call. Your goal is to keep as many players in the pot as you can, so you can maximize your winnings on subsequent betting rounds.

Obviously you need a very strong hand to slow-play, since you are always running the risk of offering your opponents a free or inexpensive card that just might improve their hands. Ideally, your slow-play will deceive your opponents into thinking you have a weak hand, and the free card will improve their hands, but not enough to win.

- The best time to slow-play is when the pot is relatively small and you believe that your actions will allow the pot to grow larger on subsequent betting rounds.

It is a powerful way to get maximum value for your strong hands, but you have to temper this strategy with some prudence. You need a strong hand, the strength of which should not be obvious to your opponents.

- You should never slow-play if a free card might give an opponent a better hand than yours.

Let's suppose you hold 4-4 in your hand and there are four players in the hand with you. The flop is 4-4-K, and two of the cards on the flop are suited. The pot is small on the flop. There is little chance of someone beating your quad fours, and if a third suited card falls, someone might make a flush and think it the best hand. All slow-playing requires is checking if no one has bet, or quietly calling if someone has bet. Hope with all your might that someone improves, and if they do you can bet on the turn, try for a check-raise, or raise if an opponent comes out betting.

By the time your opponents realize what you're up to, it's usually too late, and they will have already paid the price for your deception. But don't slow-play with hands that are not really strong. Free cards are a dangerous gift to offer your opponents.

NOTE: *A hand this strong can be slow-played. Give people who flopped two pair or a flush draw a chance to catch up.*

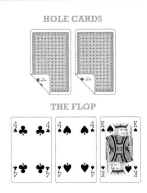

HOLE CARDS

THE FLOP

Reading Your Opponents

Reading hands is a powerful poker tool. The better you become at reading hands, the more difficult it becomes for opponents to deceive you.

Generally, weak players are tough to read because there is little structure to their play. The range of hands they can play is so broad that they could have anything. Good players are easier to read because their play is usually logical. But expert players are difficult to read because they'll add enough deception to their play to throw you off.

The most common hand reading process involves assigning a variety of potential hands to your opponents based on whether they call, raise, or reraise. You eliminate possible hands based on their actions as cards appear on the board from one betting round to the next. You can also read hands by working regressively. In a later betting round, you can assess an opponent's play in earlier rounds to deduce what cards he might be holding.

> **NOTE:** *Unless you know your opponents well, or have studied them thoroughly for several hands, you will be guessing as to what a call or a raise from them might mean. A reraise like that from Player 6 is a good way to test their hands.*

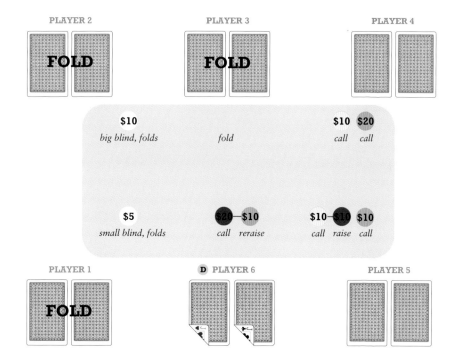

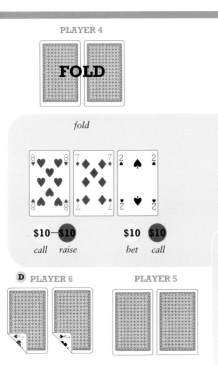

PLAYER 4

FOLD

fold

$10—$10 $10 $10
call   raise   bet   call

NOTE: *Player 4 was obviously playing with two cards that weren't helped by the flop, as he did not reraise before the flop and quickly folded after. Player 5 could have three sevens or three eights, or be a true gambler drawing to a straight. If he had a pair of aces or kings, he probably would have reraised pre-flop.*

$20—$20 $20 $20 $20—$20
call   raise   call   bet   call   reraise

Ⓓ PLAYER 6   PLAYER 5

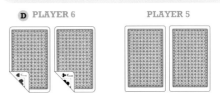

NOTE: *Player 5 has now reraised. The straight is looking awfully probable.*

The number of players in the pot can bear heavily on your analysis. If you suspect a bluff by an opponent who has been betting, but he's been called by another opponent, at least one of them should have a legitimate hand. It's tough to bluff and call simultaneously. While you can bluff by betting and by raising, calling is indicative of a real hand. A call is tantamount to saying, "I've got a real hand, and if we show our cards down right now, I'll probably be the winner."

But reading your opponents is not always enough. You need a stronger hand to call a bet, and especially to call a raise, than to bet or raise in the first place. Like semi-bluffing, betting or raising gives you two ways to win. Your opponent might release a better hand than yours or you might have or make the best hand. But if you call, there's only one path to victory: showing down the best hand. So make sure you have a strong hand if you're going to call a bettor, or overcall a bettor and another player who calls.

OMAHA

Omaha poker, particularly the one-winner version in which the high hand wins the entire pot, is extremely popular among European poker players. It's usually played as a pot-limit game, but there is no reason why this game cannot be played using fixed betting limits or as a no-limit game. Although this form of Omaha is rarely spread as a cash game in North American casinos, it is popular in the United States as a tournament offering in which the betting structure is usually pot-limit.

Omaha and Texas

With the increasing popularity of poker played in cyberspace at Internet casinos where opponents can be located anywhere in the world, there is no shortage of Omaha games online—even for those who live in areas where Omaha is seldom spread in a casino.

PLAYER 2 has a full house, kings over sevens. Two kings in his hand and a king and two sevens on the board.

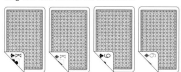

> **NOTE:** *Players must use two and only two cards from their hand. If the board does not pair, no player can make a full house. If three suited cards do not appear on the board, no player can make a flush.*

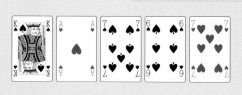

PLAYER 1 has a spade flush. Jack and four in his hand and the king, seven, and six on the board.

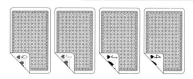

PLAYER 3 has two pair, kings over sevens: the king in his hand and the king and two sevens on the board.

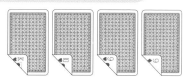

Omaha and Omaha/8 were both derived from Texas hold'em. The mechanics of both Omaha games are the same as hold'em, with one major difference: Omaha players must use exactly two cards from the four private cards they are dealt, along with three of the five community cards, to form the best five-card poker hand. Because players start with four private cards, winning Omaha hands tend to be much bigger than their Texas hold'em counterparts. The reason should be obvious. It's a lot easier to make bigger hands when you have nine cards to work with rather than just seven, and hands that the board makes possible are usually quite probable in Omaha. Whenever the community cards contain three cards of one suit, a flush is a lot more likely than it would be when you're playing hold'em. When the board contains a pair, you'll need to be wary because you might be up against a full house.

Your Position in the Betting Order

Position conveys power in all forms of poker. Just as in Texas hold'em, position in Omaha is fixed throughout the entire hand. When you're the last player to act before the blinds on the initial betting round, you'll also have the advantage of acting last on every betting round during the course of that hand.

Acting early is always a disadvantage, and acting late is an advantage—some hands that you might be better off folding in early position can be raising hands in late position.

Position in the betting order is also important because some hands play better against a few players, while others fare better against a large field. Suppose you've been dealt A-A-T-9. If you're facing only one or two opponents, your aces might end up being the best hand. But with four or five opponents to contend with, a pair of aces is frequently bested. Even if you were to flop a set of aces, someone might have a big straight or flush draw and take that pot away from you.

Pairs can be problematical against all but the smallest number of opponents. Unlike hold'em, where big pairs can survive a flop that does not help them as long as no higher-ranked cards appear on the board, in Omaha, pairs either need to flop three-of-a-kind or the hand should be released at the first sign of a bet by an opponent, who presumably has been helped by the flop. If that's not enough of a cautionary note, a set in Omaha is not nearly as powerful as it is in hold'em. Straights and flushes are much more common when you're playing Omaha, and sets can be thought of as drawing hands—they usually have to improve to win the pot. With small or medium sets, players must be wary of losing to a bigger set. And if you make a small full house, you might well lose to a bigger full house or four-of-a-kind. Although hands like these are still rare birds, they are not nearly as rare in Omaha as they are in hold'em.

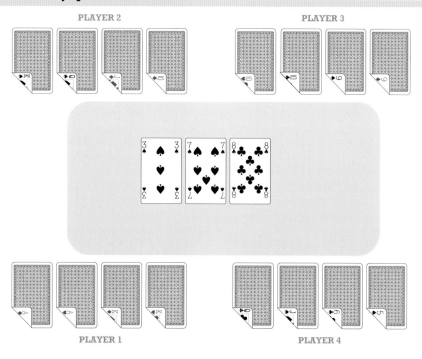

PLAYER 2 PLAYER 3

PLAYER 1 PLAYER 4

Position gives power because when you act last, you already know how many of your opponents are still active in the hand, and whether they've checked, bet, called, or raised. When you have to act first, or from an early position, you're forced to guess about these things. Since players tend to raise less frequently in Omaha than they do when they're playing hold'em, raises from players who act before you provide a great deal of information about the real or purported strength of their hands. A raised hand before the flop generally means a big pair, probably ace, and possibly kings, or even queens, and the holder of that hand is trying to win the pot before the flop or else play the hand against one or perhaps two opponents at the most.

NOTE: *Player 1 looked to have a strong hand before the flop. But after the flop straight draws are possible and someone might even catch two suited cards and make a flush.*

When you are forced to act before you have this kind of information at your disposal, you're flying blind. As a consequence, an early position raise is generally indicative of a very strong hand—or a very bold bluff—because the raise is essentially telling you that they don't care how many opponents call their raise. They may be indicating that they have a very big hand, but no matter what, you have to pay to play.

Odds and Outs

Figuring odds in Omaha is straightforward. As with Texas hold'em, Omaha is simplified by the fact that similar situations arise again and again. This means that it's easy to memorize the odds for common situations, so you don't have to perform calculations during the game—something few of us are good at.

Pot odds

Without the ability to figure pot odds you have no way of knowing whether the odds against making your hand are offset by the cost of playing the hand and how much money you're likely to win if you catch the card you need. By understanding the relationship between the mathematical odds against making your hand and the money you might win if you get lucky, you can play skillful, high-percentage poker.

For example, each and every time you hold four cards to the nut flush on the turn in an Omaha game, the probability is identical. There will be 44 unknown cards: 52 cards comprise the deck, minus your four private cards and the four visible on the board. Of those 44 cards, 35 won't help you, but those other nine cards are the same suit as your flush draw and any one of them will give you the nut flush.

The odds are 35-to-9, or 3.8-to-1 against making your draw. Percentage poker players will call a bet in this situation only if the pot is four times the size of the bet. In a game with betting limits of $20–$40 the pot would need to contain at least $160 to yield a positive expectation in the long run. Alternatively, you'd have to be able to count on winning at least a total of $160 from future calls.

Here's an example of how to count

NOTE: *There are only nine cards in the deck that will make your flush, and two of these (the king and the ten) will make a full house possible for some other player.*

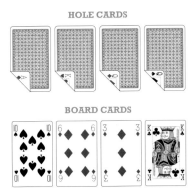

HOLE CARDS

BOARD CARDS

Cards that will complete the flush

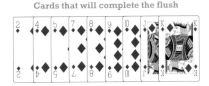

your outs and use that knowledge to determine how best to play your hand. Suppose the turn card gave you the best possible flush with no paired cards on the board. Your opponent flopped a set and now there's only one more card to come. You will win if the board does not pair, but you'll lose to a full house or quads if the board pairs. Once you know that, you can count your outs with certainty. At this point there are 40 unknown cards, 10 of which will pair the board and allow your opponent to win the pot, whereas 30 will not pair the board and you will be the one raking in the chips. In the long run, you figure to win this kind of confrontation three times out of four, or 75 percent of the time.

When you have the best of it and figure to win the majority of the time, your strategy should be predicated on continuing to build the pot. While that last river card will determine the eventual winner, its appearance will also constrain the betting. So the time to get more money in the pot is when there is still a reason for anyone with a drawing hand to stick around and chase his chances for a win—and a set is a drawing hand in Omaha, particularly when there are three suited cards on board.

The winning hand is frequently determined on the river, but preparation for the river determines the size of the pot. This means getting more money into the pot and driving the betting when you have the best hand. It also means playing on the cheap when you're the one with nothing more than a handful of hope and the odds are stacked against you.

How Omaha differs from Texas hold'em

If you've been playing Texas hold'em and are now learning to play Omaha, there is one area in which the games differ dramatically: the quality of straight draws. In fact, some straight draws are so powerful that in many situations they are mathematically favored over made hands.

In hold'em, if you have Q-J in your hand and the board is 10-9-4, you've flopped an open-ended straight draw and either a king or an eight will complete your hand. As the deck contains four kings and four eights, you have eight outs. But in Omaha, a straight draw with only eight outs is dwarfed by many other straight draw possibilities.

Lets say you hold 9-8-7-6 and the flop is 10-5-4. Here are the cards that will complete your straight: 4 threes, 3 sixes, 3 sevens, or 3 eights. You have 13 outs with this hand.

But it gets better than that, suppose you hold 8-6-4-2 and the flop is Q-7-5. You can complete your straight with any of 4 nines, 3 eights, 3 sixes, 3 fours, or 4 threes. Now you have 17 outs.

And there's more, suppose you are holding 10-8-6-5 and the flop is 9-7-4. Now you can make a straight with any one of these cards: 4 jacks, 3 tens, 3 eights, 3 sixes, 3 fives, or 4 threes. That's a total of 20 outs altogether.

If you flop a draw with 20 outs, you will complete your straight by the river an astonishing 70 percent of the time. You have a powerful straight draw and that makes you a big favorite over a smaller made hand.

ADVICE ON STRAIGHT DRAWS

Let's put some of this information about straight draws into perspective.

- Just as in war, you are much better off when you can surround your enemy. The number of potential straights is higher if you have the flop surrounded by possessing the cards immediately above and immediately below the flop. In the example above we had 9-8-7-6 when the board showed 10-5-4. We did not have the board surrounded, so we had only a 13-out straight.

- If you have 9-8-5-4 and the flop is 7-6-2, you have a wrap-around straight draw with 4 tens, 3 nines, 3 eights, 3 fives, 3 fours, and 4 threes, for a total of 20 outs. Wraps are incredibly good gambling opportunities. Not only are you an odds-on favorite to complete your straight, but if you are confronting an opponent with two pair or a set you stand a good chance of getting a lot of money into a pot that you are favored to win.

- Everything else being equal, your straight draw is much more powerful if some of your private cards are higher in rank than the flop. This won't increase your number of outs, but you could have the nut straight when you hit it. In the example above, where you have 9-8-5-4 and the flop is 7-6-2, if an eight comes you'll complete your straight, but there's always a chance that one of your opponents makes a higher straight with a 10-9 in his hand, and that will cost you some chips.

- Another advantage of holding higher cards than those on the board is that you might make a straight plus a draw to an even bigger straight. If that's the case, and an opponent has the same straight you do on the turn, you might get lucky and make a bigger one on the river. Poker players refer to this as freerolling. You can win the pot or split it, but your opponent can only split it or lose it entirely. That's a nice position to be in.

HOLE CARDS

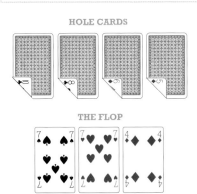

THE FLOP

The cards that will make the straight

NOTE: *Some straight draws in Omaha can have as many as 20 outs.*

But before you get too carried away it's important to remember that having a large number of outs doesn't necessarily mean you'll win the hand. It's possible that the card that completes your straight might result in a bigger straight for an opponent. Or the suit of your straight card might match that of two on the board, making a flush a real possibility. And if you make your straight but the board pairs in the process, you might be looking at a full house or better. There's a big difference between outs to your hand and outs to the nuts. The latter is a lot more important.

Calculating the odds

The following chart shows the outs, odds, and percentage chances of improving your hand on the flop. For example, if you've flopped four to a flush you have nine outs, which translates into a 36 percent chance of completing your flush. Another way of saying it is that the odds against you making your flush are 1.8-to-1.

By now you've probably reached the conclusion that odds, outs, and probabilities are all variations on a theme. We don't want to needlessly complicate things, but it's important to realize that each way of expressing the relationship between the chances of making and missing the hand you are aiming at has its own uses.

Odds give you the bad news first. With eight outs on the flop, the odds tell you that you are a two-to-one underdog. In other words, you will fail to make your hand twice for each time you do make it. Odds are useful because it is easy to compare the odds against making your hand to the money odds offered by the pot. By comparing your odds against improving to the dollar odds offered by the pot, you can make

rational decisions about whether to fold, call, raise, or reraise.

If you don't examine the odds against making your hand in light of the odds offered by the pot, you're simply looking at odds in a vacuum. Is a 2-to-1 underdog a good deal, or is it something to be avoided completely? It depends. If the pot is offering $60 for a $20 call and you are only a 2-to-1 underdog, that's a good thing. The pot odds of 3-to-1 exceed the 2-to-1 odds against making your hand. If you repeated this situation over and over, you'd have the best of it by calling a bet in this situation. But if the pot were only offering $20 on a $20 call, you'd be better off folding, because an even money wager is a bad bet if you figure to win only once every three tries.

Once you reach 14 or more outs, the odds are no longer against you. In fact, with 14 outs or more you are an odds-on favorite to make your hand. And when you're an odds-on favorite it seems easier to look at percentages rather than odds. If you're a 2-to-1 underdog the picture is quite clear and easy to understand by considering the

OUTS, ODDS, AND PERCENTAGES

Outs	Percentage chance of making your hand by the river	Odds against making your hand by the river
4	17%	4.8-to-1
5	21%	3.8-to-1
6	25%	3.0-to-1
7	29%	2.4-to-1
8	33%	2.0-to-1
9	36%	1.8-to-1
10	40%	1.5-to-1
11	43%	1.3-to-1
12	47%	1.1-to-1
13	50%	1.0-to-1
14	53%	0.9-to-1
15	56%	0.8-to-1
16	59%	0.7-to-1
17	62%	0.6-to-1
18	65%	0.5-to-1
19	67%	0.5-to-1
20	70%	0.4-to-1

NOTE: *The odds against this hand making the nut flush, without pairing the board, are 2.4-to-1. If another player bets $40, the pot would have to contain at least $96 to warrant a call.*

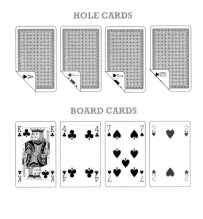

HOLE CARDS

BOARD CARDS

odds against you. But when the odds are in your favor, for example if the odds of you making your hand are 0.4-to-1, it can be easier to express it as having a 70 percent chance of making your hand.

Percentages are also useful whenever you want to combine the probabilities of independent events. You can't do this by multiplying the odds against each event happening, but you can multiply percentages. Outs are essential to the basic poker calculation: How many cards will help me?

The outs, odds, and percentages shown above are the same for Omaha/8 as they are for Omaha. However, if you're playing Omaha/8 you have to account for the fact that calling a $40 bet into a $96 pot may win only half of it for you. While the price to call a bet doesn't differ between games, the pot size usually does, and you have to take that into consideration.

Implied Odds

How big must the pot be to justify a call? Many pundits will tell you that the size of the pot has to offset the odds against making your hand. In other words, if it will cost you $20 to call an $80 pot, that's okay as long as the odds against catching the card you need are 4-to-1 or less. If the pot will reward you with $80 if you call a $20 bet and get lucky, that kind of wager has a positive long-term expectation if the odds against making your hand are only 2-to-1.

Sometimes the size of the pot won't offset the odds against making your hand. What then? Is the anticipation of future bets enough to justify a call even though the size of the pot right now is not large enough to offset the odds against making your hand? That's what implied odds are all about. They serve as a comparison of your total expected win to the cost of calling a current bet.

In Omaha, especially when you have a large number of opponents and a hand like a big straight draw or a set that might improve to a full house if you get lucky, it often pays to call or even bet if you suspect that the pot might continue growing if you stay involved in the hand.

One word of caution: Many poor players are fond of using estimates of implied odds as excuses for continuing to play a hand where the odds are long and the size of the pot is too small to offset them. Estimates, after all, are really just educated guesses. If you deceive yourself with uneducated guesses just because you feel like mixing it up in a pot in which you really don't belong, you'll only lose more money in the long run.

> **NOTE:** *To figure implied odds for a hand, try to assess how many of your opponents are likely to be calling all bets to the river.*

PLAYER 1

$20 + $20 + $40 + $40 = $120

PLAYER 2

$20 + $20 + $40 + $40 = $120

PLAYER 3

$20 + $20 + $40 + $40 = $120

TOTAL POT $360

IMPLIED ODDS ADVICE
Make good, accurate estimates that are reflective of what others seem likely to do. Don't pick numbers out of thin air simply because they provide a rationale that allows you to justify what's really an untenable play.

Deception

Good players are the easiest to deceive. Experts will sniff you out, while poor players will be so totally unaware of what you're doing that it will just pass them by as if they weren't there.

While you should attempt to deceive good players, straightforward play is usually all that's needed against weak, ineffective players who call with hands they shouldn't play and make woefully weak plays in a wide variety of situations. Fancy plays and trickery are wasted on these players and will usually cost you money in the long run. Bluffing is rare in lower-limit Omaha games, and if you can't tell whether opponents are bluffing, you're usually better off giving them credit for the hand.

Your goal should be to play straightforward poker most of the time and reserve your bag of tricks for good opponents, small pots, small fields, and those few occasions when you have a powerhouse hand and can afford to let your opponents improve just enough to get themselves into trouble.

Semi-bluffing

Every skillful player semi-bluffs. It's a far better strategem than plain old bluffing, and it's better than not bluffing at all. A semi-bluff is a bet made on a hand that can win if it improves but is not currently the best hand.

Semi-bluffs differ from pure bluffs because they offer two ways to win. The semi-bluffing bettor hopes to win the pot immediately if his opponent folds, but if he's called, he can still win should his hand improve to its obvious potential. It's an easy way to add some deception to your game, and that has value in and of itself. Betting with a four-flush or an open-ended straight draw are classic examples of semi-bluffs.

But take heed: There's nothing to be gained by semi-bluffing an opponent who calls all the time, because the guaranteed call eliminates one of the two ways you have to win the pot.

Bluffs will fail against opponents who call too frequently. Semi-bluffing is also not that savvy an idea when you're last to act, since you might as well take a free card if everyone else has checked.

At the end of the day, semi-bluffing is a good strategy because it provides two ways to win. It allows you to be the bettor instead of the caller, and that's usually a good thing too. Sometimes you might bet thinking you're semi-bluffing when you actually have the best hand. When that's the case, your semi-bluff—which in all actuality is a bet with the best hand—prevents your opponent from getting a free card. In fact, your bet may convince him to fold.

Semi-bluffing is more aggressive than passively checking a drawing hand, but it's not foolish, unmitigated aggression. It's aggression that provides a way to win the pot even if the hand you hope to make never materializes. As long as there's a chance your opponent will fold, you have two ways to win the pot, while sowing seeds of doubt and confusion in your opponent's mind.

Semi-bluffing is far more effective than a pure bluff and, when used in moderation, is tough to defend against. It's a strategy you'll familiarize yourself with as you gain more experience playing poker.

NOTE: *Player 1's bet is a semi-bluff, because although he only has a pair of queens, he has a straight draw and might even have the best hand at the moment.*

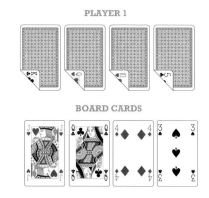

PLAYER 1

BOARD CARDS

Defending

What you don't spend, you don't have to earn, and playing good, sound, defensive poker is often just as important as playing aggressively with the best hand.

Every time you're in the small blind in an Omaha game, you'll have to decide whether to defend it at the cost of a partial bet. If you're in the big blind and someone's raised you'll have to mull that one over, too. If you come out betting from any other position and an opponent raises, you'll have to decide whether to fold, play defensively, or stay aggressive. This can be tough going for Texas hold'em players who are just taking up Omaha. Hold'em players will seldom, if ever, fold middle or bottom sets and that unwillingness to play defensively can be quite costly.

Poker requires a balance of offense and defense, between being aggressive and conserving your chips. Striking the proper balance is a combination of figuring the odds and understanding your opponents' playing styles. The right decision against one player can be a very wrong decision against another. This is where the art of poker comes into play, and it's a skill you'll develop and improve only with lots of practice and experience at the table.

Raising

Raising the pot in Omaha is not much different from raising in other games. Here are a few reasons you might want to raise.

1. RAISING TO GET MONEY INTO THE POT
This is the primary reason that most players raise. Suppose you've got a powerhouse hand and someone bets. Now it's your turn to act. What should you do? Raise! Whenever you have a lock on the pot, or the best hand now with a draw to an even better one—this happens when you make the best possible straight along with a draw to a flush, or a flush with a draw to a full house—you should raise at every opportunity because every chip in the pot could be yours at the hand's end.

2. RAISING TO ELIMINATE OPPONENTS
If you're holding A-A-Q-J, you'll want to raise if you figure it will prevent other opponents from entering the pot after you. While a pair of aces will need to improve to win against a large field, it stands a good chance of winning without improvement against only one adversary. If you flop a set, you'll want to raise to make it too costly for drawing hands to play against you.

3. RAISING TO GET A FREE CARD ON A MORE EXPENSIVE STREET
Let's say you are holding K-Q-J-7 and are last to act. The flop was 10-9-4 of mixed suits and you're facing three opponents. The player who is first to act bets, and is called by the others. You can raise. If the turn card is not the king, queen, jack, or eight you're looking for, the fact that you raised may enable you to see the river for free in hopes of catching one of the 13 cards that will make your hand—if the original bettor and subsequent callers all check the turn. And if you make the nut straight on the turn, well, you have added money to a pot that looks like it will soon belong to you.

4. RAISING TO PREVENT A FREE CARD
Just as it is correct to raise on the flop in order to gain a free card on the turn, raising to prevent your opponents from getting a free or relatively inexpensive card can also be the right course of action in other situations.

For example, let's say you hold A-10-9-6 in fifth position. Only three other players are active on the flop: the big blind and seats seven and eight. The flop is A-T-9. The big blind bets, but you're not sure what he's holding. He might have a better hand than yours, such as a set, but he's more likely to be drawing for a straight. Although you can out draw him if your hand improves to a full house, it's still your job to make him pay for the privilege of trying to improve his hand.

Raising can be risky: Sometimes you should raise even though you're not certain that you have the best hand. You'll also encounter some opponents who take raising so personally that their response is simply to raise back—even when their hands don't warrant it. But you can't let the fear of a reraise stop you from raising—if you do, you'll leave money on the table because you aren't absolutely sure about how the value of your hand stacks up.

Free Cards

If everyone checks on a given betting round, you'll get a free card. That's the good news. The bad news is that your opponents will get a free card, too. And if you have the best hand, you might also have cost yourself some money by not betting.

The general rule about free cards is straightforward: be very reluctant to give your opponents a free shot at catching a miraculous card that might beat you if you have the best hand. On the other hand, when you're the one holding something less than the best hand, you'd always prefer a free card to one you'd have to call a bet to receive.

There are some exceptions to most rules, and here are the exceptions to the free card rule: Give a free card when you have a very strong hand and want your opponents to build a hand that's strong enough to call your bets on future rounds. Suppose you flopped four-of-a-kind, or even a big full house. If you bet, it's unlikely that any of your opponents will have been helped enough by the flop to call—if they've been helped at all. But if the flop contained two cards of the same suit, or two cards in ranks that were in close proximity to one another, you can afford to let your opponents catch up a bit. If a flush card comes, or a card that gives one or more of your opponents a straight or a draw to a straight, they are now going to keep calling, even though they are drawing dead.

If the pot is small when you give away that free card, so much the better. There's nothing really satisfying about winning a very small pot with a very big hand. You're usually better off trying to win a bigger pot than a small one, even if there's some chance you might lose the whole thing. Besides, the next card

> **NOTE:** *Unless you've flopped a super hand like four-of-a-kind, don't give opponents free cards.*

PLAYER 1

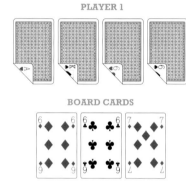

BOARD CARDS

might give your opponent a second-best hand that's good enough to bet. When that happens you can raise or try for a check-raise if you're first to act.

When you're the one still hoping to make a good hand, you'll want a free card anytime you can get it. That's not something you have total control over, but by betting on the flop you might be able to convince opponents to check on the turn. In essence, you're trading a small bet on the flop for an opportunity to save a larger one on the turn. If your hand improves on the turn you can bet; if not, you can check and take a free card if your opponents also check.

Slow-playing

Deception is an essential element in poker, and slow-playing is a form of deception with a strong hand. When you play a very strong hand weakly on an inexpensive betting round, you're slow-playing, and your goal is to lure your opponents onto the more expensive betting rounds.

To slow-play, just take no action beyond what is required to stay in the pot. If no one has bet, you check. If someone wagers, you call. Keep as many players in the pot as you can, in order to maximize your winnings on subsequent betting rounds.

A very strong hand is the first requirement to slow-play. Under no circumstances should you slow-play if it gives your opponents a free draw to a hand better than yours.

Slow-playing can deceive your opponents into thinking you have a weak hand, while you're hoping that they will improve their's, but only enough to make them second best. Slow-playing offers a powerful way to get maximum value for your strong hands, but you must be prudent. You need a very strong hand and the strength of your hand should not be obvious to your opponents. And remember: You should be cautious about slow-playing if a free card can give an opponent a better hand than yours.

Suppose you flop four-of-a-kind and there are four players in the hand with you. Two of the cards on the flop are suited. The pot is small on the flop. The chance of someone beating you is miniscule, and if a third suited card falls, someone might make a flush and think it the best hand. Just sit back and hope someone improves. If they do, you can bet on the turn, try for a check-raise, or raise if an opponent comes out betting.

It's not complex. By the time your opponents realize what you're up to it's usually too late. They will already have paid the price. But don't slow-play hands unless they are extremely strong. A free card can be a dangerous gift to offer opponents and you should only do so under the best of circumstances.

HOLE CARDS

THE FLOP

THE TURN

NOTE: *You have flopped quads and you are virtually unbeatable, but you need to keep the game going, so don't discourage your opponents. Slow-play this hand to keep those with two pair or a draw to a flush in the game. With a third suited card on the turn, an opponent may make his flush, and the size of the pot could increase dramatically.*

Reading Your Opponents

Reading your opponents in Omaha is an exercise in always knowing what the best possible hand is, and assessing what your opponents have by their betting patterns in prior and current betting rounds. The better you are at deducing what your opponents are holding, the better your results will be.

Reading opponents is a mixture of skill and art, and requires observing them in action. By examining an opponent's betting patterns against the hands he ultimately shows down, you'll learn a lot about his playing style. Does he bet his drawing hands aggressively, or does he check and call until he completes his hand? Does he come out betting when he makes a big hand, or is he a tricky player who tries to get you to do his betting for him, so he can trap you by checking and then raising after you bet?

Good players are easier to read because their actions are usually logical and consistent. Excellent players will deceive you, and poor players often don't know why they play as they do, so there's not much to look for other than

> **NOTE:** *Player 3 raises before the flop, so it looks like he's holding a big pair—aces or kings—or four big cards.*

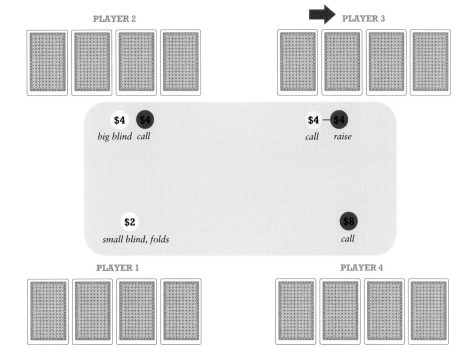

the fact that bad players usually call too frequently and enter pots with weak hands. The easiest way to read opponents is to assign them a variety of possible hands and then refine those hands according to their play and the cards that appear on the board in subsequent betting rounds.

Let's say your opponent raises before the flop. Since many Omaha players raise when they hold a pair of aces, you think that's one of the hands he might have. He also might have a pair of kings, or even four big cards with the rank of ten or higher. He checks a flop of Q♥-J♥-4♦, but comes out betting when the 9♠ appears on the turn. It's now easy to assume he's holding a ten and a king, or else he's flopped a set of queens or jacks and is trying to make it

costly for someone with a flush draw to see the river. He might even have A-K-T-9 with two hearts, giving him a straight with redraws to a bigger straight and the nut flush.

> **NOTE:** *Player 3 checked on the flop but bets on the turn. He wants to make it expensive for his opponents to see the river. You would now figure him to hold 10-K or 10-8, both of which make a straight, or a set of queens or jacks, or possibly A-K-T-9 with two hearts. There's also some possibility of a set of nines or fours. If you don't have a straight, you can't beat a set no matter how big or small it may be.*

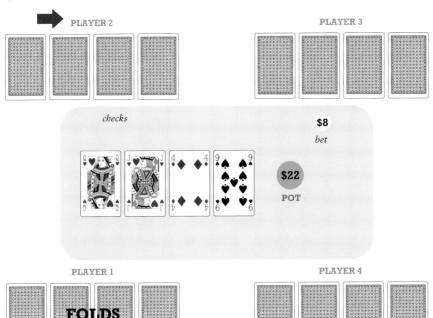

OMAHA/8

Just as in Texas hold'em and Omaha, position in Omaha/8 is fixed throughout the entire hand. Similarly, acting early is a disadvantage and acting late is an advantage—some hands that may have been folded in early position are raising hands in late position, so you want to have that dealer button.

Your Position in the Betting Order

Some hands play better against a few players, while others do better against a large field. Suppose you've been dealt A-A-6-5. If you're facing only one or two opponents, your aces might be the best high hand, allowing you to win at least half the pot and you have three low hands that will let you escape with half of the pot if you have the only low hand, although it's a very weak low hand against three or more callers. With a gaggle of opponents, a pair of aces is frequently bested too. Even if you were to flop a set of aces, there'd be at least one low card on the board— the ace—that would encourage opponents with two or more low cards in their hand to stick around in hopes of snatching half of the pot from under your nose. When you can play this hand from late position, you have a better idea of how many hands you are up against.

Here's another example. If you're in late position with A-4-5-9 and no one has called, you probably have a draw to the best low hand. But if the pot is full of opponents, at least one of them figures to have a better low draw than you. Because your chances of making a good high hand are slim as well, you might not want to play this hand at all.

The only way to be sure your hand can be played aggressively, or to guarantee that you'll be able to see the flop for only one bet, is to know how many opponents are in the pot with you. When you play a hand from late position you'll always know this. When you play from early position, you'll be forced to guess on both accounts.

In Omaha/8 pairs either need to flop three-of-a-kind or the hand should be released at the first sign of a bet by an opponent, who has presumably been helped by the flop. That's a huge difference with hold'em, where big pairs in particular can survive a flop that does not help them as long as no higher-ranked cards flop. If that's not bad enough, a set in Omaha/8 is not nearly as powerful as it is in hold'em, for two reasons:

- Straights and flushes are much more common in Omaha/8, so much so that sets can be thought of as drawing hands—they usually have to improve to win the pot.
- Even with a big set, you have to be wary of losing half of the pot to a low hand, or all of it to a low hand that may also make a straight or a flush and win the high half of the pot as well as the low end.

One of the things you'll quickly realize about Omaha/8 or any game in which

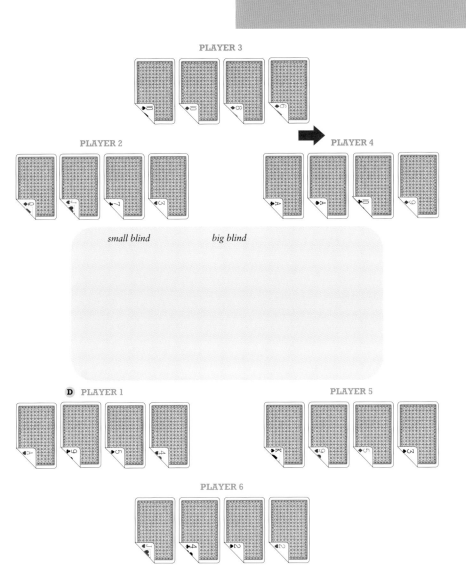

NOTE: *Player 4 must act first with no idea how many players will see the flop. Player 1 will at least know if Players 4 through 6 are still in the hand.*

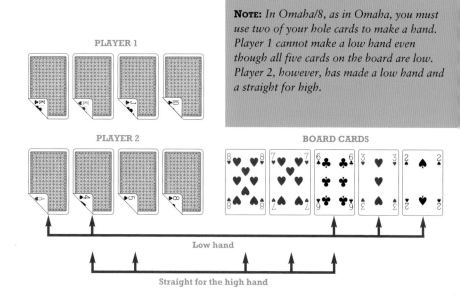

PLAYER 1

NOTE: *In Omaha/8, as in Omaha, you must use two of your hole cards to make a hand. Player 1 cannot make a low hand even though all five cards on the board are low. Player 2, however, has made a low hand and a straight for high.*

PLAYER 2

BOARD CARDS

Low hand

Straight for the high hand

the best high hand splits the pot with the best low hand is that it is much easier for low hands to morph into high holdings than vice versa. After all, low hands often grow into straights and flushes, but full houses never shrink.

Position provides information about the number of opponents you're playing against and about the cost to play a particular hand. Players raise less frequently in Omaha and Omaha/8 than they do in hold'em, and raises from players who act before you provide a great deal of information about their hands. A raised hand before the flop generally contains three very low cards, such as A-2-3-X, or it can be a hand like A♣-A♥-2♣-3♥ where one or two aces are suited to a smaller card. It can even be a hand like 5-4-3-2 and the owner is hoping that an ace will fall to give him the best low draw.

POSITIONAL ADVICE FOR ANY FORM OF POKER

Acting last or in late position lets you know:
- How many opponents will be contesting the pot with you
- The real or purported strength of your opponents' hands
- The cost to play the hand

A raise from early position generally is indicative of a very strong hand— or a very bold bluff. An early position raise tells you:
- I don't care how many opponents will call my raise
- I have a very big hand, confront me at your peril
- You have to pay to play

Odds and Outs

In Omaha/8, it's easy to memorize the odds for common situations. This eliminates having to perform calculations during a game.

Pot odds

The ability to figure pot odds is a vital skill for any poker player. By understanding the relationship between the mathematical odds against making your hand and the money you figure to win if you get lucky, you can play skillful, high-percentage poker, instead of treating the game like some form of gambling. In Omaha/8 many pots are split, and whenever you're trying to figure whether the size of the pot makes calling worthwhile, you have to be realistic about assessing your chances to scoop the pot or only win half of it.

For example, whenever you hold four cards to the nut flush on the turn in an Omaha or an Omaha/8 game, there will

be 44 unknown cards—52 minus your 4 pocket cards and the 4 cards on the board. Of those 44 cards 35 won't help you, but the remaining 9 cards are the same suit as your flush draw and any one of them will give you the nut flush.

The odds are 35-to-9, or 3.8-to-1, against you making your draw. Percentage poker players will call a bet in this situation only if the pot is four times the size of the bet.

In a game with betting limits of $20-$40 the pot would need to contain at least $160 to call a bet if you figure to win all of it. If you figure to win just half of the pot, the pot's total would have to be $320 to justify calling.

PLAYER 1

BOARD CARDS

Cards that will complete the flush

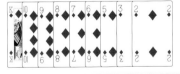

NOTE: *The pot here should be about four times the size of the bet for Player 1 to call.*

Cards that will not complete the flush

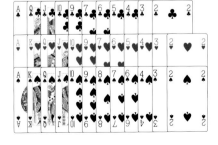

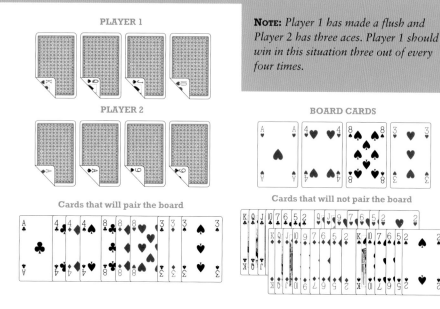

PLAYER 1

NOTE: *Player 1 has made a flush and Player 2 has three aces. Player 1 should win in this situation three out of every four times.*

PLAYER 2

BOARD CARDS

Cards that will pair the board

Cards that will not pair the board

Making the best possible hand

One of the major differences between Omaha and Texas hold'em is that more information is available to you in Omaha. In loose Omaha games, and that includes most of the lower-limit games you'll encounter, Omaha is a game of making the best hand possible given the five community cards that appear on the center of the table.

It's like this: If you're chasing the low end of the pot with a deuce and a trey in your hand, don't be shocked if one of your opponents shows up with ace-trey and another with ace-deuce. After all, you were chasing with the third-best possible low, not the best possible low. That's not the way to play this game. If you've made the best possible flush but the board contains a pair, you shouldn't be surprised to see one of your opponents turn up a full house or even

four-of-a-kind. That happens in Texas hold'em too, but not often enough to substantially diminish the value of a flush. It's much more common in Omaha/8, because with each player having four starting cards the possibilities of making big hands increases substantially.

There's no need to despair, however, because in this game you can know with some degree of certainty what your chances of winning the pot are, and you can manipulate the size of that pot by betting and raising. To do this you need to know something about your chances of succeeding.

Suppose the turn card gives you the best possible flush with no paired cards on the board. Your opponent has flopped a set and there's one more card to come. If you assume that you will win if the board does not pair, but you'll lose to a full house or quads if the board does pair, you can count your outs with absolute certainty.

At that point there are 40 other cards that are unknown. Ten of them will pair the board and allow your opponent to win the pot. The other thirty will not pair the board and you will be the one raking in the chips. In the long run, you're likely to win this kind of confrontation three times out of four.

When you're likely to win the majority of the time, your strategy should be to build the pot. The river card will determine the eventual winner, but it also confines the betting, so the time to get more money into the pot is when there is still a reason for anyone with a drawing hand—and a set is a drawing hand in Omaha/8, particularly when there are three suited cards on board—to stick around and chase their chances for a win.

While the winning hand is usually determined on the river, it's preparing for the river that determines the pot. When you have the best hand try to get more money into the pot, but when you have only a hopeful hand play wisely and keep your contribution cheap.

If you've been playing Texas hold'em and are now learning to play Omaha/8, the difference in the quality of straight draws is dramatic. In Omaha/8 some straight draws are so powerful they are mathematically favored over made hands in many situations.

In hold'em, if you have 8-7 in your hand and the board is 6-5-K, you've flopped an open-ended straight draw and either a nine or a four will complete your hand. Because there are four nines and four fours unaccounted for, you have eight outs. But in Omaha/8, a straight draw with only eight outs is dwarfed by many other straight draw possibilities.

Let's have a look at some examples of straight draw possibilities in Omaha/8. Suppose you hold 9-8-7-6 and the flop is 10-5-4. Here are the cards that will complete your straight: 4 threes, 3 sixes, 3 sevens, 3 eights. That's 13 outs.

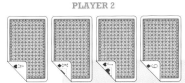

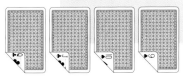

NOTE: *Player 1 has made a straight on the turn. However, Player 2 was able to make a higher straight when the ten fell.*

Say you hold 8-6-4-2 and the flop is Q-7-5. You can complete your straight with any of 4 nines, 3 eights, 3 sixes, 3 fours, and 4 threes. You have 17 outs.

If you are holding 10-8-6-5 and the flop is 9-7-4, you can make a straight with any one of these cards: 4 jacks, 3 tens, 3 eights, 3 sixes, 3 fives, and 4 threes. That's a total of 20 outs. If you flop a draw with 20 outs, you will complete your straight by the river an astonishing 70 percent of the time—and that makes you a big favorite over a smaller made hand. However, having a large number of outs doesn't mean you will always win the hand. The card which completes your straight might complete a bigger straight for an opponent. If there are three cards of one suit on the board, the chance of a flush is now a real possibility. Or, if you make your straight, but the board pairs in the process, you might be looking at a full house or better. There's a big difference between *outs to your hand* and *outs to the nuts*. The latter is a lot more important, particularly when you've got a one-way hand and are likely to win only half the pot at best.

STRAIGHT DRAWS IN OMAHA/8

From a probability perspective straight draws in Omaha/8 are identical to those in the Omaha version that's played for high only. What is different, however, is whether you are drawing for the entire pot or just half of it.

- The number of straights is higher if you have the flop surrounded, by possessing the cards immediately above and immediately below the flop. In one example above we had 9-8-7-6 when the board showed 10-5-4. We did not have the board surrounded, and had only a 13-out straight draw.

- If you have 9-8-5-4 and the flop is 7-6-2, you have a wrap-around straight draw with 4 tens, 3 nines, 3 eights, 3 fives, 3 fours, and 3 threes, for a total of 20 outs. Wraps are incredibly good gambling opportunities. Not only are you an odds-on favorite to complete your straight, but if you are confronting an opponent with two pair or a set you stand a good chance of getting a lot of money into a pot you are favored to win.

- All else being equal, you are much better off if your straight draw contains cards that are higher in rank than the flop. While it won't increase the number of outs you have, you figure to have the nut straight when you hit it. The exception to this is when your straight draw can be completed by cards that will also give you the best low hand.

- Another advantage of having bigger cards in your hand than the cards on the board is that you might make one straight and have a draw to an even bigger one. If that's the case and an opponent has the same straight as you on the turn, you might get lucky and make a bigger one on the river. You are free-rolling. You can either win the pot or split it, but your opponent can only split it or lose it entirely.

Chasing the low pot

When you have a low hand—even the nut low hand—you won't always win your side of the pot outright. It's not uncommon for two players to be dealt A-2, and when that happens, you'll wind up quartered. It doesn't happen all that often, but a little protection is always a good thing to have. In fact, if you were dealt A-2-3-X and flopped the nut low, you'd hope for an ace or deuce to fall on the next card. That way, any opponent holding acey-deucey is counterfeited and you'd win the entire low side of the pot. In addition, the card that counterfeit's your opponent's low cards might just be the card that turns your holding into a high straight as well as a low hand.

The chart, which is the same for Omaha, shows the outs, odds, and percentage chances of improving your hand once you've seen the flop. For example, if you've flopped four to a flush you have nine outs, which translates into a 36 percent chance of completing your flush. The odds against you making your flush are 1.8-to-1.

As you can see, odds, outs, and probabilities are all variations on a

theme. However, it's important to remember that each way of expressing the relationship between the chances of making and missing the hand you are aiming at, has its own uses.

Outs	Percentage chance of making your hand by the river	Odds against making your hand by the river
	OUTS, ODDS, AND PERCENTAGES (post flop)	
4	17%	4.8-to-1
5	21%	3.8-to-1
6	25%	3.0-to-1
7	29%	2.4-to-1
8	33%	2.0-to-1
9	36%	1.8-to-1
10	40%	1.5-to-1
11	43%	1.3-to-1
12	47%	1.1-to-1
13	50%	1.0-to-1
14	53%	0.9-to-1
15	56%	0.8-to-1
16	59%	0.7-to-1
17	62%	0.6-to-1
18	65%	0.5-to-1
19	67%	0.5-to-1
20	70%	0.4-to-1

NOTE: *Odds are 2-to-1 against you making your straight. You need to know you will win at least double the amount it costs you to call a bet.*

HOLE CARDS

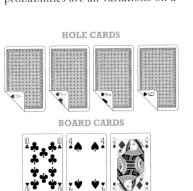

BOARD CARDS

OUTS

Odds provide the bad news first. For example, with eight outs on the flop, you will fail to make your hand twice for each one time you are successful. Odds make it easier to compare the odds against making your hand with the money odds offered by the pot. By comparing your odds against improving to the dollar odds offered by the pot, you can make rational decisions about whether to fold, call, raise, or reraise.

Without this relationship, you have no frame of reference. Is 3-to-1 a good deal, or a bad investment? It depends. If the pot is offering $80 on a $20 call and you are only a 3-to-1 underdog, that's a good thing, because the pot odds of 4-to-1 exceed the odds against making your hand.

If you repeated this situation over and over you'd have the best of it by calling a bet in this situation. But if the pot were only offering $20 on a $20 call, you should fold.

With 14 or more outs the odds are no longer against you, and you are an odds-on favorite to make your hand. When you're an odds-on favorite it's easier to look at percentages rather than odds. While the picture is quite clear and very understandable when you're a 2-to-1 dog, somehow it's easier to understand that you have approximately a 70 percent chance of making your hand, rather than stating that the odds against that event occurring are 0.4-to-1.

Percentages make it easy to combine the probabilities of independent events. You can't do this by multiplying the odds against each event happening, but you can multiply percentages. And outs are useful in this basic poker calculation: How many cards will help me?

There are some percentages that you should know, which are helpful whenever you're drawing for the low end of the pot in an Omaha/8 game.

NOTE: *Both players have a draw to a low, but the third low card in Player 2's hand provides insurance against being counterfeited.*

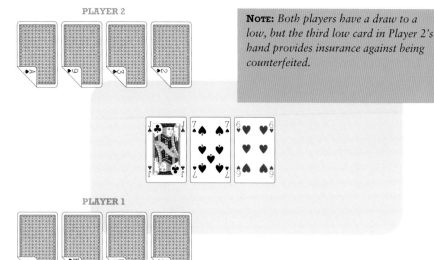

- If you hold A-2 and two unpaired low cards flop that do not counterfeit your hand, you have a 59 percent chance of making a low hand, and a 49 percent chance of making the nut low.
- If you hold A-2-3 and two unpaired low cards flop that do not counterfeit your hand, you'll make a low hand 72 percent of the time, and 69 percent of the time you'll make the nut low.

These odds are pretty good regardless of how you look at them. But if you happen to have a trey in your hand to accompany your acey-deucy, not only do your odds increase substantially, but you'll find yourself rooting for an ace or a deuce to fall once you've made your low hand. An ace or a deuce on the board will unceremoniously counterfeit any of your opponents who might be drawing to a naked A-2.

Implied Odds

Pot odds aren't always sufficient to offset the odds against making your hand, but the likelihood of future bets might be enough to justify playing.

Winning money in addition to what's in the pot right now is what implied odds are all about.

Although you can never be certain how many opponents will call your future bets or raises if you make your hand, implied odds are a way to compare your total expected win to the current cost of calling a bet.

Deception

As discussed in other games, better opponents are more susceptible to your deceptive play than weaker ones. Poor players are usually unaware of any "messages" you're sending by virtue of your betting patterns. Against weak opponents, straightforward play is all you need.

Bluffing is rare in lower-limit Omaha/8 games because such play can be costly. There are often so many players in the pot that you'd probably be better off if you never bluffed at all.

More poker players suffer from being too deceptive than they do from not being tricky enough. You should play straightforward poker most of the time and save your deceptive play for good opponents, small pots, small fields, and those few occasions when you have such a great hand that you can afford to let your opponents improve enough to get themselves into trouble.

Semi-bluffing

Every skillful player uses semi-bluffing as a playing strategy, even if he is not aware of the term. You're semi-bluffing whenever you bet a hand that's probably not the best one, but one that can win if it improves.

Semi-bluffing gives you two ways to win. Your opponent might fold, but if called, you can still win if your hand improves. Semi-bluffing also provides an opportunity to add some deception to your game, and that has value in and of itself. Betting on the come, which many players routinely do when they flop a four-flush or a straight draw, is a very common semi-bluff.

Despite their advantages, there are some cautionary measures too. You shouldn't semi-bluff an opponent who calls all the time, because your bluffs are doomed to fail against opponents who call too frequently. Semi-bluffing is also not all that savvy an idea when you're last to act, since you might be better off just taking a free card.

But when all is said and done, semi-bluffing provides two ways to win and it allows you to be the bettor instead of the caller, and that's usually a good position to be in. Sometimes you might even bet thinking you're semi-bluffing when you actually have the best hand. When that's the case, your semi-bluff—which in all actuality is a bet with the best hand—prevents your opponent from getting a free card. In fact, your bet may convince him to fold.

Semi-bluffing is a strategy you'll familiarize yourself with as you get more and more experience playing poker. It is usually far superior to a pure bluff and is tough to defend against when used in moderation.

NOTE: *Player 1 bets with only a pair of fours on the flop, but with draws to the nut flush and the nut low. The bet is a bluff, but with a good chance to scoop the pot it is more of a semi-bluff.*

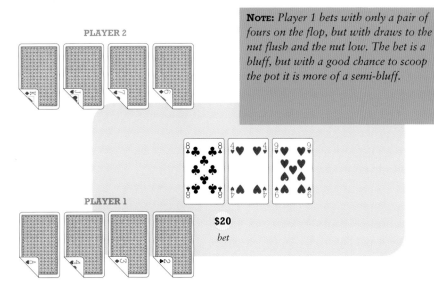

PLAYER 2

PLAYER 1

$20

bet

Defending

Because pots are split between high and low hands in Omaha/8, many players eagerly contribute chips to each pot. But money saved is the same as money won, and playing defensively is just as critical as playing aggressively with the best hand.

While aggressive play is generally winning play, it can't be unmitigated. Poker is always a balance of offense and defense, particularly in Omaha/8, where the cost of a full bet might only garner half of the pot. Refraining from raising with less than a draw to the best low, not betting two pair, and treating sets—particularly low sets—as made hands instead of drawing hands are common situations in Omaha/8 where too much aggression can be very costly.

Raising

Reasons to raise the pot in Omaha/8 are similar to those in Omaha, though the split pot can have an influence.

1. GET MORE MONEY IN THE POT

This is the most common reason to raise, and the most enjoyable too. Let's say you have a powerhouse hand. Someone bets and three players call. Then it's your turn to act. You should raise. If you have a lock on one side of the pot in Omaha/8 and more than one opponent whom you suspect is going in the opposite direction, you should raise at every opportunity. After all, you stand to win fifty cents of every dollar they contribute to the pot.

2. ELIMINATE OPPONENTS

If you've been dealt a hand like A-A-2-4 you should raise if you think it will prevent other opponents from entering the pot after you. A pair of aces will need to improve to win the high side of the pot against a large field, but it stands a good chance of winning without improvement against only one opponent. If a low board develops, you also stand a good chance of scooping the pot. Raising makes good sense any time you've got a hand that plays better against fewer opponents.

3. GET A FREE CARD ON A MORE EXPENSIVE STREET

You're last to act with a K-Q-J-8. The flop was 10-9-4 of mixed suits and you're facing three opponents. If the player who is first to act bets and is called by the others, you can raise. If the turn card is not the card you're looking for, and there are 13 of them (4 sevens, 3 eights, 3 kings, and 3 queens), the fact that you raised may enable you to see the river for free. If you make the nut straight on the turn, you will have increased a pot, which by all appearances will soon be yours.

4. PREVENT A FREE CARD

The example below shows that raising can also be a good way to prevent your opponents from getting a free or relatively inexpensive card.

You hold A-10-9-6 in fifth position. On the flop only three other players are active: the big blind, and seats eight and nine. The flop is A-9-7. The big blind is first to act and bets, but you're not sure what he's holding. He might have an ace

with two low cards, and if he's hoping for a low hand to develop on the last two betting rounds, it's your job to make him pay for the opportunity to draw to a low-percentage hand. He may also be betting with A-7, in which case you have an opportunity to punish him for betting a dominated hand.

While you have some idea about the players in seats eight and nine, you're not certain you have the best hand.

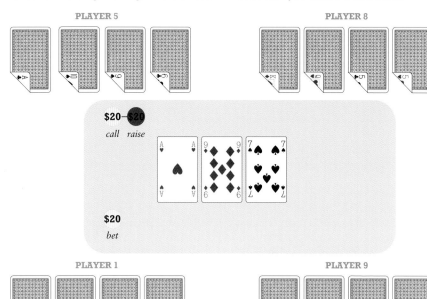

PLAYER 5

PLAYER 8

$20—$20
call   raise

$20
bet

PLAYER 1

PLAYER 9

NOTE: *Player 1, the big blind, bets. Player 5 raises because he thinks he might have the best high hand. He also wants to drive out any players who might be waiting for their low hand to develop—he doesn't want to give them a free card.*

Someone might have flopped a set of nines or sevens. What should you do in this position? While calling is not a bad idea, raising is probably better.

If your raise forces seats eight and nine to fold, you are now heads-up against the blind, and you have the added advantage of acting last on the turn and the river.

Raising can be a difficult proposition and sometimes you'll raise without knowing for sure that you have the best hand. Sometimes you'll encounter opponents who respond to any raise by raising back—even if their hands don't warrant it. If you're going to be a selectively aggressive player, you can't let the prospect of a reraise stop you from raising when strategy calls for it. You can't leave money on the table just because you weren't absolutely certain that you had the better value hand.

Free Cards

Free card situations occur when everyone checks. Each player gets another card without having to pay the cost of a bet. Those times that you have the best hand, you don't want to give your opponents a free card that might snatch the pot right out from under your nose. On the other hand, most of the time you're holding less than the best hand, and you'd prefer a free card to one you'd have to call a bet to receive.

There are some exceptions. Sometimes you have a hand so strong that it's worth giving a free card to your opponents in the hope that they'll build a hand strong enough to call your bets on future rounds. If you bet a big hand you're lucky enough to flop, such as four-of-a-kind or a full house, it's unlikely that any of your opponents will have been helped enough by the flop to call, if they've been helped at all. But if the flop that has given you such a powerhouse hand contains two cards of the same suit, or two cards in ranks that are in close proximity, you can afford to let your opponents see another card for free. If a flush card or one that gives one or more of your opponents a straight or a draw to a straight comes, they are likely to call a bet.

If the pot is small when you give out that free card, so much the better, since winning a very small pot with a very big hand is not what you're after. Instead, try to win a bigger pot, even at the risk of losing the whole thing. Besides, if there's some chance the next card might give an opponent a hand that's good enough to bet, you might get a chance to raise, or try for a check-raise if you're first to act.

If you're the one hoping to make a good hand, a free card is always welcome. That's not something you have total control over, but by betting on the flop you might be able to convince opponents to check to you on the turn, when betting limits double. Once the turn card is exposed you can always bet if your hand has improved sufficiently, or check and see the river card for free.

Slow-playing

To slow-play, you should take no action beyond what is required to stay in the pot. If no one bets, you check. If someone bets, just call. Keep as many players in the pot as you can so you can maximize your winnings on subsequent betting rounds.

Slow-playing in Omaha/8 is trickier than it is in games where there's only one winner. If you have the best high hand, under no circumstances should you slow-play if it gives your opponents a free draw to a low hand that might capture half the pot.

Under ideal conditions your slow-play will deceive your opponent into thinking that you have a weak hand and the free card will improve his hand, but only enough to make it second-best. The best time to slow-play is when the pot is relatively small and you believe that your actions will allow it to grow larger on subsequent betting rounds, thereby getting maximum value for your strong hands. But temper this strategy with some prudence. Make sure that the strength of your hand is not too obvious to your opponents, and don't slow-play if a free card can give an opponent a better hand than yours.

Suppose you hold 4-4 and there are four players in the hand with you. The flop is 4-4-K and two of the cards on the flop are suited. The chance of someone beating your quad fours is minimal, but if a third suited card falls on the turn or river, someone might make a flush and think it the best hand. If no one has bet when it's your turn to act you should check, or if someone has bet, call. If someone improves on the turn and bets, try for a check-raise, or raise if an opponent comes out betting.

By the time your opponents realize what you're up to it's usually too late,

> **NOTE:** *When you flop four-of-a-kind, you can afford to slow-play and let the others complete their flushes and full houses.*

HOLE CARDS

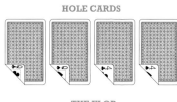

THE FLOP

and they will have already paid the price earned by your deception. But don't slow-play with hands that are not really strong. Free cards are rather dangerous gifts to offer your opponents, and you should only do so under the best of circumstances.

Reading Your Opponents

Reading opponents is a mixture of skill and art.

The easiest way to read a player is to assign a variety of possible hands to him and reduce these possibilities based on a combination of his play and the cards that appear on the board from one betting round to the next.

Here's an example. Your opponent raises before the flop. Since many Omaha/8 players raise when they have an ace and a deuce and one other low card in their hand, this is one of the hands you think he might be holding. He also might have a pair of aces or four big cards with the rank of ten or higher. Your opponent checks a flop of Qh-6h-4d, but comes out betting when the 8s appears on the turn. At this point it is pretty easy to assume he's holding an ace and a deuce in his hand, giving him the best possible low, because he raised before the flop. If you have A-3 in your hand now is the time to fold, because you'll be beaten unless a deuce on the river were to counterfeit his low hand. But if you were holding A-3-7-5 you could raise, because your straight is the best possible high hand. If your opponent does not have an ace and deuce among his four hole cards, you will probably win at least three-quarters of the pot and possibly all of it.

> **NOTE:** *By assigning Player 3 a variety of possible hands and then eliminating them on the basis of his actions, you figure on the turn that he is holding A-2. You are holding A-3-7-5, the best possible high hand, so you raise.*

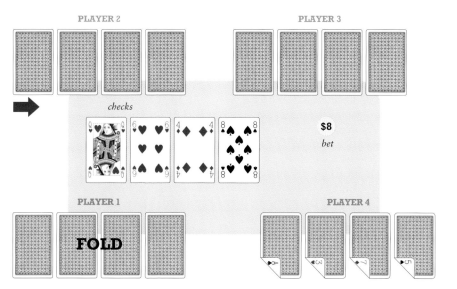

PLAYER 2   PLAYER 3

checks $8
bet

PLAYER 1   PLAYER 4

FOLD

SEVEN-CARD STUD

Seven-card stud is a dramatically different card game compared to Texas hold'em or either variant of Omaha. You'll hear poker players refer to hold'em and Omaha as *flop* games while they refer to seven-card stud and its derivatives, such as seven-stud/8, as *board* games. Flop games feature communal cards turned up in the center of the table that belong to all the players. Anyone who is active in the hand may combine these community cards with their own private cards to form the best five-card poker hand they can. That's not the case in board games, where each player is dealt his or her own cards and must use these and only these to form the best five-card poker hands that can be made according to the rules of the game.

Board versus flop

There are big differences between board games and flop games when it comes to calculating odds and outs. In hold'em or Omaha the number of cards you need can easily be ascertained. These games are structurally constant regardless of the number of players that are actively involved in any given pot, which makes it easy for the poker player to determine which cards will improve your hand and how many of them remain potentially available in the deck.

Here's an example that will help explain things. If you flop four to a flush in hold'em, there will be two or three suited cards in the flop and you'll hold either two or one similarly suited card in your hand. As there are 13 cards of each suit in a 52-card poker deck, 9 of your suit remain in the deck and it's easy to figure the odds or the percentages that apply to your hand's potential for improvement. It doesn't matter how many opponents are still active in the pot, or how many have folded, because the cards held by each player are unknown until the end of the hand, and maybe forever.

In seven-card stud things are different. You get to see some of your opponents' cards, but not all of them. As in every poker game, some opponents will fold on the very first betting round and others will fold on later betting rounds as the hand is played out. Their decision to fold or keep playing depends on how they assess their chances of winning the pot versus the cost to keep drawing for the cards they need.

TRACKING CARDS
Every hand is unique. Sometimes you'll get to see more exposed cards than others. If you have five or six opponents still involved in the hand by fifth street, you'll have seen a lot more exposed cards than you would if the majority of your opponents folded on the first betting round. All savvy seven-card stud players know how to keep track of exposed cards, because knowing which cards were folded and are therefore no longer available to you will help you accurately assess your chances to improve. But that's not all. You'll have

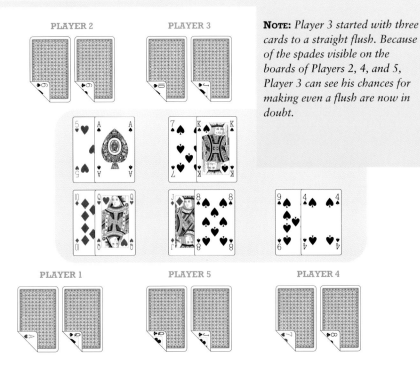

PLAYER 2

PLAYER 3

NOTE: *Player 3 started with three cards to a straight flush. Because of the spades visible on the boards of Players 2, 4, and 5, Player 3 can see his chances for making even a flush are now in doubt.*

PLAYER 1

PLAYER 5

PLAYER 4

to track your opponents' cards, too. If you're drawing for a straight and your opponent with three diamonds showing seems to be going for a flush, it's nice to know how many diamonds have already been lost. If you haven't seen a single card of the suit needed by your opponent, he stands a good chance of completing his hand. But if you knew that five diamonds were already out of his grasp, then his chances of making a flush are severely compromised and should you make your straight, it is likely to survive any chances he has for completing a flush.

DRAWING OUT YOUR OPPONENT

Another difference between seven-card stud and Texas hold'em is that it is

NOTE: *Player 2 is ahead with a pair of jacks, but Player 1 can take the lead by catching an ace, king, or five.*

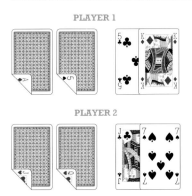

PLAYER 1

PLAYER 2

Playing Your Hands / Seven-Card Stud

easier to draw out on your opponent in seven-card stud. Because of the shared nature of the cards in hold'em, draw outs are less common. If there's a pair of fives on board it belongs to everybody, and the only one who really benefits from that pair in most cases is the player who has a five in his hand. But in seven-card stud your cards are your own, and each draw is made on its own merits. So

if you start with a small pair and a live ace for a side card and pick up another large, live side card on the next betting round, you can afford to chase someone who has a pair bigger than yours. If you get lucky and pair either of your large, live side cards, you'll have made two pair—hopefully bigger than your opponent could possibly make given the cards he is holding.

Your Position in the Betting Order

Knowledge is power in poker. Your position in a hand provides you with information. Seven-card stud is no exception. When you act last you won't have to guess about the number of opponents you're competing against. Some hands, such as big or *premium* pairs, fare better against one or two opponents. Flush and straight draws—long shots under most circumstances—need large fields of opponents to provide the number of customers needed to compensate for the nature of your draw.

In Texas hold'em and other flop games, position is fixed throughout the entire hand. That's not the case in seven-card stud, where the betting order can change dramatically from round to round. The only certainty you'll have in this game is that your betting position will be the same on the river as it is on sixth street. Other than that, it is subject to change depending on which board is lowest on third street's first round of betting and which board is highest on each succeeding round. As with other games, acting late is beneficial and some hands you will have to fold if you're forced to act early, because you won't know

whether you'll face a raise or how many opponents will contest the pot with you.

Some hands play better against fewer players and others fare better against a larger field. Suppose you've been dealt

> **NOTE:** *At the start of betting on third street, Player 1 is the low card and must act first. On fourth street Player 2 must act first because of his higher board. Player 1 pairs on fifth street and now must act first. Player 2 makes a higher pair on sixth street and now acts first.*

PLAYER 1   PLAYER 2

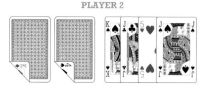

A-A / K. If you can reduce the field by raising, you'll stand a good chance of winning against only one or two opponents, because you can win without improvement. Against a large number of opponents, however, your hand will probably have to improve to win the pot. On the other hand, if you were dealt J-T / 9 of mixed suits, you'd like to play that hand against a big field, and play for only a single bet. If you're forced to act early you have no way of knowing whether you'll get the right number of callers your straight draw requires, nor will you have any way of forecasting whether you can see the next card for a single bet. But if you're fortunate enough to act last, you'll know the answers to both of these questions and your decision will be a lot more informed.

Position provides you with information about the number of opponents you'll confront, as well as information about the cost to continue playing a particular hand. In the example below, Players 2 and 6 have the same hand (though they don't know it). Player 2, however, wary of two big door cards that act after he does, will probably release his hand. Player 6 will certainly release his hand if Player 3 or 4 is aggressive. But he'll raise if neither the king nor the ace play, because if the king and the ace fold, his pair of jacks is almost certainly the best hand.

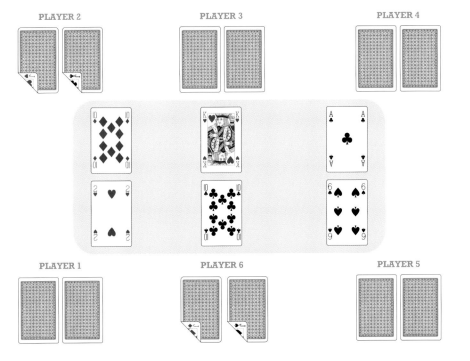

Odds and Outs

Figuring odds in seven-card stud and similar games such as seven-stud/8 is complicated, because the number of exposed cards differs from hand to hand. This makes each calculation unique to the hand being played.

We're never going to suggest that you work out calculations at the poker table. There are some math people who can do that, but they are fewer and further apart than you might expect. The vast majority of seven-card stud players don't juggle numbers and perform calculations at the poker table.

Counting cards

There are some rules of thumb, which were discussed in the Starting Hands section that will help your game playing. Although you don't have to perform calculations, you still have to count cards. It's important to realize that seven-card stud is a game of live cards. You always need to be aware of whether the cards you need are actually available to you and how many are unavailable, because you've seen them in an opponent's hand.

The rule of three is applicable here. If you begin with a flush or straight draw, you can safely get rid of your hand if you see that three or more of your cards are no longer available to you. As you go through subsequent betting rounds, you have to account for two things:

• How many more of my cards are no longer available to me?
• How many more opportunities do I have to catch the card I need?

Even if you started with three suited cards and no other cards of your suit have been exposed by fifth street, it's still a long shot to complete your hand, because you're running out of opportunities.

Getting a feel for the game

Although you won't have time to do arithmetic while you're playing, we'd be remiss if we didn't put all of this into a perspective that will enable you to quickly develop a feel for how often you can expect certain events to occur when you're playing seven-card stud. Odds, outs, and probabilities are all variations on a theme. Each is a way of expressing the relationship between the chances of making and missing a hand, and each has its own uses.

ODDS

Odds present the bad news first. For example, if you begin with three suited cards and catch a fourth card of your suit on the next round, the odds against making a flush are only 1.5-to-1 against you. But they can change dramatically if the next card you are dealt is not of your suit. When that happens the odds against making that flush jump all the way to 8.5-to-1 and your chances have gone from pretty good to very bad.

ODDS AND ENDS ABOUT SEVEN-CARD STUD

These odds put seven-card stud in perspective. They assume that all the cards you need to complete the hand you're drawing to are live. If cards you need are exposed, they are unavailable to you, thus lengthening the odds against making your hand.

424-to-1	Odds against being dealt three-of-a-kind.
5-to-1	Against being dealt any pair on your first three cards.
18-to-1	Against being dealt three suited cards.
3.5-to-1	Against making a full house if your first four cards make two pair.
5-to-1	Against making a straight if your first three cards are sequenced.
4.5-to-1	Against making a flush if your first three cards are suited.
1.2-to-1	In favor of improving to at least two pair if you start with a straight flush like 10♦ J♦ Q♦.
1.4-to-1	Against making two pair if you start with a pair in your first three cards. The odds are 4.1-to-1 against making three-of-a-kind or better.
1.5-to-1	Against making a flush if you begin with three suited cards and catch a fourth card of your suit on the next round.
4-to-1	Against making a full house if you hold three-of-a-kind and three other cards on sixth street.

When the odds are 1.5-to-1 against you, it means you have a 40 percent chance of success. Odds are a ratio of failures to successes; in this case there will be 1.5 failures for every 1 success. By adding the failures to the successes we get a universe of 2.5 events (1.5 + 1 = 2.5). When we divide the expected wins (1) by the universe (2.5 events), we discover that we have a 40 percent chance to make our hand. But when the odds jump all the way to 8.5-to-1, it's a different equation altogether. When we divide our single chance of winning by the universe of 9.5 events, we are shocked to see that the chance of making our flush is only 10.5 percent.

How did it get so bad so quickly? Two things happened at once:
• You didn't catch the card you needed.
• You now have one less opportunity to catch the card you need. On third

street you had four opportunities to catch two more cards of your suit. Now you still have to catch two suited cards, but this time you have only three shots at them.

PERCENTAGES
Changing percentages to odds is very simple. All you need do is subtract the percentage from 100 and divide the result by the same percentage. For example, if you knew the chances of making a flush were 10.5 percent, just subtract 10.5 from 100 percent (100 – 10.5 = 89.5) and divide that result by 10.5 (89.5 / 10.5 = 8.5). Now you know that odds of 8.5-to-1 against an event occurring equate to a 10.5 percent chance of success, and you've learned enough poker player's mathematics to convert one to another and back again with ease.

Implied Odds

The size of the pot isn't always sufficient to offset the odds against making your hand. But that doesn't mean you shouldn't play your hand. Sometimes you can still continue playing when you consider the implications of future bets you might win if you make your hand. If you find yourself in this position, just ask yourself this:

• Are potential future wagers substantial enough to justify playing this hand, even though the size of the pot right now is not large enough to offset the odds against making my hand?

Winning money over and above what's in the pot right now is what implied odds are all about. While you can never be certain about just how many opponents will call your bets or raises if you make your hand, implied odds are a comparison of your total expected win to the current cost of calling a bet.

> **NOTE:** *Player 3 has a live flush draw. If he picks up a fourth club on fourth street he has a 40 percent chance to make a flush.*

LIMIT $10-$20

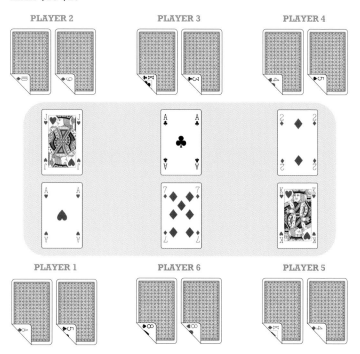

In seven-card stud, pots can grow quite large because there are five betting rounds. You'll find that it often pays to chase an opponent holding a high pair when all you're holding is a small pair, but only as long as you have big, live side cards. It also pays to draw to your flushes, especially when you're up against a large number of opponents. After all, if you catch a fourth suited card on the second betting round, the chance of making your flush if all your cards are live is about 40 percent. So it often pays to call—or even to come out betting—if you suspect that the pot might continue growing while you're still involved in the hand. All of those bets you figure to win if your flush comes in should more than offset those times you start with three suited cards only to see your chances of winning devolve to 10.5 percent on fourth street, when you fail to catch a fourth suited card and have to toss your hand away.

Deception

While poor players are easily beaten if you play solid, straightforward poker, better players are more susceptible to your deceptive play. The better your opponents, the more you'll find yourself attempting to deceive them. Weak, ineffective players tend to call with hands they shouldn't play and make woefully weak plays in a wide variety of situations, so deception on your part isn't necessary against them.

In seven-card stud, bluffing, with certain exceptions, is rare in lower-limit games, but becomes a lot more frequent at higher-limit games.

Your goal should be to play straightforward poker most of the time and reserve your bag of tricks for good opponents, small pots, small fields, and those few occasions when you have a powerhouse hand and want to let your opponents increase the pot.

Nevertheless, there are certain occasions when a bluff may be required, even against players who call too frequently.

- If you have four cards of the same suit showing on your board and your opponent looks to be playing a lesser hand, such as a pair, go ahead and bet as though you made your flush already. Unless he has a good hand, he'll probably toss his hand away.

- If you have an ace showing and are in late position on third street, and no one has yet called the bring-in, you must raise. Not only will your opponent fear you have a big pair, but you probably have the best hand. Remember, the odds are 5-to-1 against the bring-in—or anyone else—being dealt a pair on their first three cards.

NOTE: *Player 2's board is so weak and Player 1's so strong that a bet by Player 1 will probably win the pot immediately.*

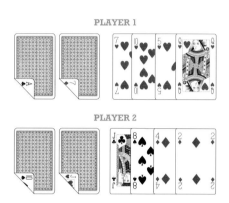

Semi-bluffing

Semi-bluffing is a strategy that every skillful player uses. It is a bet made on a hand that's probably not the best hand at the time the bet is made, but one that can win if it improves. A pure bluff only has one way to win, but a semi-bluff has two—making the opponent fold or improving your hand's potential.

If your first three exposed cards are of the same suit, you can bet. When you bet, you'll be representing a flush, even if you don't have one. If your opponent is analytical, one of the hands he'll think you might have is a flush or a big flush draw. If you catch a fourth suited card on sixth street you should come out betting again. Now your opponent really has to assume that you've made a flush, and if he's smart, he'll toss away any hand that can't beat a flush right now and has no possibility of improving to a full house on the river. But even if

he calls with one or two pair, you can still make a flush on the river, so your semi-bluff provides two ways to win: Your opponent might fold the best hand or you might catch the card you need and leapfrog over him to win the pot on the strength of your hand.

Although semi-bluffing is a terrific tactic, you shouldn't carry it to extremes by making this play against opponents who call all the time. If you do, you will have eliminated one of the two ways you can win the pot. If an opponent always calls to keep you honest, then be honest. Don't bluff him, but bet for value instead. Since he'll always call, you can bet into him any time you think you hold a hand that's even a smidgen stronger than his hand, and he'll pay you off each time. Another time you might not want to semi-bluff is when you're last to act, since you might as well take a free card if everyone else has checked. Do this when you figure your chances of helping your hand with a free card look better than the chances that all your opponents will fold to your semi-bluff.

Semi-bluffing allows you to be the bettor instead of the caller, and that's usually a good thing too. Sometimes you might bet, thinking you're semi-bluffing when you actually have the best hand. When that happens, your semi-bluff—which in this case is a bet with the best hand—prevents your opponent from receiving a free card. In fact, your bet may convince him to fold. Semi-bluffing is aggression that provides an additional way to win the pot even if the hand you

NOTE: *This hand started as a flush draw but became a middle pair on fourth street. A bet here would make any opponent think before calling, as the board combined with the bet suggests trip eights. This player can still make a strong hand with the appearance of an ace, queen, eight, or two more hearts.*

HOLE CARDS   BOARD CARDS

hope to make never materializes. As long as there's a chance your opponent will fold, you have two ways to win the pot while sowing some seeds of doubt and confusion in your opponent's mind.

Defending

In most sports it's the offense that gets the glory, but it's the defense that usually wins championships. It's no different in poker. Every time you're the bring-in you'll have to decide whether to defend your hand if someone completes the initial bet. If you've called the bring-in and someone raises, you'll have to think that over too. If you come out betting from any other position and an opponent raises, you'll have to decide whether to fold, play defensively, or stay aggressive.

Seven-card stud is always a balance between offense and defense, between being aggressive and conserving your chips. Striking the proper balance is a combination of figuring the odds and understanding your opponents' playing styles. The right decision against an aggressive, loose player might not work against a timid opponent. This is where the art of poker comes into play, and it's a skill you'll develop and improve only with lots of practice and experience at the table.

Raising

Here are a few reasons to raise the pot in a seven-card stud game.

1. RAISING TO GET MONEY INTO THE POT

Whenever you have a big hand, say a pair of poker aces, or three-of-a-kind, or the best hand now with a draw to an even better one—for example, if you start out with three-of-a-kind and can improve to a full house—you can raise at every opportunity, because each dollar your opponents contribute to the pot will come back to you in the end and it demands more money from your opponents.

> **NOTE:** *A pair of aces plays much better against fewer opponents. A raise is always the right play here.*

HOLE CARDS   **BOARD CARD**

2. RAISING TO ELIMINATE OPPONENTS

If you've been dealt a hand like A-A / Q, you'll want to raise if you figure it will prevent other opponents from entering the pot after you. While a pair of aces will need to improve to win against a large field, it stands a good chance of winning without improvement against only one or two adversaries.

3. RAISING TO GET A FREE CARD ON A MORE EXPENSIVE STREET

You're last to act with A♥-9♣ / Q♠-9♦. You raise when an opponent showing a jack comes out betting. Although he might have a better hand than you do at this juncture, you can raise as long as your ace and queen are live cards. Even if you're up against a pair of jacks, your opponent is not likely to reraise because he must consider the possibility that you have a pair of queens, especially if another queen has not been exposed.

This is also a semi-bluff because you're raising with a hand that might not be the best hand right now. If you

pair your ace or queen your two pair will be better than his. If you catch a nine he won't suspect you of trips until it's too late. Moreover, if he doesn't hold the hand he's representing, he might fold right then and there and you'll win the pot without any further ado. If the next card you're dealt doesn't improve your hand, the fact that you raised on fourth street may enable you to see subsequent cards for free. When you need to improve your hand, betting or raising on fourth street in hopes of seeing a free card on fifth street—when the cost of betting doubles—is a sound idea anytime your opponent is likely to "check to the raiser." And if you happen to catch a card that improves your hand, your raise on the preceding betting round represents more money in a pot you figure to win.

PLAYER 2

$20
bet

$20 $20
check   call   raise

PLAYER 1

4. RAISING TO PREVENT A FREE CARD

Just as it is correct to raise on third or fourth street in order to gain a free card on the more expensive betting rounds that begin on fifth street, raising in certain situations to prevent your opponents from getting a free or relatively inexpensive card is also the right course of action.

Here's an example. Let's say you hold A♣-J♦ / T♥-A♥. One opponent shows X-X / T♠-4♠ and the other shows X-X / Q♣-6♦. The player showing a queen comes out betting and is called by the opponent showing two

spades. You figure one of them for a pair of queens and put the other player on a spade flush draw. Now you raise. Your pair of aces figures to be ahead of the player who is representing a pair of queens, and you want to make it as costly as possible for your third opponent to continue to chase his flush draw. Although you can't be absolutely certain of what either of your opponents is holding—and there's a chance that you're not in the lead at all—you should still make your opponents pay for the chance to complete their hands.

Free Cards

The general rule about giving or receiving a free card is fairly straightforward to remember: Whenever you have the best hand you should be very reluctant to give your opponents a free chance to catch a miraculous card that might beat you. But when you're the one holding a hand in need of help, you'd always prefer a free card to one you'd have to call a bet to receive.

There are some exceptions. Sometimes your hand is so strong that it's worth giving a free card to your opponents in hopes that they'll catch up enough to call your bets on future rounds. Suppose you were fortunate enough to make four-of-a-kind on fourth or fifth street, or even a big full house. If you bet, your opponents may not have been helped enough by that juncture to call. But you can afford to let your opponents catch up a bit, and you should. If cards that portend a flush or straight appear to have helped one or more of your opponents, they'll be eagerly tossing money into the pot too. And that's a good thing, because your adversaries will be drawing dead.

If the pot is small when you give out that free card, so much the better. There's nothing really satisfying about winning a very small pot with a very big hand. You're usually better off trying to win a bigger pot—even if there's some chance you might lose the whole thing—than trying to win a really puny pot. Besides, if there's some chance that the next card might give an opponent a second-best hand, but it's one that he deems good enough to bet, you might get a chance to raise, or try for a checkraise if you're first to act.

If you're the one hoping to make a good hand, then you'll want a free card anytime you can get it, and by betting or raising on third or fourth street you

NOTE: *You are most likely winning with this hand at the moment, but if you let opponents have free cards, they can catch you with straights, flushes, and three-of-a-kind.*

HOLE CARDS   BOARD CARD

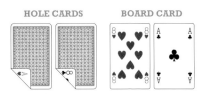

might be able to convince opponents who act before you to check on the fifth street, when the betting limits double. You can always bet if your hand improves, or you can check and take a free card if your hand doesn't improve and all your opponents check to the raiser.

Slow-playing

Playing a very strong hand weakly on an inexpensive betting round is called slow-playing, and the idea is to lure your opponents on to the more expensive betting rounds, where you'll spring the trap. To slow-play, just take no action beyond what is required to stay in the pot. If no one bets, you check. If someone bets, you call. Keep as many players in the pot as you can to maximize your winnings on subsequent betting rounds.

A very strong hand is required to slow-play because you always run the risk of offering your opponents a free or inexpensive card that just might improve their hands. The time to slow-play is when it gives your opponents an opportunity to build hands that still can't win.

Under ideal conditions, slow-playing a powerhouse will deceive your opponents into thinking you have a weak hand. You're also hoping that the free card your opponent receives will improve his hand, but only enough to make it second best. Slow-playing is a powerful way to get maximum value for your strong hands, but you have to temper this strategy with some prudence. You need a very strong hand to do this, and the strength of your hand should not be obvious to your opponents. And remember: Never slow-play if a free card can give an opponent a better hand than yours.

It's not complex. By the time your opponents realize that you've slow-played by giving them a harmless free card, it's usually too late. They will have already paid the price garnered by your deception. But don't slow-play hands unless they are extremely strong. Free cards are a dangerous gift to offer your opponents, and you should only do so under the best of circumstances.

NOTE: *If you bet this hand on fifth street, there are not too many other players who would call. You won't lose much by giving opponents free cards in the hope they make their straights, flushes, or full houses.*

HOLE CARDS   BOARD CARDS

Reading Your Opponents

Seven-card stud provides a lot of opportunities for card reading because of the large number of exposed cards. It's a game made for those who can develop their powers of deductive reasoning. The better you are at deducing what your opponents are holding, the better your results will be. To read them accurately, you'll have to observe them in action, and examine their betting patterns while cataloguing the exposed cards that might help you to deduce your opponent's hand. When you examine the hand he ultimately shows down, you'll learn quite a bit about his playing style, too.

Good players are easier to read than weak opponents, because a good player's actions are predicated on logic and there's usually some consistency to his play. As with other games of poker, the easiest way to read a player is to assign a variety of possible hands to him and then winnow your assessment down based on a combination of their play and the cards that are dealt to each opponent from one betting round to the next. You can also work recursively by examining later plays in terms of how your opponent played his hand on earlier betting rounds.

NOTE: *Player 3 raises the bring-in. At this stage you assign him several hands, from a big, premium pair to a smaller pair with a live, big kicker, or even three straight flush cards, or rolled-up jacks.*

PLAYER 2   PLAYER 3

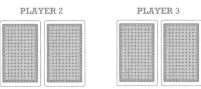

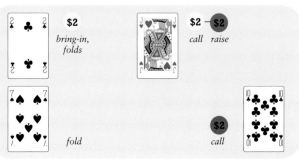

PLAYER 1   PLAYER 4

Here's an example. Your opponent raises on third street. Since many seven-card stud players raise when they have a big, premium pair in their hand, that's one of the hands you think he might be holding. He also might have a smaller pair with a live, big kicker, or even three straight flush cards, such as 9♥-T♥ / J♥ or rolled-up jacks. He catches the 8♥ on fourth street and checks and calls, but bets when the Q♥ appears on his board on fifth street. When you look at his hand, you'll see X-X / J♥-8♥-Q♥. At this point it's pretty easy to assume he's holding one or two big pair, or a set of queens or jacks, and he is trying to make it very costly for someone with a higher flush draw to see the river. He might even have made a flush already, or completed a straight, or even a straight flush. If he hasn't, he might easily have a big, live draw to one of these hands. Now is the time for you to fold, because you'll be beaten unless you get very lucky indeed on the next card. And even if you catch the card you're hoping for, it won't be enough if he's made a straight flush.

NOTE: *Player 3 checked and called on fourth street, but bets on fifth street. At this point you would think that he's holding one or two big pair, or a set of queens or jacks. He may even have a flush, a straight, or a straight flush. If he hasn't, he might easily have a big, live draw to one of those hands. If he hasn't beaten you already, then almost any card on sixth street that's seven or higher will help his hand. You should fold because even if you do get a seven or a ten on sixth street, it won't beat a straight flush.*

PLAYER 2   PLAYER 3

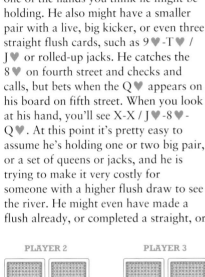

FOLD

PLAYER 1   PLAYER 4

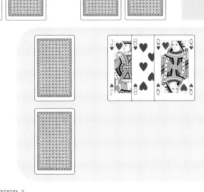

FOLD

SEVEN-STUD/8

Seven-card stud eight or better, hi-lo split, more easily abbreviated as seven-stud/8, is a form of stud poker in which pots are split between the best high hand and the best qualifying low hand. A player can make the best high hand, the best low hand, or make both the best high hand and the best low hand, thereby *scooping* the whole pot.

Procedures are nearly identical to seven-card stud, with just two small differences. In seven-stud/8, you can't make a double bet when there's a pair showing on fourth street, as you can in seven-card stud. And, of course, the pot is split whenever there's at least one qualifying low hand at showdown.

• In seven-stud/8 the best high hand and the best *qualifying* low hand split the pot. In order for a low hand to qualify, it must contain five unpaired cards with the rank of eight or lower. No qualifier is required for a high hand, which ensures there's always one, but there won't always be a low hand. For example, if your seven cards were A♦-J♦-9♦-7♦-5♦-4♠-2♣, your high hand would be an ace-high flush, composed of A♦-J♦-9♦-7♦-5♦. Your low hand would be called a *seven-low*, made up of 7♦-5♦-4♠-2♣-A♦.

Highs and lows

Games in which high and low hands divvy up the money often result in very large pots, which probably accounts for their popularity in traditional casinos as well as online and as tournament offerings. Because the pot is frequently divided, players who ordinarily wouldn't be in the hand are in there slugging it out. But because many of these players shouldn't be in each pot, skilled players have a great opportunity to win their money!

Your aim when playing should be to scoop the pot, winning both the best high hand and the best low hand. Short of that, your hand at showdown ought to be the best low or the best high hand, to claim at least half the pot. If there's no qualifying low hand, the high hand scoops the entire pot.

Aces are unique in this game because they are playable as both the highest and lowest card in the deck. When you're dealt an ace it's like receiving two cards for the price of one, and that's worth remembering. Aces are valuable!

Seven-stud/8's five rounds of betting often result in large pots simply because some players are trying to make a high hand while others are hoping to make the best low hand. There are generally more players involved in most hands than you'd find in a game with only a single winner. As in seven-card stud, the best players are cognizant of both live cards and cards that have been folded.

This game requires a lot of patience. Many people love playing high-low split games because they think they can play more hands. But the best seven-stud/8

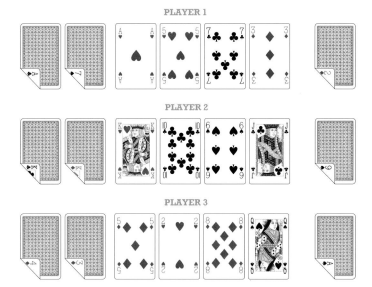

PLAYER 1

PLAYER 2

PLAYER 3

players play few hands and generally look for those with two-way possibilities. After all, the objective is to scoop the pot, not split it. Skilled players release many hands on third street.

Most savvy seven-stud/8 players will advise newcomers to play low hands rather than high ones, because low hands can evolve into high hands a lot more easily than high hands can become low ones. After all, if you begin with three low cards and two or three of them are suited, you might make a flush or a straight in addition to a low hand. But if you decide to get into the action with a hand like K♦-K♥ / 4♠, you have very little chance of ever making a low hand, so you're playing a one-way hand with no guarantee that it will hold up for even half of the pot. If you were to play a pair of kings against a player who's showing an ace and you knew with complete certainty that your opponent was drawing for a low hand,

NOTE: *Player 1 has a high hand of two pair (aces over sevens) and a qualifying low hand of 7-5-3-2-A. Player 2 has a high hand of three kings but no qualifying low. Player 3 has a high hand of a straight with the A-2-3-4-5 and the nut low with 5-4-3-2-A. Player 3 has scooped the pot with both the winning high and low hands.*

it's still possible that he could pair his ace and beat your high hand. Against a large field of opponents the conventional wisdom is correct. It's a good idea to try for low, especially if your low hand might morph into a high hand too. That gives you a chance to scoop the pot, and in seven-stud/8, whenever you have some opponents going low and others going high, pots

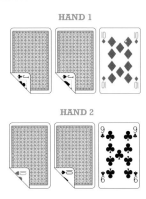

HAND 1

HAND 2

NOTE: *Starting hands like these might be okay in seven-card stud, but not in seven-stud/8. They can never make a low, plus they can easily be beaten for high if another player pairs a higher card.*

can grow quite large, and it doesn't take too many scoops to ensure a good day at the tables.

So how good does your low hand have to be to play it? It all depends on

what your opponents' hands look like. An eight-seven low can be a terrific hand, as long as all opponents have face cards showing and are heading off along the high road. But an eight-low is a terrible starting hand if you look around the table and see a garden of likely low draws staring back at you.

Figuring odds

Seven-stud/8 is a lot like seven-card stud when you're trying to figure the odds. Just as in seven-card stud, you'll see some of your opponents' cards, but not all of them. A few opponents will fold on the very first betting round, while others will fold on subsequent betting rounds as the hand develops.

Each hand is unique. Sometimes you'll see more exposed cards than others. If you have five or six opponents still involved in the hand by fifth street, you'll have seen a lot more exposed cards than you would if the majority of your opponents folded on the first betting round. Your skill in tracking exposed cards will help you assess your chances to improve.

But the cards you need are only part of the story. You'll have to track your opponents' cards too. If you're drawing for a straight and your opponent has

three diamonds showing, it's nice to know how many diamonds have already been lost. By the same token, if you're building a low hand, you'll have to be aware of how many low cards still remain that won't pair those in your hand. If you're holding 7-6 / 3-2 and figure you'll have to make a seven-low to win half of the pot, but most of the low cards remaining are sevens, eights, and sixes, and not the fives, fours, and aces you need, you're probably drawing dead or close to it and should probably throw your hand away. But suppose you noticed that a disproportionate number of eights were discarded, as well as some low cards that would pair your hand, but you haven't seen a single ace, five, or four? Now you've got a great opportunity to capture half of the pot and if you get very lucky, you might back into a straight for a high hand too.

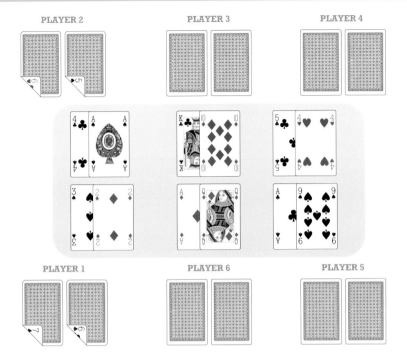

DRAWING OUT

In seven-stud/8, as in seven-card stud, your cards are your own. Each draw is made on its own merits. That's not the case in Texas hold'em or Omaha, where the communal nature of the cards makes it more difficult to draw out on someone. However, in seven-card stud, when you're chasing an opponent, you're likely to win the entire pot if you catch him. With many seven-stud/8 hands, your draw will be for half the pot, not all of it. And whenever you're chasing half the pot and having to invest a full bet to do so, many of the situations that make it cost-beneficial to draw in seven-card stud are just not worthwhile in seven-stud/8.

NOTE: *Players 1 and 2 are both going for the best low hand but from the cards they can see, Player 2 is in better shape. Player 1 needs an ace to have a shot at the best low, but three aces are already visible in other players' hands. Player 2 needs a two, three, seven, or eight to complete what should be the winning low, and from the cards he can see, 14 of those 16 cards are live.*

Your Position in the Betting Order

Position provides you with important information regardless of the form of poker you're playing, and seven-stud/8 is no exception. Acting late will let you know the number of opponents you'll confront, and the cost to continue playing.

As with seven-card stud, the betting order often changes from round to round in seven-stud/8, depending upon which player's board is lowest on third street and which player's board is highest on each succeeding street.

Acting early is a disadvantage, in all forms of poker, because you're forced to make decisions in the dark. Some hands should be folded if you're forced to act early, because you won't know if you'll face a raise or how many opponents will contest the pot with you. This is particularly true if you are thinking of

playing a big pair like queens or kings and see someone with an ace poised to act behind you. When it's your turn to act you won't know whether the ace represents a high hand, a low one, or a hand like A-3 / A that can veer off in either or both directions.

Against a large number of opponents your hand will have to improve to win the pot. Plus, if you fail to knock out potential low hands, you might wind up with only half the pot instead of all of it. On the other hand, if you were dealt 5-4 / 6 of mixed suits, you'd like to play

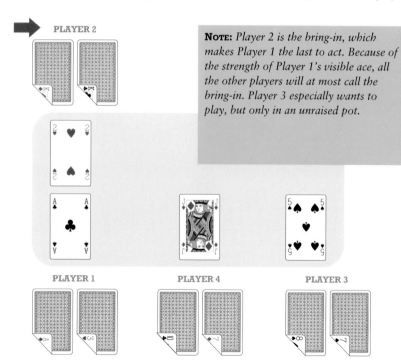

NOTE: *Player 2 is the bring-in, which makes Player 1 the last to act. Because of the strength of Player 1's visible ace, all the other players will at most call the bring-in. Player 3 especially wants to play, but only in an unraised pot.*

that hand against a big field, but for a single bet. If you're forced to act early you have no way of knowing whether you'll get the right number of callers your straight draw requires, nor will you have any way of forecasting whether you can see the next card for a single bet. When you act last you'll know the answers to both questions, and your decision will be a lot more informed than it could ever possibly be if you had to act in early position.

A raise from a player in early position usually indicates a very strong high hand or a draw to the best low hand. Otherwise it would be a very bold bluff—since your opponent's raise is essentially telling you:

• I want to eliminate opponents.

• I have a hand like A-2 / A. It's a two-way hand with scoop potential and I want to knock out as many opponents as I can right now.

• I have a very big hand right now, not a draw. Confront me at your own peril.

• If you're holding a marginal draw to a low hand, you'll have to pay to play and there's no guarantee that yours will be the best low hand even if you complete it.

NOTE: *If you're Player 4 you have a real dilemma. If you call and are raised by Player 6, his ace may indicate three cards to a low hand, but it may also represent a pair of aces. Even if Player 6 has a low draw, he might pair his ace and be ahead of you for high. Aces are really two cards in one—the best low and the best high cards in the deck. Confront them at your own peril.*

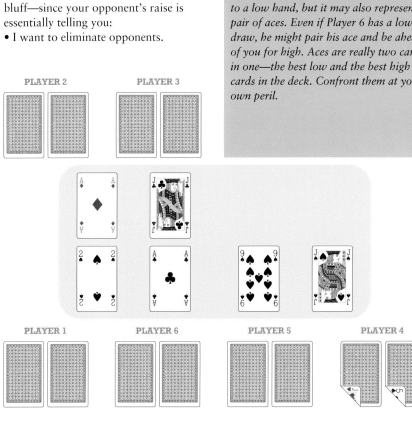

Odds and Outs

In seven-stud/8, as in seven-card stud, the number of exposed cards differs from hand to hand, making each calculation unique to the hand being played, so figuring odds is difficult.

We don't suggest that you work out calculations at the poker table. You've got more than enough on your mind without having to figure odds and percentages. The vast majority of seven-stud/8 players don't fancy juggling numbers and performing calculations at the poker table. Most seven-stud/8 players use the rules of thumb, discussed in the section dealing with starting hands. These rules are based upon counting cards rather than on performing calculations. Seven-stud/8 is a game of live cards, and you must always know whether the cards you need are actually available to you and how many may have already been removed from your universe of helpful cards because you've seen them in an opponent's hand.

Playing beyond third street

If you decide to play past third street, your next key decision point occurs on the very next betting round. If you're going for low but catch a high card on fourth street, you've hit a rut in the road. But if you catch a fourth low card, you stand a good chance of completing your draw.

If you start with a three-card low draw and catch another low card on fourth street, while an opponent who also has a low draw stumbles by

TAKE THESE FIVE CONCEPTS TO HEART

- Just because you've got three unpaired low cards—all of the eighth rank or lower—doesn't mean you have a playable hand.
- You do have a playable hand, even with a weak holding such as 2-7-8, if it's the only low hand against at least two opponents with obvious high hands.
- If you have only one opponent and yours is a one-way low hand that can't scoop the pot, the best you can do is break even, so why would you want to invest money in a hand like that? The worst-case scenario finds you failing to make even a low hand while your opponent scoops the pot. That's ugly.
- You don't have a playable hand if opponents have better low draws, unless you have a two-way hand with a good chance at the high side.
- When two or three players begin with low draws, don't be surprised to catch high cards because the deck is probably short on babies at that point.

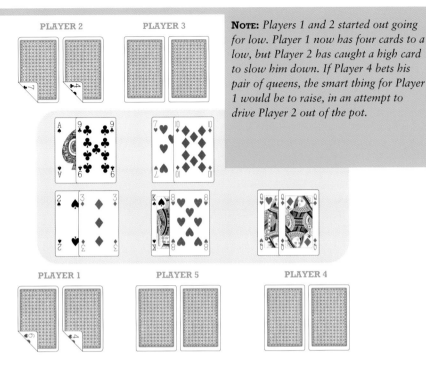

catching a high card, you can raise if someone bets. That will make it tough for the other low draw to call, because he's now dragging the heavy anchor of a high card attached to three babies. If you're able to raise and drive out all other low draws, it no longer matters how good your low is, because you'll be rewarded with half the pot if you make any low hand at all.

If you find yourself on third street facing opponents who have deuces, treys, fours, fives, or sixes showing, you can assume they're drawing for low. But an opponent with an ace showing could be going high or low, or even have a two-way hand like A-2 / A. Whenever you make a two-way hand that already has a lock on half the pot, you should jam the pot by raising or reraising at

every opportunity. You'll scoop the pot if you get lucky, but even if the pot is split, each additional bet is profitable provided there are multiple opponents.

If you're dealt a big pair early, your hand already has some intrinsic value. If you start with three low cards, however, all you have is a drawing hand and as good as it looks there's always a chance it won't get there. But if you make the only low hand by fifth or sixth street, along with a chance to improve to a high hand too, you already have half the pot won. Now you can bet or raise with complete safety.

If you make a small straight or any other good high hand to complement your low hand, you may scoop the pot. Even if your high hand is still just a wannabe, as long as you hold the best

DRIVING AND BRAKING IN SEVEN-STUD/8

Keep these points firmly in mind. They are the rules of the road for driving and braking in seven-stud/8:

- Drive your high hands until fifth street, or until it appears your opponent has made a low hand. Then apply the brakes—fast.
- If you have a draw to a low hand, draw inexpensively. There's no guarantee you'll complete your hand, so why make it more costly?
- An exception is when you have the only low draw against two or three high hands. If you start with three low cards and catch another on fourth street, go ahead and bet—or raise!
- When you have the only low draw against several high hands, bet or raise to get their money into the pot. Some players contesting the high side will probably fold later in the hand.
- Seven-stud/8 is a game that requires a certain amount of gambling, and situations where it looks like the size of the pot will exceed the odds against making your hand are prime opportunities.
- Avoid gambling when you're not sure yours will be the best low hand even if you make it. Better opportunities to invest your money will come along.

possible low hand there's no cost or risk in drawing for the high hand. This is a situation where you have everything to gain and nothing to lose. Poker players call this freerolling. Although it doesn't happen often, it's a wonderful feeling when it does!

If you have a high hand you should bet and raise early and often. You need to make it as expensive as possible for anyone drawing to a low hand to stay in the pot. After all, you want to avoid splitting the pot, and you'd also like to avoid the indignity of an opponent's low draw backing into a better high hand than yours, thus scooping the entire pot right out from under your nose. This happens more often than you might think, so be careful.

If it's your opponent and not you who makes a low hand, you have a problem. Once you suspect you're up

against a made low hand, it's time to stop driving and apply the brakes. At best you've become the player who's chasing half the pot. At worst you'll get scooped if your high doesn't hold up. Since that's the case, what earthly reason could you have for betting into this pot?

If you've seen the hand through to the river, call any bet if you think you can escape with half the pot. If your opponent appears to have a low hand, even a paltry pair can sometimes capture the high side. If you're heads-up and you have a high hand while your opponent appears to have made a low hand, there's no point in betting. At best you'll just split the pot. At worst, he'll have a hidden high hand to complement his low and might scoop the entire pot.

NOTE: *This hand is in good position to be the best low. But it can also become a flush for high if another spade falls, or a straight if a three comes.*

Taking a chance

The odds are the same in seven-stud/8 as they are in seven-card stud. But while the math is the same, the money can be very different, particularly when you're asked to call a full bet to win only half the pot. The odds against making a flush if you begin with three suited cards and catch a fourth card of your suit on the next round are only 1.5-to-1 against you, the same as they are in seven-card stud, but they can change dramatically if the next card you are dealt is not of your suit. When that happens the odds against making that flush jump all the way to 8.5-to-1 and your chances have gone from pretty good to very bad.

HOLE CARDS

BOARD CARDS

EIGHT TIPS FOR WINNING PLAY AT SEVEN-STUD/8

Master these tips and you'll be on the way to becoming a winning seven-stud/8 player.
• Steal the antes: If you've got the only ace showing, and no one has entered the pot on third street by the time it's your turn to act, you should raise to steal the antes.
• This game requires patience, especially on third street. If you don't have three low cards, the best high hand, or a draw to a straight or a flush, save your money.
• Fourth street is a major decision point. If you begin with a low draw and catch another low card on fourth street, you have a good chance to make a low hand. But if you catch a bad card here, it can easily be too costly to continue.
• Once the cards have all been dealt and your opponent comes out betting, you should call with any hand that stands a chance of winning half the pot.
• Like its cousin seven-card stud, this game demands strong powers of observation to know whether the cards you need are live or dead.
• You also must be able to determine whether you have the best hand in your preferred direction, and whether you have a chance to scoop.
• Drawing hands offer great promise, but your cards must be live.
• Low draws are more playable than high draws because they offer the chance to make both a high hand and a low hand to scoop the pot. High hands seldom become low hands too.

Odds of 1.5-to-1 against you mean that you have a 40 percent chance of success. Odds are a ratio of failures to successes. By adding the failures to the successes you have a universe of 2.5 events (1.5 + 1 = 2.5). When you divide the expected wins by the universe of events (1 / 2.5), you discover that you have a 40 percent chance to make your hand. But when the odds jump all the way to 8.5-to-1 it's a different story altogether. When you divide your one chance of winning by 9.5 events, you are shocked to see that the chance of making your flush is only 10.5 percent—quite a disastrous change in only a single betting round.

If that seems like a drastic drop in your chances, remember that two things happened at once:

- You didn't catch the card you needed.
- You now have one less opportunity to catch it.

To change percentages to odds, simply subtract the percentage from 100 and divide the result by the same percentage. If you knew the chances of making a flush were 10.5 percent, just subtract 10.5 from 100 percent (100 − 10.5 = 89.5) and divide that result by 10.5 (89.5 / 10.5 = 8.5). Now you know that odds of 8.5-to-1 against an event occurring are just another way of saying that you have a 10.5 percent chance of success.

PERSONAL SKILLS REQUIRED TO WIN AT SEVEN-STUD/8

Becoming a winning seven-stud/8 player requires more than technical poker skills. It also takes strength of character, determination, and grit.

- Be patient: If you lack patience, you'll never become a good seven-stud/8 player, regardless of how much knowledge you acquire.
- Be observant: If you don't pay close attention to visible cards, you'll have a hard time winning consistently. If you're not aware of discards, it's easy to lose money drawing to hands you probably won't make. Do take notes when you're playing online—nobody will see!
- Be determined: Play live hands, and play low hands. Don't throw money away on longshots.
- Be studious: Since you'll throw away most of your starting hands, there's plenty of downtime you can put to good use. Observe your opponents: Learn the kinds of hands they play and how they bet them.
- Be aggressive: Don't be afraid to raise or even reraise if you think you have the best hand or the only hand in your direction.
- Be judicious: Don't play every hand dealt to you. You won't start with three low cards very often, but even some of those holdings are not playable, particularly when an ace raises on third street. Wait for better opportunities.

Implied Odds

Although the pot may be too small to offset the odds against making your hand, you don't always need to fold. Sometimes you can play when you consider future bets you might win if you make your hand. There are two questions you must ask yourself before making a decision:

- Are potential future wagers big enough to justify playing a hand even though the current size of the pot is not enough to offset the odds against making my hand?
- Does my hand have realistic potential for morphing into a two-way hand that can scoop the pot?

Implied odds are all about winning money over and above what's in the pot right now. Although you can never be certain about how many opponents will call any future bets, implied odds are a comparison of your total expected win to the current cost of calling a bet.

That's why two-way hands are so important in seven-stud/8. If you're playing against two opponents and yours is a one-way hand, each dollar you invest in the pot will return $1.50 if you win your side of the pot—a profit of fifty cents on the dollar. But if you have a two-way hand and scoop the pot, each dollar invested will return $3, for a profit of $2 for every dollar

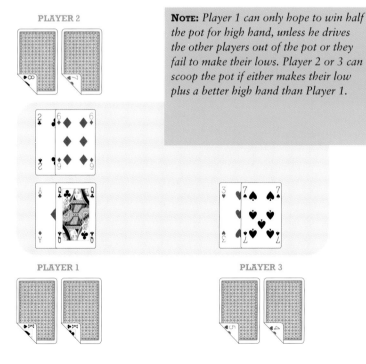

PLAYER 2

NOTE: *Player 1 can only hope to win half the pot for high hand, unless he drives the other players out of the pot or they fail to make their lows. Player 2 or 3 can scoop the pot if either makes their low plus a better high hand than Player 1.*

PLAYER 1

PLAYER 3

invested—four times the profit! The possibility of scooping a pot in split-pot games such as seven-stud/8 is really a practical application of implied odds.

In seven-stud/8 pots can grow quite large because there are five betting rounds and players going in one direction are often oblivious to the actions of opponents who are headed the other way. If you can make a winning hand in one direction while you have a hidden winning hand in the other, you stand a great chance of dragging a huge pot. Because of opportunities like these, it often pays to play two-way hands as long as the cards you need are live.

The concept of implied odds is nothing more than a sophisticated name for something you do all the time while playing poker: You estimate the amount of money you're likely to win if you get lucky and assess those chances against the cost of trying to make your hand. It's that simple.

One word of caution, though. Many poor players are fond of overestimating implied odds to provide an excuse for playing a hand where the odds are long and the size of the pot is too small to offset it. You'll see examples of this all the time, particularly when a player enters the fray with a draw to a weak low hand, or a player calls on third street with a king showing while an ace is visible and ready to act after he does. Estimates are educated guesses. If you deceive yourself with uneducated guesses just because you feel like mixing it up in a pot you don't really belong in, it will cost money you needn't have lost had you been a bit more realistic about your chances.

Deception

In split-pot games such as seven-stud/8 you can't expect a bluff to work if you appear to have a low hand and your opponent has a high one. He'll quickly see that you're headed off in the opposite direction and your bluff won't bother him at all. But you can often bluff early in the hand, especially when you have an ace showing, because your ace is simultaneously the highest and lowest card in the deck. As long as that's your only card showing, your opponent won't have any idea whether you're headed high or low.

Suppose you've been dealt A-K / A and you notice that there's just one low card showing. Because you can presume he's the only player chasing the low end of the pot, you should bet or raise when it's your turn to act in hopes of inducing him to toss away his low draw for fear that yours is far better. If you can eliminate everyone who might be going low, you will scoop the entire pot if you win it with your high. If your opponent was heading low with a hand like 8-7 / 3, your raise with an ace might be just enough to send him packing. Even if he calls on third street, he'll probably release any marginal low draw as long as you catch another small card on the next betting round. He might be seeing X-X / A-4 as your hand, and if he has something like 8-7 / 3-5 he can't feel too

HOLE CARDS   BOARD CARD

NOTE: *A bet or raise with just an ace showing early in the hand can put confusion and doubt in all opponents.*

good about his chances. He'd feel even worse if he had caught a nine or higher instead of a five, or any card that paired him. He knows that he probably won't win the high side of the pot and that his low draw stalled when he paired or caught a big card. Now if you bet, representing a low draw instead of a pair of aces, your opponent will almost surely release any weak low draw.

But don't get too tricky in this game. After all, more poker players suffer from being too deceptive rather than not being tricky enough. Your goal should be to play straightforward poker most of the time and reserve your bag of tricks for good opponents, small pots, small fields, and those few occasions when you have a powerhouse hand and can afford to let your opponents improve—just enough to get themselves into trouble.

Bluffing can be advantageous

There are certain occasions when a bluff is required, and it may even succeed against players who call too frequently.

- If you have four cards of the same suit showing on your board and your opponent looks to be playing a lesser high hand such as a pair, go ahead and bet as though you've made your flush already. Unless he has a good hand, he'll probably toss his hand away. However, if you have nothing but a flush draw and are facing two opponents, one of whom looks to have a low hand and the other a weak high, don't try this. If you knock out the high hand, your only accomplishment might be to pass the high end of the pot to the low hand, who might after all have a pair or some other middling high holding that's strong enough to

topple your (unimproved) hand.

- If you have an ace showing in late position on third street and no one has yet called the bring-in, you must raise. Not only will your opponent fear you have a big pair, but you probably have the best hand right now. Remember, the odds are 5-to-1 against the bring-in—or anyone else—being dealt a pair on their first three cards. If your opponent has a weak low hand, he'll fear you have a better low draw and may release his hand too.

Semi-bluffing

Semi-bluffing is not a familiar term to all players, but it is a strategy that they will probably use. A semi-bluff is a bet made with a hand that's probably not the best one at the time the bet is made, but one that can win if it improves. Unlike pure bluffs, they have two ways to win. A bettor can win the pot if his opponent folds, but if the bluff fails and he's called, he can also win if his hand improves. Semi-bluffing adds some deception to your game. Betting with a four-flush or an open ended straight draw are classic examples of semi-bluffs.

If your first three exposed cards are the same suit, you can bet. You'll be representing a flush, even if you don't have one. If your opponent is sharp, one of the hands he'll think you might have is either a flush or a big flush draw. If you catch a fourth suited card on sixth street you should bet again. Your opponent should assume that you've made a flush, and he'll probably toss away any hand that can't beat a flush and has no possibility of improving to a full house on the river. Even if he calls with one or two pair, you still might make a flush on the river, so your semi-bluff provides two ways to win: Your opponent might fold the best hand or you might catch the card you need and leapfrog over him to win the pot on the strength of your hand.

Sometimes you can come out betting as though you have a flush when all you have is a low hand. If you figure to win the low end of the pot anyway, you might be fortunate enough to back into the best high hand and scoop the pot. You can also do this if you've made a flush with a hand like Q♣-K♣ / 4♣-2♣-6♣. While you don't have a low hand it sure looks like you do, and if you bet representing a low or a flush—isn't it nice when your hand scares opponents regardless of the direction they're heading in—you might dissuade

NOTE: *Betting out or raising with this hand is a good semi-bluff. Other players will see your potential nut low, flush, straight, and straight flush. Even if they don't fold, you have chances to make a powerful hand in the next two cards.*

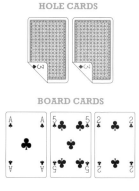

HOLE CARDS

BOARD CARDS

any weak low hands from continuing to draw against you, enabling you to scoop the pot rather than splitting it with a low hand.

Semi-bluffing is a strategy you'll grow into as you gain experience playing poker. It's far more effective than a pure bluff and tough to defend against when used in moderation.

Defending

A bet saved is as good as a bet won, so defense is just as vital as playing aggressively. Every time you're the bring-in you'll have to decide whether to defend your hand if someone completes the initial bet. If you've called the bring-in and someone raises, you'll have to mull that one over too. If you come out betting and an opponent raises, you'll have to decide whether to fold, play defensively, or stay aggressive.

If you're playing correctly, you'll usually enter pots with low hands, but not all low hands are equal. Even though three low cards aren't dealt to you that often, sometimes you can't even play the three low cards you've been dealt. Suppose you notice other potential low hands with door cards lower than yours. If some of the cards that will improve your low draw are in your opponents' hands, your chances of catching the cards you need are reduced. If you've got a poor low draw that has no chance of morphing into a high hand, such as a 7-6-2 of mixed suits—you probably won't make a straight or a flush—and an opponent showing an ace raises, you're already behind for high and might have a worse low hand too. These hands can be safely released most of the time.

Raising

Here are a few reasons to raise the pot in a seven-stud/8 game.

1. RAISING TO GET MONEY INTO THE POT

Building a pot is the most common reason to raise and the most enjoyable too. Whenever you have a big hand, such as a flush and a low, or a wheel (which is also a 5-high straight), you can raise at every opportunity. Each dollar your opponents contribute to the pot figures to migrate over to your stack of chips by hand's end. You should always raise whenever you've got a lock on half the pot and a chance to scoop all of it. Even if you only have a one-way hand but know you cannot lose your end of the contest, you should bet or raise whenever you have two or more opponents who are heading off in the other direction.

2. RAISING TO ELIMINATE OPPONENTS

If you've been dealt a hand like A-Q / A you'll want to raise if it's likely to prevent other opponents—particularly those with marginal low draws—from entering the pot after you. A pair of aces generally needs to improve to win against a large field, but it stands a good chance of winning without improvement against only one or two adversaries.

3. RAISING TO GET A FREE CARD ON A MORE EXPENSIVE STREET

You're last to act with A ♥-6♣ / 4 ♥-8 ♥. You raise when an opponent showing two high cards comes out betting. Although he might have a better hand than you do at this juncture, you can raise as long as hearts are live and you have a shot at making the best low hand too. Opponents are not likely to reraise because they must consider the possibility that you have a flush draw, a low draw, or both.

This is also a semi-bluff, because you're raising with a hand that might not be the best hand right now. But if you catch another low card, especially if it's a low heart, you'll have made a low hand and picked up a flush draw. And if that's not enough, you even have an opportunity to better your low hand. Your opponents might decide to fold, and if they do you'll win the pot right there. If they call and the next card is not to your liking, you can always take a free card if everyone checks to you.

4. RAISING TO PREVENT A FREE CARD

Raising can be a dicey proposition, but on a more costly betting round, raising to prevent your opponents from getting a free or relatively inexpensive card can be the right course of action.

Here's an example. You hold A♣-A♥ / 3♥-2♥. One of your two opponents shows X-X / 8♠-4♠ and the other shows X-X / 7♣-6♦. The player showing a seven comes out betting and is called by the opponent with two spades. You figure one for a low draw and assume the other is drawing to a spade flush. You raise, because your unseen pair of aces is probably a higher hand than the one held by the player representing the flush draw and you want to make it as costly as possible for your third opponent to continue his draw to a low hand. Although you can't be absolutely certain of what either of your opponents is holding—and there's a chance that you're not in the lead at all—it's still your job to make your opponents pay for the privilege of improving their hands.

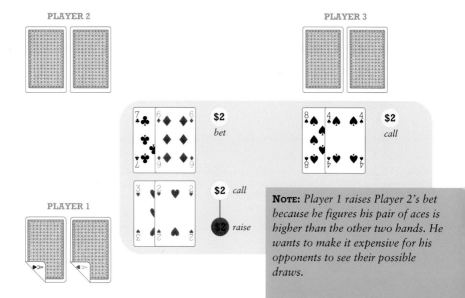

PLAYER 2

PLAYER 3

PLAYER 1

$2 *bet*

$2 *call*

$2 *call*

$2 *raise*

NOTE: *Player 1 raises Player 2's bet because he figures his pair of aces is higher than the other two hands. He wants to make it expensive for his opponents to see their possible draws.*

Free Cards

Sometimes you want a free card, sometimes you don't. The general rule about giving or receiving a free card is very straightforward.

With the best hand, you should be reluctant to give your opponents a free card that might win the pot for them. If you have a high hand you have to make it expensive for anyone with a low draw to capture half the pot. If you've got the best low hand with even as little as a pair or a flush or a straight draw for high, bet at every opportunity. When you have half the pot in hand, make your adversaries pay dearly for a chance to win the other half of it. On the other hand, when you're the one holding something less than the best hand, you'd always prefer a free card to one you'd have to pay for by calling a bet.

There are always exceptions. Sometimes you have a hand so strong that it's worth giving a free card, in the hope that your opponents will catch up a bit by building strong enough hands to call your bets on future rounds.

If you're the one hoping to make a good hand, you'll want a free card anytime you can get it. That's not something that you have total control over, but by betting or raising on third or fourth street you might be able to convince opponents acting before you to check on fifth street, when the betting limits double. You can always bet if your hand improves, or you can check and take a free card if your hand doesn't improve and all your opponents check to the raiser.

PLAYER 2

PLAYER 1

Slow-playing

Slow-playing is representing a very strong hand weakly on an inexpensive betting round. Your objective is to lure your opponents on to the more expensive betting rounds, where you'll trap them for additional, expensive bets. To do this, just take no action beyond what is required to stay in the pot. If no one has bet, you check. If someone bets, you call. Keep your opponents in the pot in order to maximize your winnings on subsequent betting rounds.

Slow-playing requires a very strong hand because you run the risk of offering your opponents a free or inexpensive card that just might improve their hands. If you have the best high hand, don't slow-play if it gives your opponents a free draw to a better hand. The time to slow-play is if it gives your opponents an opportunity to build hands that look good, but still can't win. Under ideal conditions, you're hoping that the free card your opponent gets will improve his hand, but only enough to make it second-best. The best time to slow-play is when the pot is relatively small and you believe your actions will allow it to grow larger on subsequent betting rounds. Slow-playing requires a strong hand that is not obvious to your opponents. Never slow-play a hand when a free card could give your opponents a better hand than yours, or give them a free chance to catch a card that will win one side of the pot for them. In seven-stud/8, your goal is to scoop a pot whenever possible, not to split it.

NOTE: *These two hands are strong enough to be slow-played. Anything weaker and you could find yourself in trouble at the showdown.*

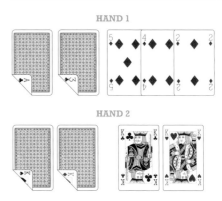

HAND 1

HAND 2

REMEMBER
Free cards are always a dangerous gift to your opponents, and should only be offered under the best of circumstances.

Reading Your Opponents

If you knew your opponents' cards you'd almost never lose, because you'd always make correct decisions. However, you don't have that information, so the better you are at deducing what your opponents are holding, the better your results will be. Reading seven-stud/8 opponents is usually straightforward if all you're trying to determine is whether they are going high or low. An exposed ace is difficult, however, because your opponent can be headed off in either or both directions. Low hands can also grow into straights and flushes too, so you'll have to be aware of those possibilities as the hand progresses.

Good players are easier to read than weak opponents, because a good player's actions are usually consistent and logical. To read a player, you assign a variety of possible hands to him and then reduce those hands to a few, based on their play and the cards dealt to each opponent from one betting round to the next. You can also examine later plays in terms of how your opponent played his hand on earlier betting rounds.

In this example your opponent raises on third street. Since many seven-stud/8 players raise when they have what they assume is the best low draw, that's one of the hands you think he might be holding. He also might have a hidden pair of aces with another very low card,

or even three straight flush cards, such as 7♥-6♥ / 5♥. He checks and calls on fourth street when he catches the Q♥, but raises an opponent when the 2♥ appears on fifth street. When you look at his hand, you'll see X-X / 5♥-Q♥-2♥. At this point it's pretty easy to assume he has a flush draw. He might even have made a flush already and he might also hold four low cards.

> **NOTE:** *On fifth street this player appears to have a flush draw or four low cards. Unless you can beat whatever hands your opponent appears to have, you might want to save your money for a better opportunity.*

PLAYER 1

GLOSSARY

all in (adj) When all your chips are in the pot, you are said to be "all in." When you are all in, you can win only as much as you have put into the pot, but you can win this amount from every other player. For example, if you are all in with $100, you can win up to $100 from each of your opponents, but no more. An all-in player cannot win any amount from side pots that develop after going all in.

all-in bet (n phrase) A bet made by a player in which he puts all his chips into the pot.

ante (n) A mandatory bet made before any cards are dealt.

banana (n) In seven-stud/8, a card with a rank of nine or higher. It does not help a low draw.

bet (n) A wager of any sort. (v) The action of a player whose turn it is to act and who is the first person in that betting round to wager money on his poker hand.

betting round (n phrase) The phase in a hand in which each active player has the option to fold, bet, call, or raise. This phase almost always follows the appearance of a new card or cards in players' hands or on the board. A standard betting round allows one bet and three or four raises, depending on the house rules.

blind bet (n) A bet made by a designated player or players in games, such as Texas hold'em and Omaha, before the initial deal. A blind becomes part of that player's bet if he comes into the pot, as compared to an ante, which is a separate bet.

bluff (v) To bet a weak hand in hopes of causing your opponents to fold. (n) The act of bluffing. "John made a good bluff and everyone folded."

board (n) 1. The five community cards in hold'em and Omaha. 2. A player's four exposed cards in seven-card stud or seven-stud/8.

brick (n) A card that does not increase the value of a player's hand. In hold'em or Omaha, a useless card that hits the board. (v) "The dealer bricked me."

bring-in, or forced bet (n) The mandatory opening bet paid by the player with the lowest card showing in the first betting round in a stud game. In some versions, the highest card showing pays the bring-in.

button (n) Disc of no value, used to denote the player last to act in games like hold'em and Omaha. Each player gets the button for one hand and then must pass it on to the player on his left.

call (v) To match a bet made by another player, which is required in order to stay in a hand.

check (v) To refrain from betting, permitted only if no bet has been made before you in the current betting round.

check-raise (v) To check initially and then raise an opponent who has bet behind you.

chip (n) A clay or plastic disc used to represent cash when betting at the poker table. Chips are also called checks, or poker chips.

community cards (n phrase) The cards that are dealt face up on the table and which belong equally to each player active in the hand, as in Texas hold'em or Omaha.

connector/s (n) Cards sequenced in rank, such as a nine and an eight, or a queen and jack.

counterfeited (adv) In Omaha/8, you are counterfeited if the rank of one of your low hole cards is duplicated on the board. For example, you hold a three and another three hits the board. Being counterfeited can ruin your low hand by making a better low hand for an opponent.

crying call (n phrase) A call made reluctantly, usually accompanied by a sigh or a whining complaint about how the caller believes he is now beaten.

cut-off seat (n phrase) The seat immediately to the right of the button in games like Texas hold'em and Omaha.

dangler (n) A card that doesn't fit or coordinate with a player's other cards.

dealer button see **button**

deuce (n) Another name for a card with the rank of two.

door card (n phrase) In stud games, the first exposed card in each player's hand.

down card (n phrase) Any card dealt face down to a player; a hole card, or a private card.

draw (n) An as-yet incomplete and thus valueless hand—usually four cards to a flush or straight.

draw out (v phrase) To beat a player by catching a card to propel your (second-best) hand into the lead.

draw-out (n phrase) The act of drawing out.

expectation (or return) (n) The average profit or loss of a specific bet in the long run.

expected value (EV) (n phrase) Expectation expressed in dollars. For example, if your chance of winning a $100 pot is 50 percent, your expected value in that pot is $50.

fit the flop (v phrase) How a player's hole cards work with the first three board cards in games like hold'em and Omaha.

flop (v) To make a hand using your hole cards and the first three community cards in games like Omaha and hold'em, as in "He flopped a flush." (n) The first three board cards in games like hold'em and Omaha.

fold (v) To throw away your cards and withdraw from the current hand.

free card (n phrase) A card obtained by a player or players who did not have to call a bet in the immediately preceding betting round.

full of (adj phrase) Used in describing the pair of a full house, such as three kings and two deuces, which would be called "kings full of deuces."

gut shot straight (n phrase) A straight that can be completed only by the addition of a single rank. If you draw to a 4-5-7-8 and catch a 6, you have made a gut shot straight.

hand reading (n phrase) Deciphering an opponent's hand through the use of deductive reasoning, by analyzing betting patterns in connection with any cards that are visible to you. Also called "putting an opponent on a hand."

heads-up (adj or adv phrase) Playing one-on-one, head-to-head, mano-a-mano; when there are exactly two players left in a game, such as in a tournament.

hitting the flop (v phrase) When a player's hole cards are greatly helped by the first three board cards in games like hold'em or Omaha.

hole cards (n phrase) Any cards dealt face-down to a player and which are for that player's use only; a down card, or a private card.

implied odds (n phrase) The ratio of what you estimate you will win on a particular hand compared to the cost of a current bet or call, based on money likely to be wagered on future rounds as well as money currently in the pot.

kicker (or side card) (n) An unpaired card that comes into play when two or more players have made hands of otherwise equal value; for example, the same one or two pair.

miracle card (n) A card that gives a player a big hand in the face of terrible odds against it happening.

nut flush (n phrase) The highest possible flush. In games like Omaha and hold'em, the cards on the board are crucial for determining the potentially highest flush.

nut low draw (n phrase) In any high-low game, four cards to the best possible low hand.

nuts, the (n) The best possible hand at any given point in a pot.

Omaha (n) A variant of hold'em in which players must use two of their down cards in combination with three of the community cards. Players each receive four down cards.

Omaha/8 (n) A form of Omaha in which the best high hand and the best qualifying low hand split the pot. To qualify, a low hand must be made up of five unpaired cards with a rank of eight or lower.

on a hand see **put someone on a hand**.

on tilt (adv phrase) Poor play when emotionally upset, often occurring when a player has a good hand beaten by an opponent's inferior starting cards. Also called steaming, having one's nose open, opened up, unglued, flying open, and being wide open.

outs (n) Cards that will improve a hand that is generally not winning at the moment.

overcards (n) 1. In hold'em, Omaha, or Omaha/8, community cards higher than a player's pair. "I started with a pair of eights but had to fold when Tom bet because there were two overcards on the board." 2. In hold'em, Omaha, or Omaha/8, a card in a player's hand that's higher than any of the community cards. "Phillip bet and I called, hoping that I'd pair one of my overcards on the next betting round." 3. In seven-card stud and seven-stud/8, a down card that is higher than any card showing among your opponents' cards.

playing zone (n phrase) Refers to cards in a range that most players are fond of playing. In Texas hold'em this includes cards with ranks of eight or higher. In a split-pot game, such as Omaha/8, the playing zone would include cards with a rank of ten or higher as well as those with a rank of five or lower.

pocket pair (n phrase) A pair contained among one's hole cards in Texas hold'em, Omaha, Omaha/8, seven-card stud, or seven-stud/8.

poker (n) A card game in which players wager that their own five-card hand outranks the hands of their opponents, and in which players attempt to convince other players to surrender hands that may, in fact, be better than their own.

pot (n) The chips that have been wagered and become part of the prize during a given hand.

pot-limit (n phrase) A betting structure in which the size of a player's bet is limited only by the current size of the pot.

pot odds (n phrase) The ratio of the size of the pot compared to the size of the bet a player must call to continue in the hand. For example, if the pot contains $10, and you must call a $5 bet; this gives you pot odds of 2-to-1.

premium pair (n phrase) In seven-card stud, this phrase usually refers to a pair of tens or higher dealt to a player before the first betting round.

private cards (n phrase) In games with community cards, private cards are those dealt to each player face down, prior to the initial round of betting. They are for the recipient alone to use. Also known as down cards or hole cards.

put someone on a hand (v phrase) To attempt to determine an opponent's hand through analysis of the exposed cards, and the player's bets and raises on previous betting rounds, as well as his or her playing style.

qualifier (n) A holding in a split-pot game that a player must have to win the low half of a pot; usually five unpaired cards with a rank of eight or lower, with the ace counting as a one.

quartered (adj) Winning one-fourth of a pot, usually in a split-pot game, when the low half of the pot is divided between two players.

raise (v) To increase the bet. (n) The money, or chips, that comprise this bet.

reraise (v) The act of raising the bet of a player who has already raised. Generally, a reraise must be at least equal to the size of the raise that preceded it.

the river (n) The final card that precedes the last round of betting in a given hand.

rolled-up (n phrase) The first three cards being three of a kind.

scare card (n phrase) A card that appears on the board of a player or a community board that can make players think an opponent has a big hand.

scoop (v) To win the entire pot in a high-low split poker game.

semi-bluff (n) A bet made on a hand that is not currently winning but which can grow into the best hand. If the bet causes everyone else to fold, it succeeds as a bluff; if not, the hand can still improve on succeeding betting rounds.

set (n) Three cards all the same rank, as in three kings. To flop a set in hold'em means that a player started with a pair and one of those cards appeared in the flop.

seven-card stud (n phrase) A poker game with two cards dealt face down, four cards dealt face up, and one final card dealt face down, with betting commencing on the third card and continuing with each round of cards. At the showdown, a player uses the best five of the seven cards to form the best poker hand.

seven-stud/8 (n) A variation of seven-card stud in which the best high hand and the best qualifying low hand split the pot. To qualify, a low hand must be composed of five unpaired cards with a rank of eight or lower, with the ace counting as a one.

showdown (n) The point in a hand when all the betting is over and the players still vying for the pot turn their cards face up to determine the winning hand or hands.

slow-play (v) Playing a strong hand as though it were weaker in order to lure opponents further into the pot. Slow-playing usually consists of trapping opponents for additional bets by not raising with a powerful hand, then either betting or check-raising on a subsequent betting round.

street (n) A betting round in poker following the introduction of a new card or cards during a hand.

tell (n) A physical mannerism, whether voluntary or involuntary, that gives other players clues about your hand.

ten-point cards (n phrase) Tens, jacks, queens, and kings. By implication, lower cards are assigned their face value.

Texas hold'em (or hold'em) (n phrase) A form of poker with two cards dealt face down to each player, and five community cards dealt face up in the center of the table. The game has four betting rounds: one after the first two down cards, one after the first three community cards are simultaneously revealed (the flop), one after the fourth community card (the turn), and one after the fifth (the river).

toke (n) A tip, given to the dealer by a player when he wins a pot.

top pair (n phrase) In Texas hold'em, when a player pairs one of his hole cards with the highest card on the board. For example, if Abby's hole cards are Q-9 and the flop is 9-7-3, she has flopped top pair.

trey (n) A card with the rank of three.

trips (n) Three cards all the same rank; three-of-a-kind.

the turn (n) The fourth community card to be revealed in games like Omaha and hold'em.

weak-tight (adj) A term that describes a player who loses because of tight, timid play; that is, a player who is reluctant to raise and quick to fold.

wheel (n) A five-high straight and the nut low 5-4-3-2-A in split-pot games. Also known as a bicycle.

World Series of Poker (WSOP) (n phrase) A prestigious poker tournament series held in Las Vegas each spring. Among its many events is the original no-limit hold'em tournament with a buy-in of $10,000.

wrap-around (n) When your four down cards in Omaha or Omaha/8 combine with two of the three flop cards to form five consecutive cards so that a large number of cards on the turn or river can give you a straight.

wrap hand (n phrase) In Omaha a wrap hand occurs whenever your four down cards combine with two flop cards to form five consecutive cards, so that either 13, 17, or 20 cards on the turn or river give you a straight.

RESOURCES

You'll find lot of information available to help you at poker in a variety of locations.

Bookstores

ConJelCo: www.conjelco.com
Gambler's Bookstore: www.gamblersbook.com
Playersbooks.com: www.playersbooks.com
Borders: www.borders.com
Amazon.com: www.amazon.com
Gamblers General Store:
   www.gamblersgeneralstore.com
High Stakes: www.gamblingbooks.co.uk

Playing Poker Online

Royal Vegas Poker: www.royalvegaspoker.com
Poker Stars: www.pokerstars.com
Party Poker: www.partypoker.com
Paradise Poker: www.paradisepoker.com
College Poker Championship (for students at
   colleges and universities only):
   www.collegepokerchampionship.com

Magazines

Card Player: distributed every other week for free
   in casinos and card rooms or available via
   subscription. www.cardplayer.com.
Poker Player: a biweekly that is distributed in
   numerous casinos and card rooms.
Poker Europa: free of charge in Europe with
   subscription copies available in Italy, Hungary,
   the U.S.A., Thailand, and Brazil.
Live Action Poker: for sale at news-stands and
   distributed free of charge in card rooms and
   casinos. www.liveactionpoker.com.
All-In Magazine: published six times annually and
   available through news-stand and subscription
   sales. www.allinmagazine.com.
www.loukrieger.com: Not really a magazine, but
   you can visit this website to read numerous
   articles that should help improve your game,
   and for links to all of Lou's other books and lots
   of other information.

Poker Discussion Sites and Forums

Rec.Gambling.Poker: www.recpoker.com
All Poker: www.allpoker.org
Gutshot Poker Collective: www.gutshot.co.uk
Live Action Poker.com: www.liveactionpoker.com
Poker Clan: www.pokerclan.com
Poker in Europe: www.pokerineurope.com
Poker Pages: www.pokerpages.com
Poker Savvy: www.pokersavvy.com
Poker Strategy Forum:
   www.pokerstrategyforum.com
Poker Strategy.Org: www.poker-strategy.org
Poker News.com: www.pokernews.info
Two Plus Two: www.twoplustwo.com
United Poker Forum: www.unitedpokerforum.com

INDEX

Note: Explanations of poker terms are on the pages shown in bold type, e.g. all-in bet **248**

A

aces 88, 93, 104, 118, 150, 155
 ranking of 30
all in **248**
all-in bet **248**
ante/s 15, 26, **34**, 68, 74, **248**
ante stealing 144–145, 237

B

banana/s 149, **248**
best possible hand 200–202
best starting hands 107, 121
bet **34**, **248**
betting 48–49, 56–57, 62–63, 68, 74
betting order position 158–160, 181–182, 196–198, 214–215, 232–233
betting patterns 36–37
betting round/s **34**, 50–53, 58–61, 64–67, 75–79, **248**
bicycle (wheel) 14, 32, **251**
blind/s **34**, 56, **248**
 see also ante
bluff/bluffing 13, 37–38, 241, **248**
 see also deception; semi-bluff; slow-play
board **34**, **248**
board games 212–215
 see also seven-card stud; seven-stud/8
body language 36–39
brick/s 149, **248**

bring-in (forced bet) 26, 27, **34**, 68, 74, **248**
bug (joker) 13, 30
button (dealer button) **248**

C

call/calling 12, 17, **34**, **248**
character, of winning players 15
cheating 45
check **34**, **248**
check-raise **34**, **248**
chip/s 13–14, **248**
community cards 20, **34**, 56, 212, **248**
connector/s 86–87, 90, 94, **248**
counterfeiting **248**
counterfeits 127
counting cards 216
crying call **248**
cut-off seat 118, **248**

D

dangler/s 100–101, **248**
dealer button (or button) **248**
deception 167–168, 189, 205, 219–220, 240–241
 slow-play 133, 177, 193, 210, **251**
decisions 17, 84
defending 169–170, 190, 207, 221, 243
defining hands 173–174
deuce **248**
door card **35**, 68, **248**
double-suited hands 107
down card **35**, **248**
draw **248**
drawing out **249**
draw-out/s 213–214, 231, **249**
draw poker 30

E

early position 90–91
etiquette 44–45
expectation (return) **249**
expected value (EV) **249**

F

fifth street 71, 77
fit the flop 110, 120, **249**
fixed-limit 26, 48, 49, 62, 68, 74
flop/flopping 129, **249**
flop games 212–215
 see also Omaha; Texas hold'em
flop, the **35**
 Omaha 58, 111–113
 Omaha/8 64, 103, 125
 Texas hold'em 50–51, 55, 89
flushes 30, 31, 90, 111, 139–140
fold/folding 13, 17, **35**, 110, 120, **249**
forced bet (bring-in) 26, 27, **34**, 68, 74, **248**
four-of-a-kind 31
fourth street 70, 76, 237
free card 176, 192, 209, 224, 245, **249**
 on a more expensive street 173, 191, 207–208, 222, 243–244
 preventing 174–175, 191, 208, 222–223, 244
freerolling 102
full house 31, 101–102
full of **249**

G

gapped cards 86, 87, 94
gut shot straight **249**

H

hand rankings 30–34
hand reading 36–39, 42–43,
   249
   Omaha 194–195
   Omaha/8 211
   seven-card stud 130,
      226–227
   seven-stud/8 247
   Texas hold'em 178–179
hands
   best playing 200–202
   defining 173–174
   double-suited hands 107
   mid-ranging 99
   playable 84, 123–124
   premium drawing 90
   rankings 30–34
   selection of 110, 124
   starting 29, 84–155
   two-way 152–153, 154
   unplayable hands 108
   very best starting 107, 121
   very good 108, 122
   wrap hands 108, 122
   see also high hands; high and
      low hands; low hands
heads-up **35**, **249**
high hands 81, 152–153, 155
high and low hands 14, 30–34
   seven-card stud 28–29
   seven-stud/8 81, 152–155,
      228–230
history of poker 6, 14
hitting the flop **249**
hold'em see Texas hold'em
Holden, Anthony 15
hole cards **35**, 68, **249**

I

implied odds 165–166, 188,
   205, 218–219, 239–240,
   249
internet poker 7, 9, 14, 180

J

jacks 89, 94
joker (bug) 13, 30

K

kicker (side card) 135, 136,
   249
kings 88–89, 94, 105

L

late position 93–94
live cards 26, 216
long shots 162–163
lowball 30
low hands 81, 99, 127–128,
   154, 202–203

M

middle pairs 89, 91
mid-ranging hands 99
miracle card **249**
multiple options/draws 126

N

no-limit 48–49, 166
no pair 33
nut flush 19, 90, 102, **249**
nut low draw **249**
nuts, the 19, 112, 129, **249**
nut straight 102

O

odds, calculating 163–164,
   186–187, 230–231, 234
odds and outs 161–164,
   183–187, 199–205,
   216–217, 234–238
Omaha 19, 22–23, 56–61, **249**
   playing hands 180–195
   starting hands 96–113
Omaha/8 19, 24–25, 62–67,
   249
   playing hands 196–211
   starting hands 114–130

on a hand 42–43, **250**
one pair 33
on tilt **249**
opponents 36–39, 41–42, 113,
   129
   eliminating 171–172, 191,
      207, 222, 243
   preventing 174–175, 191,
      208, 222–223, 244
   see also hand reading
outs **249**
overcards 142, **250**

P

pairs 85, 88–89, 93, 132–138
   middle 89, 91
   no and one pair 33
   pocket pair **250**
   premium 132–138, **250**
   in seven-card stud 27
   top pair **251**
   two pair 32
percentages 187, 203,
   204–205, 217
playable hands 84, 123–124
playing zone **250**
"Pochen" 14
pocket pair **250**
poker **250**
poker skills see strategies
"Poque" 14
pot 12, 129, **250**
pot limit **35**, 48, 56, 166, **250**
pot odds **35**, 42, 161,
   183–184, 195, **250**
premium drawing hands 90
premium pair/s 132–138, **250**
private cards **250**
put someone on a hand 42–43,
   250
   see also hand reading

CREDITS

Quarto would like to thank and acknowledge the following for supplying illustrations and photographs reproduced in this book:

p6 Universal / The Kobal Collection
p7 David Butow / CORBIS SABA
p9 Royal Vegas Poker
p14 Bettmann / CORBIS

All other illustrations and photographs are the copyright of Quarto Publishing plc. While every effort has been made to credit contributors, Quarto would like to apologize should there have been any omissions or errors—and would be pleased to make the appropriate correction for future editions of the book.

Dedication

This book is dedicated to my wife, Deirdre Quinn, who took a circuitous route from Sligo, Ireland, all the way to Montana and then to the state of Washington, before settling in Palm Springs. We had the good fortune to meet at the very confluence of Irish and Jewish cultures—over a plate of corned beef at Sherman's Deli, where we wagered our hearts on love and were lucky enough to win.

I also wish to thank the editorial staff at Quarto, especially Penny Cobb and Paula McMahon, who were a great help to me in combining some terrific artwork with my writing and pulling it all together into this wonderful book.

ADVICE
Although poker is fun and exciting, make sure that you wager only what you can easily afford to lose. And if you suspect that you have a gambling problem, be sure to seek immediate professional help.

NOTE
Throughout the text, the author uses "he" or "him" when referring to poker players. This is a convention that has been adopted to save space and aid clarity, and no gender bias is intended.

Q

qualifier 228, **250**
quartered **250**
queens 89, 105

R

raise/raising **35**, **250**
  Omaha 113, 191
  Omaha/8 129, 207–209
  seven-card stud 222–223
  seven-stud/8 243–244
  Texas hold'em 171–175
reading *see* hand reading;
    selection
reraise **35**, 118–119, **250**
return (expectation) **249**
river **35**, 53, 61, 66, 73, 79, **250**
rolled-up **250**
royal flush 30

S

scare card **250**
scoop/scooping 24, 29, 228,
    250
selection of hands 110, 124
semi-bluff 168–169, 189–190,
    206, 220–221, 242, **250**
set **250**
seven-card stud 19–20, 26–27,
    68–73, **250**
  playing hands 212–227
  starting hands 130–145
seven-stud/8 28–29, 74–81,
    251
  playing hands 228–248
  starting hands 146–155
seventh street 73, 79
showdown **35**, 61, 67, 80–81,
    251
side card (kicker) 135, 136,
    249
sixth street 72, 78
slow-play/playing 133, 177,
    193, 210, 225, 246, **251**

split-pot games 14, 30
    see also Omaha/8; seven-
      stud/8
spread-limit 48
starting hands 29, 84–155
Sting, The (film) 6
straight 32, 111, 141–143,
    184–186, 202
straight flush 30, 138–139
strategies 16–17, 36–38
  Omaha/8 124–125
  seven-card stud 132, 135,
    137
  seven-stud/8 234, 236, 237,
    238
  Texas hold'em 84, 94–95
  see also bluff; deception;
      decisions; defending;
      selection; semi-bluff;
      slow-play
street/s 26, **35**, 69–73, 75–79,
    251
stud games *see* seven-card
    stud; seven-stud/8
suited cards 85, 86–87, 90, 92,
    107
Swift, Jonathan 15

T

television poker 6
tell/s 36, 39, **251**
  see also hand reading
ten-point cards **251**
terms **34**
Texas hold'em 18, 20–21,
    48–55, **251**
  playing hands 158–179
  starting hands 84–95
third street 69, 75, 234–236
three-of-a-kind 32
three to a straight flush
    138–139
toke/toking 45, **251**
top pair **251**

trey **251**
trips 131–132, 155, **251**
turn **35**, 52, 65, 103, **251**
two pair 32
two-way hands 152–153, 154

U

unplayable hands 108
unsuited cards 85, 86–87,
    90–91, 94

V

very best starting hands 107,
    121
very good hands 108, 122

W

weak-tight **251**
wheel (bicycle) 14, 32, **251**
winning 15, 54–55, 238
World Series of Poker (WSOP)
    8, **251**
wrap-around **251**
wrap hands 99, 105–106, **251**

KEY TO DIAGRAMS

A quick reference guide to the diagrams and notations is given below. For clarity of presentation, cards are shown with suit and rank at all four corners. When playing, you will most likely encounter cards with suits appearing in the upper-left and lower-right corners only.

For an explanation of the most-used technical terms, turn to page 34, and there's a full glossary on page 248.

For an explanation of the most-used technical terms, turn to page 34, and there's a full glossary on page 248.

THE POKER TABLE

$ A bet made before cards are dealt

$ First bet or call

$ First raise or call of that raise

$ Reraise or call of that raise

$ An incomplete pot

$ The total money in the pot at the beginning of a round of betting

$ The total amount of money in the pot at the finish of the game

‒‒‒‒   When chips are linked, they are part of the same move. A player must match previous bets before raising.

AROUND THE TABLE

D
Dealer button

Player designated to start the betting

Player folded

Player's hole cards

Blue circles show which cards make the final hand

HAND RANKINGS

Royal flush	Ace-high straight flush.
Straight flush	Five sequenced cards, all of the same suit.
Four of a kind	Four cards of any rank, plus one unrelated card.
Full house	Three cards of any given rank with a pair of another.
Flush	Five cards of the same suit.
Straight	Five sequenced cards, not of the same suit.
Three of a kind	Three cards of the same rank plus two unrelated cards.
Two pair	Two cards of one rank, two cards of another, and one unrelated card.
One pair	Two cards of one rank plus three unrelated side cards.
No pair	Five unrelated cards.

KEY TO DIAGRAMS

Use this handy pull-out key as a quick
reference to the diagrams used in this book.